D1623789

Why
Young
MEN

JAMIL JIVANI

WHY
YOUNG
MEN

THE DANGEROUS ALLURE OF
VIOLENT MOVEMENTS AND
WHAT WE CAN DO ABOUT IT

ALL
POINTS
BOOKS

www.allpointsbooks.com

Designed by Ellen Cipriano

Library of Congress Cataloging-in-Publication Data

Names: Jivani, Jamil, author.
Title: Why young men : the dangerous allure of violent movements and what we can do about it / Jamil Jivani.
Description: New York : All Points Books, [2019] | Includes bibliographical references and index.
Identifiers: LCCN 2019001772| ISBN 9781250199898 (hardcover) | ISBN 9781250199904 (ebook)
Subjects: LCSH: Young men—Psychology. | Young men—Social conditions. | Identity (Psychology) | Oppression (Psychology) | Alienation (Social psychology) | Radicalization.
Classification: LCC HQ799.6 .J58 2019 | DDC 155.6/5—dc23
LC record available at https://lccn.loc.gov/2019001772

Our books may be purchased in bulk for promotional, educational, or business use. Please contact your local bookseller or the Macmillan Corporate and Premium Sales Department at 1-800-221-7945, extension 5442, or by e-mail at MacmillanSpecialMarkets@macmillan.com.

First Edition: June 2019

10 9 8 7 6 5 4 3 2 1

Pam, Jasmine and Janine—
you'll never walk alone

CONTENTS

FOREWORD

■ ■ ■ ■ ▬▬▬▬▬▬▬▬▬▬▬▬▬▬▬▬▬▬

During my first days at Yale Law School, I distinctly remember meeting two people. The first was the girl who would eventually become my wife. The second was Jamil Jivani, the author of the book you now hold in your hands.

Jamil and I didn't obviously share much in common. He was a black guy from Canada; I was a white guy from America. He grew up in a big city, and I grew up in a small town. He didn't understand why I liked guns, and I didn't understand why "about" sounded like "aboot" when he pronounced it.

But appearances can be deceiving, and Jamil and I quickly realized our similarities. We were both patriotic, and loved and admired our home countries, despite their imperfections. We both owed much of our lives' opportunities to women—my grandmother, his mother—who stepped up when others let us down. We both felt a strong connection to our communities back home even as we lacked a certain comfort with the elite environment of Yale. Neither of us came from families with money. And we both knew very personally the feeling of loss and shame that comes from growing up without your father around.

Early during that first year of law school, Jamil and I found ourselves in a large group eating at a late-night chicken joint. As everyone filed out, Jamil and I both noticed the terrible mess we'd left and stayed behind to clean everything up. "We are probably the only people here who've ever had to clean up someone else's mess," I said. Jamil just nodded in agreement.

Jamil would eventually become one of my best friends. Years later, at my wedding, I chose Jamil to read my favorite verse from the Bible, from Saint Paul's letter to the Philippians: "Finally, brethren, whatsoever things are true, whatsoever things are honest, whatsoever things are just, whatsoever things are pure, whatsoever things are lovely, whatsoever things are of good report; if there be any virtue, and if there be any praise, think on these things."

I am proud of Jamil. Proud mostly of the man he has become and strives to become each day. Proud of his dedication to his beliefs. Proud of this book he has written, published for the first time in my home country. In it, Jamil asks the question, as the title indicates, "Why young men?" Why do young men seem to be struggling so much in our modern society? Why are young male immigrants less able to assimilate into their new homes in the West? Why are so many young men in the inner city caught up in gang activity? Why is it that so much of the violence, social dysfunction and misery in our societies disproportionately exists and flows from our young men?

His answer is that today's world throws more traps and

temptations in front of young men than ever before with even fewer ladders out of the ditches they end up in. From their families, their neighborhoods, their communities and even their countries, young men find themselves a little more disconnected and isolated than ever before. Moreover, there are fewer sources of legitimate and productive meaning available. Thus, there's a temptation to take the easy or fun way out of situations. Tragically, of course, the easiest way out of a given crisis is often the most destructive.

Jamil's way of answering that question is insightful and engaging. It's impossible to do justice to a book—or indeed, a man's life—in a brief foreword. But Jamil brings perhaps the three most important qualities to this task: a brilliant intellect, a life of experiences and insights and real moral courage. Jamil does not avoid tough questions, or make the most ideologically or politically convenient arguments. He takes the world as it is. He allows experience and data to inform and guide him. And he tackles this extraordinarily difficult topic with grace and compassion. I am biased, of course, but I believe that this is an important book.

One of the things I admire most about my friend is that he has not lost his passion for working on the things he cares about. A few years after we graduated from law school, as I thought about creating a nonprofit organization focused on the opioid epidemic that is ravaging my home state of Ohio, I called Jamil. He had created nonprofits of his own before, and I wanted his advice on how to proceed. He offered to take a sabbatical from his teaching position in Toronto and help me get the organization off the ground.

The organization we created together was low budget and leanly budgeted. We focused initially on a couple of public policy issues, especially on increasing access to kinship guardians. In

Ohio, there are so many parents incapacitated (or worse) because of their addiction, that there's an entire generation of children growing up without stable homes. And, terribly, the grandparents, aunts, uncles and other relatives who want to take care of those children can't because of various legal and financial barriers. Our organization pushed some legislation to remedy that problem. (It's still a work in progress, but we have at least acquired a number of cosponsors.)

We've also successfully brought a nationally renowned addiction expert to southeastern Ohio, where the epidemic is the worst, and funded some of her work in treating patients and researching the epidemic. At every step of the way, Jamil has thought through how to solve problems, attract resources and implement our plans. This is not a person who merely writes or thinks about our society's most troubling problems. He actually does something about them.

About a year ago, I began noticing that Jamil was often feeling ill. It was fall, and he was in a new environment, so I just assumed he was having a run of bad luck with cold and flu season. But one day he called me and told me that he had returned home to Toronto for treatment, and that his doctors thought he likely had advanced lymphoma.

There is simply nothing that can prepare you for the news that your friend—a young and healthy friend, at that—has been diagnosed with cancer. Jamil and I spoke about his treatment plan, and his progress, as weeks with cancer turned into months. I knew he was optimistic that he could beat the disease, and I knew that he drew a lot of strength from his community in Toronto, especially his church. Throughout his treatment, Jamil never gave in to pessimism or defeatism. There were certainly hard days, and both the disease and the treatments took a physical toll, but Jamil persevered. And he always checked in on our organization, doing what he had to even at the lowest points of the disease.

As I write this, Jamil has finished his cancer treatment and is hopeful that in the weeks to come he'll receive a clean bill of health. His health has given the book a new poignancy, and it's tough for me to separate this book from the disease that came into his life just as the book approached publication. But the book, like Jamil, is bigger than any health problem.

After I proposed to my wife, my favorite professor, Amy Chua, threw us an engagement party. She asked Jamil and a few others to give toasts. Jamil and I were very close, so his toast naturally focused on me. "We are," he told me (and about a hundred others), "a generation of fatherless men. For so much of our lives, we've had to figure out how to be men on our own."

In Canada and the United States, this is undoubtedly true. There are so many fatherless men out there, and we owe it to them to figure out why they struggle so much. Jamil's book, and the life he's led, helps us begin to do that.

J. D. Vance

INTRODUCTION

Paris Attacks

■ ■ ■ ■

On November 13, 2015, a series of suicide bombings and mass shootings killed or injured nearly 500 people in and around Paris, France. These violent acts were carried out by nine men who belonged to the terrorist group Islamic State of Iraq and Syria (ISIS). The president of France called the Paris attacks an "act of war" against his country.

Over the following days, news media pundits and social media influencers quickly gathered in their ideological camps to treat the attackers as faceless representatives of a religion or a race to be criticized or defended. One side blamed religion and culture for the killings, while the other expressed concern over racism in response to terrorism. These debates predictably looked the same as the famous exchange between actor Ben Affleck and philosopher Sam Harris on HBO's *Real Time with Bill Maher* following another terrorist attack the previous year. Harris, representing the "blame religion and culture" side, argued that among the billion-plus Muslims in the world, there are significant numbers who hold extreme beliefs, and among that group there are jihadists who want to wage war against nonbelievers. In response, Affleck, representing the "fear racism" side, was passionately defensive and compared Harris to people who stereotype and stigmatize black Americans because of gang violence.

Missing in these discussions was an effort to see the men beyond the monsters, to see the individual stories buried beneath headlines and left out of viral videos. The actual lives of the Paris attackers and, just as important, the communities around them were mostly ignored or only superficially examined. But as the debates went on, I learned that the young men who orchestrated these tragedies weren't as foreign to me as I'd initially thought, or as Affleck-and-Harris-style exchanges would indicate.

The masterminds of the Paris attacks, Abdelhamid Abaaoud and Salah Abdeslam, didn't lead ordinary lives before pledging allegiance to ISIS, but their lives also weren't necessarily indicative of the killers they would become. Both were born in Belgium in the late 1980s to parents who had emigrated from Morocco, and they were raised together in the Molenbeek district of Brussels. Both men had also been involved with petty crime: they were arrested together for attempting to break into a parking garage in 2010, and Abaaoud had been to prison at least three times. Abdeslam, on the other hand, had tried his luck at becoming an entrepreneur: he was the manager and part owner of a bar in Molenbeek. Neither man's background suggested that he was particularly devout or traditional in his adherence to Islam. The religion and culture of both men's parents seemed to be a distant part of their lives.

To my surprise, there were similarities between the Paris attackers and some of the young men I had grown up with in the Toronto suburbs: children of immigrants, living in a disadvantaged neighborhood, drawn into petty crime, and ambitious to a fault. Of course, none of my peers ever transitioned from petty crime to the extremes of terrorism. That doesn't mean they weren't equally vulnerable to destructive influences, however. Growing up, they were often easily persuaded by the people around them to do harmful things. Most of what they got into trouble for, such as fighting, was the result of being around people who encouraged them to be criminals.

I wondered if ISIS's success at recruiting young men in Europe was a more extreme example of what I had seen in my own life and that of my friends. And if so, why had one friend appeared on a local Crime Stoppers report for petty crimes rather than on CNN or the BBC for terrorism? Can we learn something valuable about how these young men in Europe become so disconnected from their countries that they can be recruited by a foreign enemy? Hoping to find answers to these questions, I traveled to Brussels in February 2016 to conduct the research that appears in this book.

The time I spent in Belgium after the Paris attacks marked an expansion of my activism outside of the urban centers of the United States and Canada, where I have spent more than a decade focused on young men exposed to violent criminals, ideologies that encourage conflict and other antisocial influences. Specifically, I have worked to help young men find positive influences by improving the public institutions that shape their lives, such as schools, child welfare agencies and police departments, and by empowering men to be more involved in their communities as parents, mentors and youth workers. My activism is rooted in my own journey from a supposedly illiterate high school student who considered a life of crime to Yale Law School graduate and award-winning lawyer.

On the surface, the various types of violent groups that draw young men—gangs, terror cells, extremist networks, more loosely organized criminals—are widely seen as being completely different from one another. One thing is certain: such groups thrive when enough people believe that differences of race, religion, class or neighborhood are irreconcilable. And, in my work, I've discovered remarkable similarities between young men who turn to violence in search of belonging and brotherhood. Many of these traits are also exhibited by self-destructive young men—those coping with addiction or contemplating suicide—and isolated young men, whose behavior isn't so extreme that they make the news cycle, but who have nevertheless withdrawn from the outside world. The techniques and strategies that have been shown to help one group of marginalized young men can be applied to the others.

The impetus for this book was an interview Canadian journalist Nahlah Ayed did with me when I first left Toronto for Belgium. I was nervous because Nahlah is a world-renowned journalist and I was still relatively new to being on TV. I answered most of the questions reasonably well—until I was caught off guard by her final one: Why young men?

Nahlah wanted to understand why journalists like her end up talking about young men like me so often. It is true that we appear in news headlines an awful lot, and most of the time it's not for good reasons. That day, though, I buckled under the weight of the question, overwhelmed by the number of directions it could go in. I settled on focusing on the economic pressures faced by young men, explaining that when they don't believe they'll be able to support themselves or their families, they may experience trauma that leads to extreme thinking and behaviors.

The answer wasn't very good—it was too short and too simple—and I stumbled through it. Leaving the TV studio, I felt like a failure. As a young man myself, I know the struggles and triumphs of young men. I conducted research on the topic for years as a student. My work now is designed to help alleviate these struggles and reproduce these triumphs. My answer should have reflected these personal and professional insights.

But the interview was over, so I carried the question with me. And I've written this book so I can give the world a better answer.

The following pages include what I've learned in trying to understand why young men in the West are vulnerable to falling outside the reach of mainstream morals in the countries they call home. I also want to raise some ideas that could better protect young men from the negative influences seeking them out. Above all, I want to develop the language and reference points to help families communicate about what's going on in the lives of young men.

In the stories I tell, young men come across as good guys and bad guys, victims and perpetrators, heroes and villains. I have changed some personal details and also made use of composite characters.

Most of my writing is set in majority black and Muslim communities because that's where I've lived and worked, but my hope is to transcend racial and religious differences to highlight common experiences that shape the lives of young men. I seek to highlight voices that are often underrepresented and overlooked, and which increasingly require our collective attention. I don't intend to displace or take away from efforts to discuss the experiences of young women and others whose voices must also be heard. In this respect, I am following the example set by President Barack Obama's My Brother's Keeper initiative, which focuses on the lives of young men without undermining other efforts to achieve justice and equality.

This book also outlines methods of community organizing and activism that have successfully combated various types of youth radicalization around the world. If community organizers and activists learned better from one another, shared resources and exchanged best practices, we would be better positioned to protect young men from the harmful influences seeking them out. Parents, teachers and others seeking to mentor young men can also benefit from understanding these methods of engaging youth in crisis.

Finally, a handful of important books helped facilitate my personal growth as a young man. At different points in my life, the right book at the right time challenged my worldview and changed how I thought about myself and others. I hope *Why Young Men* might do the same for other people who find themselves in a similar position.

Why
Young
MEN

1

Role Models

■ ■ ■ ■

In my family, it's tradition to grow up without male role models. My father, Ismat, didn't have a father figure for much of his childhood, and he left me in the same position. Both of us are part of the intergenerational cycle of fatherlessness that makes young men vulnerable to people posing as authorities on masculinity.

Ismat was born in 1963 at the Aga Khan University Hospital in Nairobi, Kenya. I don't know why, but his biological parents didn't take him home after he was born, so he was cared for by the hospital until the age of one, when he was adopted by people who seem to have loved him dearly. From what I've been told, however, both of his adoptive parents had tragically passed away in separate incidents by the time he turned fourteen. He was then largely on his own, with minimal to no support from his adoptive relatives. In some of his most formative years, he was without parental figures altogether.

What Ismat had going for him was his hustle and intelligence. As a teenager, he used his inheritance from his adoptive parents to put himself through cooking school. He worked as an apprentice at the Hilton Hotel in Nairobi, then pushed for a transfer to the Hilton in London. He became a chef and embarked on a successful career working in hotels.

His life up to that point is an inspiring story of what hard work can do for you. I feel proud when I tell people about my father's difficult start in life and how high he climbed before he was even twenty. But that pride fades quickly when I begin talking about what his life became as he grew into adulthood. The lack of male role models in his life caught up to him after he met my mother.

Ismat met Pam when he was twenty-two years old. He had traveled to Toronto to attend the wedding of one of his adoptive cousins, who happened to be a co-worker of my mother's. After their chance meeting at the wedding, my parents quickly got married themselves, and my father relocated to Toronto from London. They had three children, with me the first. The pressures of being a husband and father weighed on Ismat early on, meaning their relationship never really got off to a good start. By the time their second child was born, Ismat was already slipping in his responsibilities. He was at home sleeping while Mom gave birth to my sister Jasmine.

Ismat was a far more successful chef than he was a husband or father. In Toronto, he worked in expensive restaurants and built a strong reputation for himself. He even appeared on television a few times to promote the restaurants where he cooked. Meanwhile, Ismat the husband and father was largely absent. Many days he wasn't around at all. I would go to sleep most nights not having seen or spoken to him. Mom would say it was because he was working late. Eventually I was old enough to see he was choosing not to be home because he had other places he wanted to be.

An important difference between Ismat the chef and Ismat the husband or father is that he had role models to help him learn how to cook. He went to school for it. He worked as an apprentice for years under the tutelage of chefs who showed him how to wash dishes, chop vegetables, work a fryer, use a stove, boil pasta, grill a steak and bake a cake. He just didn't have the same education in being a husband or father.

As his oldest child, I've struggled to have empathy for Ismat. Certainly, I was hurt by his absence—and even more hurt by his terrible behavior when he was around. He was always yelling and bullying, as if he wanted us to be glad when he was gone. I've continued to hold a grudge against him as an adult because I've seen the consequences of his choices for my mother and sisters. I've also learned to look back at how he was as a husband and father, however, and remind myself that he, too, was a fatherless young man.

My family has one home video of us, on an old VHS tape from 1989. The video was a gift from one of Ismat's friends in honor of the birth of Jasmine. In the film are scenes from the hospital where she was born and the days after she came home. When I watched it as a kid, I loved it because we seemed like the families I saw on television. There are images of my parents together, my father sitting on the couch, me playing with a toy guitar and baby Jasmine doing what babies do.

I haven't watched the video in many years, but in my last few viewings I started to see something I'd missed as a kid. I could see Ismat's struggles: the distant look in his eyes when he was around his wife and kids, his discomfort when showing affection, the emotionless expressions on his face. Our few family photos tell a similar story of a man who just didn't know what he was doing. In a picture of the two of us sitting together on the couch, he looks like he doesn't want to be there with every fiber of his being. A picture of him with his arm around my mom captures his forced and uncomfortable body language. He looks like he is posing for a picture he wishes wasn't being taken.

Ismat's ignorance of his role in our family also played out in the few interactions we had as father and son, such as on Father's Day, which was one of my least favorite days of the year. In third grade, I came home from school with a picture I'd drawn of Ismat as a superhero, kind of like Balrog, the boxer character from the video game Street Fighter. I spent hours at school that day working on it. I tried to make my father look cool, and I knew he really liked boxing. The top of the drawing read "Happy Father's Day." I was glad he was home because I didn't often get to see him. I handed him the drawing with high hopes for how he might react. When he looked at it, he seemed confused. "What does this mean?" he said dismissively. He then put it to the side, never even making eye contact with me. Not once.

There was something phony about the whole thing. My father didn't deserve a day in his honor—nor did he deserve a gift from any of his kids. That damned teacher had set me up, I thought. She'd made me look like an idiot by forcing me to give him some gift he could toss to the side like it was worthless. And there I was, trying to reach out to him as a son, only to feel rejected once again.

Mom could see the frustration in my eyes. To cheer me up, she picked up the drawing and told me it was good. She put it on the fridge as if it was something valuable. Whenever I got upset with my father, Mom would try to fix things by showing me enough positive attention to compensate for his negative behavior. Sometimes she was successful at turning those negative moments into positive ones; other times she wasn't.

If I could go back in time, I would love to ask her, "Is this what a man is supposed to be like? If yes, why? If not, then what should I grow up to be like?" Instead of having that discussion, though, we both just left things unsaid. We moved on as if nothing happened, but these moments stuck with both of us.

There was a period of time—when I was seven or eight years old and he was thirty—that I remember Ismat coming home from work very late at night. At least twice he woke me up to talk to me. I was really happy to see him. On the first of those nights, he told me about a new handshake he was doing at work—one reminiscent of a handshake Will Smith did on *The Fresh Prince of Bel-Air*. I still remember it to this day, but I've never used it.

The situation was much more serious on the second night, when he came into my room, sat on the edge of my bed and cried. He told me he didn't know how much longer he could keep doing "this." I was scared because I didn't know what "this" meant. Was he talking about being my dad? Or working? Or coming home late? He told me that he was working so hard for his family, and that he was always tired and hurting. After a few minutes of silence, he stopped crying, said good night and left my room.

Having lacked role models to draw on as a kid, Ismat obviously didn't have those resources as a young man, either. He was struggling not just with being a father and husband but also with being a whole person. He was living a life of such emotional suppression that one of the few people he felt he could open up to was his son, who wouldn't judge or criticize him. Ismat didn't have a supportive community he could rely on to help him on his journey as a husband and father. He was struggling to figure everything out on his own.

My parents' marriage gradually fell apart. I recall both of them making comments to me about separation as early as the mid-1990s, just a few years after the birth of their third child, my sister Janine. But the state of their relationship was never quite clear to me. Ismat became increasingly absent and was away for longer periods of time, until eventually I didn't expect to see him at all. Every so often it seemed like Mom was trying to make the marriage work again—encouraging my father to be home more by getting us to do things as a family, like go out to eat—but when I was in my late teens she gave up and made it clear to me that their relationship was over.

I often thought about how Ismat's absence affected me. I listened to songs about growing up without a father to look up to. Two Jay-Z songs in particular, "Meet the Parents" and "Where Have You Been," were my favorites. I wondered if I, too, would be a disappointment to my children when I grew up. Perhaps it was fate, or something in my DNA.

Mom had a lot to think about in my father's absence as well. She wasn't prepared for the kind of dysfunction that existed in her own marriage and the family she had created with Ismat. She had been raised in a two-parent household—her Scottish father was a school janitor, and her Irish mother kept the house and kids in order. She has three siblings, including a twin sister, and the four of them went to church regularly as kids. They had, from what I can tell, a fairly stable and boring (in a good way) childhood.

Perhaps it was hard for Mom to talk to me about my father because doing so reminded her of how far the situation she found herself in was from the stability she'd grown up with. She also had to deal with the heartache my father brought into her life, which affected her greatly, in ways I'll never begin to know. What I do know is that I could see the pain in her eyes when my sisters and I asked where our father was. Mom gradually became less social and seemed to embrace loneliness. She spent so much time excusing my father's poor behavior when they were together that she probably thought that's how men are supposed to be. She gave up on the possibility of meeting someone who might be different. Both she and I struggled in silence, never talking about how my father's behavior affected us.

Just as Ismat was put on this path by the absence of his biological and adoptive fathers, I was on a similar path marked by similar challenges because of *his* absence. I didn't have him there to steer me away from the negative influences I encountered growing up. This is the cyclical nature of broken families. I've inherited his struggle in my own efforts to learn about masculinity and manhood without role models at home. I also carry a deep anxiety about what this means for my future ability to be a husband and father. I imagine my father didn't set out to be a bad parent. I bet he told himself he was going to be there for his kids in all the ways he wished his father had been for him. He probably also told himself he was going to be a good man and love his wife the way she deserved. That's also what I tell myself, and I'm concerned that those good intentions won't matter.

I can look back on my life and see where Ismat's intervention or positive example might have kept me from making bad choices. For instance, as a high school student I often got into fights, mostly because I held on to a conflict-oriented view of masculinity. To be a man was to fight, I thought. In grade eleven, I was suspended following an incident in our school cafeteria. Some older students who had been trying to assert themselves as the tough guys in our school had challenged me to a fight earlier that week. I saw one of them in the cafeteria right before lunch on a day I was ready to fight and asked if he still wanted to go at it. As we were swearing at each other a crowd gathered, which tipped off a vice principal that something bad was about to happen. The crowd scattered when the vice principal showed up, leaving no one in the cafeteria except for me and a few of the guys who wanted to fight me. The vice principal tried to single me out as the problem. I didn't want to talk to him, so he suspended me.

Mom was called to the school to meet with that same vice principal. Afterward, she tried her best to speak to me about what had happened, but she could only see the issue from the school's perspective. To her, I was wrong because I was getting into fights and disregarding an authority figure. I wasn't able to get her to see my side of the story: I needed to be tough and look tough. I couldn't refuse to fight. Nor could I just be obedient to the vice principal. To me, getting suspended wasn't as bad as going to school and having people think I was weak or a snitch.

Ismat probably would have understood what I was thinking and feeling—I'd heard stories about him getting into fights when he was young, too. He wasn't around, though, so Mom was stuck trying to figure it all out on her own. It would have helped to have a role model who could show me that being a man didn't mean being like the rappers I saw on television. Without that, moments like the one in the cafeteria pushed me further toward the Hollywood gangster subculture I was already obsessed with—and later toward other groups that offered an alternative vision for who and what men could be.

Recognizing the importance of fathers doesn't dismiss the importance of mothers in the lives of young men. It's about acknowledging that male role models are important, and that their absence has consequences. The National Fatherhood Initiative (NFI), a nonprofit organization working to end fatherlessness in the United States, claims that "there is a father factor in nearly all social ills facing America today."[1] This bold statement is backed up by research showing that fatherless children are more likely to have behavioral problems, live in poverty, experience abuse or neglect, use drugs or alcohol, repeat grades in school, become teenage parents and go to prison. NFI research also shows that adolescent boys with absentee fathers are especially likely to engage in criminal and other delinquent behaviors.

A 2013 literature review by researchers from Princeton University, Cornell University and the University of California, Berkeley, also found that fatherlessness significantly impacts children. These researchers examined forty-seven studies from both Western and non-Western countries and concluded, "We find strong evidence that father absence negatively affects children's social-emotional development, particularly by increasing externalizing behavior [such as aggression and attention seeking]. These effects may be more pronounced if father absence occurs during early childhood than during middle childhood, and they may be more pronounced for boys than for girls."[2]

University of Virginia professor W. Bradford Wilcox, the co-editor of *Gender and Parenthood: Biological and Social Scientific Perspectives*, has outlined four distinct ways that involved fathers can contribute to children's lives: (1) playing with children in ways that show how to properly use your body for play and not violence, (2) encouraging children to take risks and be independent, (3) offering physical protection or the appearance of physical protection and (4) providing firm discipline.[3] Wilcox has argued that in the absence of these contributions, sons "are more vulnerable to getting swept up in the Sturm und Drang of adolescence and young adulthood, and in the worst possible way."[4]

The challenges posed by fatherlessness are growing across the West. Divorce rates and single-parent households have been on the rise for decades in Europe and North America. The United States is the clearest example of this change, with up to 50 percent of first marriages ending in divorce and subsequent marriages failing at an even higher rate.[5] Of all American children born in 2014, 40 percent were born out of wedlock.[6] And one-third of American children live without the involvement of their biological fathers.[7] Statistics Canada reports that 12.8 percent of Canadian children live in fatherless households.[8] In the United Kingdom, more than one-fifth of families with dependent children are without fathers in the home.[9] Across the European Union 16 percent of children are growing up in single-parent households headed by the mother.[10]

Jay-Z has talked about the vulnerability to outside influences that comes from growing up without a father: "We were kids without fathers, so we found our fathers on wax and on the streets and in history." He goes on to describe this search as "a gift," because he and his peers "got to pick and choose the ancestors who would inspire the world we were going to make for ourselves."[11] Searching for father figures is, to paraphrase one of Jay-Z's album subtitles, both a gift and a curse—a gift if the inspirations you choose motivate you to make positive contributions to the world, a curse if your inspirations motivate you to make negative contributions.

Jay-Z himself is an example of that gift and curse. I know young men who looked up to the Jay-Z who rapped about selling drugs and making money at all costs. I know others who looked up to the Jay-Z who became one of America's great entrepreneurs and gave back to his community as a philanthropist. Some versions of Jay-Z negatively influenced the people I grew up with by fueling their gangster fantasies and glorifying a life of crime and violence. Other versions positively influenced some of those same people by showing them how to dress professionally or inspiring them to become businessmen.

Behind all the statistics about fatherless homes are increasing numbers of young men experiencing the gift and curse of choosing who shows them how to be men. That means we have more unpredictability about and less control over the direction our boys will take as they grow into men, and we face a greater likelihood that they'll stray from the reach of mainstream morals. For young men in these circumstances, the wider community becomes increasingly important as a source of positive role models who can set an example for how to be men and also intervene when young men adopt destructive forms of masculinity.

Traditionally, two of the most important institutions providing male role models outside of the home were schools and places of worship. These institutions formally and informally connected young men to older men who could provide examples of how to live a healthy life. Today, however, these institutions are drastically losing their influence over young men and failing to keep them engaged.

The decline of religious influence in Europe and North America has been growing for decades. The BBC reports significant downward shifts in religious observance for Christians in these regions, with some researchers identifying particularly stark drops among young adults. For instance, the number of Anglicans in Britain fell from 40 percent of the population in 1983 to 17 percent in 2014.[12] The Pew Research Center reported that there were 5.6 million fewer Christians in Europe from 2010 to 2015.[13] And the population share of Christians in the United States declined by 8.2 percent from 2007 to 2014.[14] Some of my European friends have told me that the only time they go to church is for weddings and funerals. That's mostly the same for the Christians I know in North America, too.

There are typically higher observance rates among immigrant communities because religion plays a larger role in public life in many other parts of the world. Still, the trend of young adults moving away from places of worship extends to minority communities in the West when the right religious institutions are not in place.

For example, mosques in Europe often struggle to reach Muslims there because of language barriers.[15] In many mosques, religious leaders don't speak the local language and instead offer their services in Arabic, a language that young men born in Europe may not speak with fluency. Religious leaders are often educated outside of Europe, and they make use of Islamic literature created outside of the West, in places like Saudi Arabia and Turkey. This reliance on non-Western countries is partly a result of insufficient local investment in religious education in Europe. Two Muslim parents in Belgium, Ilias Marraha and Ibtisam Van Driessche, have responded to this problem by creating children's books in languages spoken in Belgium. These books are designed to introduce young people to Islam from the perspective of European Muslim authors.

Similar efforts to invest in and grow local religious education may be a critical step in countering extremism. Richard Alexander Nielsen, a professor at the Massachusetts Institute of Technology, analyzed texts from a hundred Sunni Muslim clerics and found that the presence of strong local education networks and promising job opportunities in their communities may discourage clerics from preaching radical ideas.[16] Nielsen also found that clerics in Saudi Arabia and Egypt who are desperate for followers sometimes self-radicalize to distinguish their message from that of more established authorities.

The communities built through faith networks are today less central to the lives of many people, and young people in particular, than has been the case in the past. As those sources for possible role models disappear, they leave voids that can be filled by other influences, sometimes positive and sometimes negative. British rabbi Jonathan Sacks has argued that these voids embolden radicals, who often are "the sharpest, clearest voices" reaching out to young people from a religious perspective.[17]

The disappearance of role models from homes and religious institutions is often difficult for societies to address because of how personal questions of family and faith are. In the West, however, we do hope to standardize public education to some extent, as a way of providing a minimal level of support to all young people. Schools are publicly funded places where we send our children to be educated, nurtured and encouraged. We expect teachers, guidance counselors, peers and others in our schools to set positive examples for our young men. Sad to say, schools throughout the Western world are also failing to connect with young men, diminishing their ability to serve as a source of role models.

While males make up slightly more than half of high school students in the United States, they account for only 43 percent of postsecondary students.[18] According to an analysis of US Department of Education statistics by researchers at Lehigh University in Pennsylvania, boys receive 71 percent of school suspensions and make up 67 percent of special education students; they are also five times more likely to be labeled hyperactive and 30 percent more likely to flunk or drop out of school.[19] In England, male students are 36 percent less likely to attend university than female students; the numbers are even worse in other parts of the United Kingdom.[20]

These signs of male disengagement reflect a broader trend across Europe and North America. The Organisation for Economic Co-operation and Development (OECD), an intergovernmental economic body, has described the current state of education in its member nations, which include most of the countries in Western Europe and North America, as "the reversal of the gender gap." Male students make up just 45 percent of secondary school graduates and 42 percent of bachelor's degree recipients in OECD countries.[21]

What the OECD describes as a reverse gender gap looks different from one community to the next. In the United States, for example, black men lag significantly behind black women in educational attainment, creating a gender gap more pronounced than that in white communities.[22] This reverse gender gap among black Americans has been in place for decades, long before it began showing up in broader OECD trends. In Europe's Muslim communities, however, the reverse gender gap is a more recent phenomenon. In older generations, men performed better in school than women, but in younger generations, the reverse is true—Muslim communities in Europe are now mirroring the gender gaps found in wider society.[23]

Researchers affiliated with the Equality of Opportunity Project, a collaborative effort by professors at Stanford, Brown and Harvard, have also found evidence of the reverse gender gap in US employment rates. In a 2016 paper examining population tax records for children born in the 1980s, these researchers noted, "There is robust evidence that boys who grow up in poor families in highly segregated neighborhoods—i.e., environments of concentrated poverty—have much lower employment rates than girls who grow up in the same environment."[24] As one possible explanation for this gap, the paper points to boys turning to crime as an alternative to formal employment.

It's important to note that this reverse gender gap is limited to specific issues and generations in Europe and North America. The traditional gender gap still exists in other parts of the world, where many women continue to be denied access to equal education. And in countries where the reverse gender gap does exist, such as the United States, a gap in pay after graduation still disadvantages women.[25] Additionally, the reverse gender gap does not apply to all school subjects and professional fields. Women continue to be underrepresented in areas like math and science.[26]

If mainstream institutions aren't able to provide role models and examples of masculinity, young men will increasingly look to alternative sources for that support. Instead of attending classes or doing homework, young men are spending their time on the streets, on the internet and with their peers (who are also more likely to be disengaged from school). Young men who do have male role models, like fathers at home, are growing up alongside those who don't, and their peer groups are being shaped by these trends, making this a problem with a far greater reach than any statistic can capture.

2

New Arrivals

■ ■ ■ ■

I grew up in a mostly immigrant neighborhood near a modest shopping mall in Brampton, Ontario. Brampton started out as a small suburb northwest of Toronto, and between the early 1990s and the early 2010s grew from around 200,000 people to almost 600,000. This population growth was initially driven by waves of immigrants and new Canadians who couldn't afford to live within the city limits. These people were drawn to places like Brampton, where homes were affordable for families of more modest economic means.

Most of my neighbors were from two of Canada's biggest minority groups: black Canadians (2.9 percent of the country's population in 2011) and Sikh Canadians (1.4 percent).[1] Sikh and black communities in Canada have similar histories of fighting exclusion. Sikh activists have been at the center of some of the country's most important court decisions on matters of equality, while black activists have been the face of many political and cultural battles.

In 1989, when my family first moved to the area, the neighborhood was a mix of black, Sikh, and white families. As I got older, the white families moved away, and most of their homes were purchased by Sikhs, who wanted to live close to the nearby gurdwara, a Sikh place of worship. By the late 1990s, about ten years after we moved to Brampton, there were fewer than five white students in my grade at school. Most students were Sikh or of Caribbean background.

In our neighborhood, we all had to figure out what our identity would be in a new and rapidly changing environment. There was great diversity in our journeys, and in where we found a sense of belonging.

Most of my closest friends were black with Jamaican or Trinidadian parents. A preexisting black identity awaited us before our parents even immigrated to Canada. This identity was communicated to us through American media, which offered messages about what it meant to be a black person in the West. The dominant message we received came through rap songs and music videos, which introduced us to a captivating Hollywood gangster subculture.

Harvard University sociologist Orlando Patterson has called this subculture part of "the Dionysian trap for young black men"—a trap that includes "hanging out on the street after school, shopping and dressing sharply, sexual conquests, party drugs, hip-hop music and culture, the fact that almost all the superstar athletes and a great many of the nation's best entertainers were black."[2] I got into this trap not because I was poor or lived in a violent neighborhood but because it was there, and I wanted to fit in with friends who were in the trap, too.

This subculture took hold in my peer group once we entered

middle school in the late 1990s. One day, a group of us were walking home from school and talking about a new DMX music video from the album *Flesh of My Flesh, Blood of My Blood*. The most popular guy in my school, Rich, talked about how great it was, and how DMX was the "realest" rapper because his music videos were not about dancing. Most of us had seen the new video and agreed with everything the popular guy had to say. Some of us pretended we had seen it because we wanted to look cool. On the strength of Rich's recommendation, DMX became the standard for what type of hip-hop we gravitated to. A diverse group of rappers was pushed aside and a very narrow group—the gangsters, drug dealers, tough guys and gun-toters—remained.

Of all the types of rap music we had to choose from, it's difficult to say why we chose gangster rap, which is particularly aggressive and violent. I think we liked it so much partly because it reflected a certain anger that we had within us. We were angry because we didn't have fathers around, because our families didn't have the money we wanted and because life at home was unstable and unpleasant. I was angry for some of those reasons. Gangster rap was also some of the most dynamic and interesting music we listened to. It tapped into the rebellious, anti-authority inclinations that a lot of young people have. And we didn't have any role models to steer us away from it.

There were also economic forces that made it more likely we would find ourselves consuming and being consumed by this Hollywood gangster subculture. DMX was one of the most popular rappers in the world for much of my childhood. His music was actively marketed to people like me. Hip-hop as a whole was becoming increasingly focused on crime, drugs, violence and other gangster activities. Akilah Folami, a law professor at Hofstra University on Long Island, attributed this broader shift to changes in American telecommunications law. "The Telecommunications Act of 1996 has led to the development of huge corporate media conglomerations in radio that in turn control the radio airwaves and its content," she wrote. "The Act has made it virtually impossible for alternative voices in rap . . . to be heard on the radio, since corporate conglomerates are less concerned with diversity in ideas [than] in meeting market-created consumer demand for such lyrics."[3]

My friends and I were not just passive consumers who would mimic anything that was popular on the radio. On the other hand, we were children and had to make do with the cultural products available to us. As fewer people decided which rap songs would be promoted, the music that reached me and my friends was gradually narrowed down to just a few styles and messages. This trend was represented by DMX for me but could be associated with a range of other artists, too. Young Canadians consume a significant amount of American television and online content, as well as Canadian artists making music in the United States, such as Drake, Justin Bieber and The Weeknd. Thus, changes in American music influence Canadians, as they do many others in even more distant places, because of the broad influence of American culture.

There was a clear correlation—I'd go so far as to say a causation—between the intensity of our consumption of rap music and the behavioral changes among those in my peer group. Fighting became more frequent at my school. We adopted aspects of gang culture, including bandannas and rapper-inspired nicknames.

We even gave gang names to our friend groups. Using slang from West Coast hip-hop, we routinely began talking about marijuana. Some of us began smoking it and talking about getting it from drug dealers. We would hang out and loiter, with nothing to do but share gangster fairy tales. It became normal to speak about women in disrespectful language and to pursue sexual relationships with our female classmates as sport. For kids who didn't have much money, we became oddly obsessed with expensive clothes, particularly the kind you'd see on rappers and basketball players.

Rich led the way in the changes we all went through. He was a year older than the rest of us because he'd been made to repeat a grade after moving to Canada from Jamaica. Rich was also bigger and stronger. I knew him well, and although he was feared because of his great fighting skills, he was one of the nicest and most thoughtful friends I had. In private, he was like any other kid who wanted to have fun playing video games or sports. He liked to come over to my house and use the inflatable swimming pool in my backyard. Rich was also very kind and respectful to my mom. At school, though, he seemed to be trapped by the expectations of those who viewed him as a tough guy. He was constantly trying to mimic what we saw from rappers, and he set a certain tone that the rest of us would follow. Every time he got into a fight and won, his reputation would grow, and people would want to be more like him. By eighth grade, Rich was skipping school regularly and had found a part-time job at a nearby grocery store. He was making money while we suckers sat in a classroom all day.

Every young person goes through the process of learning what passes for cool in his social circle and struggling to fit in or risk becoming a social outcast. My friend group wasn't unique in that respect. Unfortunately, the things we decided were cool were also harmful and made it more likely that we'd hurt ourselves or others.

My best friend at the beginning of middle school, Pavan, had experiences both different from and similar to mine. He lived a few blocks away from me, and we often walked home from school together. He was from a devout Sikh family, and he proudly wore the turban and the kara (steel or iron bracelet) as symbols of his faith. The cultural differences between us weren't noticeable to me at first, but gradually I realized that he had a bond with some of our Sikh classmates that I couldn't relate to. We'd leave school on a Friday afternoon, and on Monday Pavan would be full of stories about what he did on the weekend with our classmates. I learned that he and the other Sikh kids in my class often knew one another's parents and siblings through the gurdwara or from other activities. In addition to sharing a religion and a language, my Sikh classmates also shared a mutual respect and appreciation. When we teased, as kids do, Pavan and his friends from the gurdwara were easier on each other than they were on the rest of us.

I didn't have a faith community or family network like Pavan's—nor did a lot of the black youth in the area. There was no nearby church of any denomination for us to go to, which meant we didn't have a common institution or shared traditions to bind us together. Many of us also lacked a close relationship with our fathers. Our smaller family networks meant that we didn't have the same role models to provide mentorship and guidance. We were stuck on our own—especially as young men, because it was often older men who were the missing links in our families.

Our different circumstances meant that Pavan and I faced different challenges in forging an identity for ourselves in Canada. Pavan had to figure out how to combine his new surroundings with the way of life passed down from his parents. Many people perceived him to be from another country because he visibly carried traditions from other parts of the world, such as his turban. He had to create space for himself in a country that didn't seem to understand him very well.

Pavan and his parents saw so few people who looked like them on North American television that they bought a satellite dish so they could find relatable entertainment on Indian channels. On the rare occasions when Pavan did see Indian people on North American television, they were portrayed in negative or stereotypical ways—as taxi drivers, for example, or store clerks like Apu from *The Simpsons*. Even worse, Canadian media outlets often connected the Sikh community to terrorism. When we were growing up, Sikh terrorism was a topic of discussion in Canada because of the 1985 Air India bombing, which killed 329 people, including 268 Canadians. It was the deadliest terror attack on or by an airplane before 9/11.

Nav Bhatia, the famous "superfan" of the Toronto Raptors basketball team, has talked openly about how one-dimensional representations of Sikhs in North American media have affected him, even though he's a highly successful entrepreneur. "I went [to a store] to fix my cellphone," he told the *Toronto Star*, "and this Caucasian guy, I overheard him saying, 'Honey, I have to go, my cab is here.' I guess he assumed I was a taxi driver, because I wear a turban and I have a beard."[4] Another well-known Sikh Canadian, the former amateur boxing champion Pardeep Singh Nagra, has expressed exasperation at the ongoing struggle to find a place in Canada. "At what point do I get freed and get to be seen as Canadian? . . . As long as I am not seen as a Canadian, my existence here offends people because of what I choose to wear."[5]

For me and other black youth in my neighborhood, the challenge wasn't really to create a space for ourselves in the West, but to contend with the politics and struggles attached to the black identity that absorbed us upon arrival.

To understand this distinction between Pavan's search for identity and mine, it helps to look at the use of the derogatory term "fob," short for "fresh off the boat." "Fob" is used in a variety of ways, but in the Toronto area, it most commonly refers to people who are brand-new to Canada. My Sikh friends used this term to describe new students from India. They also used it to make jokes about each other when they did things that weren't perceived as "Canadian," like pronouncing words with a heavy Indian accent (for example, saying v's like w's). I've also heard the term used in other Asian communities in the Toronto area, like the Chinese community in Scarborough.

I can't recall ever hearing the term "fob" used by my black friends. We never even thought about people being less Canadian because they'd just arrived from another country. Rich, for instance, influenced what many of us believed black Canadians should be like, and he had recently arrived in Brampton from Jamaica. If someone was black and in our neighborhood, he or she was black the same way we all were.

Despite the differences between us, a lot of my Sikh classmates were similarly drawn to hip-hop. The lack of Indians or Sikhs in pop culture left my Sikh friends searching for people to identify with. Rappers were easier for them to relate to than rockers, I suppose, because most rappers also had brown skin and talked about the struggles of minority groups. We all consumed the same media, enjoyed the same music and dressed in similar clothes. Hip-hop influenced what we all thought was cool.

Some of us were able to draw a distinction between our own lives and what we saw in music videos. Others of us weren't. With Pavan, I always sensed that hip-hop was part of who he was, but not everything he was. He wore baggy jeans and ostensibly glorified gangsters, but he was also influenced by a family network, the gurdwara and Indian culture. Pavan was not all in. Many of the other guys—including me—were, though. We saw no distinction between us and the rappers we idolized. Hip-hop was all we had. We didn't do our homework and our grades were mostly bad, and that was because we were focused on trying to be like rappers or basketball players instead of students.

American writer Thomas Chatterton Williams observed in his own life that some of his peers were able to distinguish themselves from rappers and others were not. In his school, this distinction was along racial lines. "We [black youth] tended to approach hip-hop seriously and earnestly," he explained, "striving to 'keep it real' and viewing a lifestyle governed by hip-hop values as some kind of prerequisite to an authentically black existence. Non-blacks were better able to embrace hip-hop with a healthy sense of irony."[6]

In Brampton, however, it was less about race and more about faith and family. The Sikhs in my neighborhood who didn't engage with their faith community or family networks, for instance, were more likely to fall into the Hollywood gangster traps that also caught many local black youth. The same is true in other parts of

Canada, such as British Columbia, where Sikh and black youth have been caught up in neighborhood gang wars.[7]

I asked a former classmate, Rajpal, what he thought of my observations about Sikh and black communities. Rajpal grew up not far from me and is just a few years older than I am. We met in community college but hadn't spoken in nearly a decade. After I explained to him what I recalled from growing up in Brampton, Rajpal asked me, "You know I went to prison, too, right?"

I hadn't had any idea.

"Yeah," he confirmed. "Before we met, I was in prison. I was into the wrong things, listening to the same music you're talking about."

I asked, "Why do you think you were able to change your life around?"

Rajpal credited his Sikh faith, which motivated him to go back to school, build a satisfying career and start a family. He said his transformation wasn't necessarily about religion, but rather about the identity his faith gave him. "I can relate to my Sikh gurus through image, identity and geographic location," he explained. "Above and past religion, I think it has to do with a sense of identity."

At one time, my mom was probably concerned that I'd end up in prison, too. In middle school, she'd seen my attitude change. In response, she'd encouraged me to change school districts for high school. I was initially hesitant about moving, but ultimately agreed it would be good to be in a new environment. Rich and some other friends would be moving on to a different high school anyway, because they were going to Catholic school.

With my mom's support, I transferred to a high school in Mississauga, another part of the Toronto area; I enrolled by applying to a magnet program that brings together students from different neighborhoods. This specific magnet program focused on business and technology. My bus ride went from ten minutes to over an hour. The biggest difference, however, was the change in student demographics. My new school had very few black students. Most were white or of South Asian or East Asian backgrounds.

The change in environment could have helped by connecting me with new friends, but instead I gravitated to people who were most like those I lived with in Brampton. Some of my white classmates—especially those who lived around the school and weren't in the magnet program—were heavily influenced by hiphop. These guys also thought the idea of fighting and selling drugs was cool. Like my friends in Brampton, though, most of them didn't actually fight or sell drugs. They were from working-class families, and we related to each other through our shared ambition to make money and change our economic circumstances. We skipped school together to watch gangster movies and then fantasized about launching our own criminal enterprises someday. The truth is, I spent most of my time in high school contemplating various criminal activities. Many of my friends, old and new, were connected to people who sold drugs, so I was always at most one degree removed from the drug trade. I tried to build a reputation as somebody who was strong and fearsome, somebody who could fit in with gangsters. In my backpack, I carried a police-style baton and a hunting knife so I could protect myself in fights and also intimidate people older and bigger than I was. I also kept an old Louisville Slugger wooden baseball bat in my locker. If I suspected a fight might break out at school, I would hide the baseball bat in the baggiest pair of jeans I owned and walk around with a limp. All these things made me feel cool. My friends and the older guys we knew seemed impressed by this behavior, so I kept it up. I felt as if I was investing in the future—as if this might turn into a career one day.

Looking back on those years, I'm aware of how constrained my imagination was and how few paths I saw in front of me. I had blinders on, with no idea of just how much I didn't know. I wasn't materially poor, but I was poor in imagination. To get a clear sense of what that poverty of imagination looks like, consider an example from my first semester in high school. In drama class, we were asked to talk about an actor we admired. I mostly watched gangster movies at that time, so I decided to do my presentation about the 1991 movie *Boyz n the Hood* and the lead actor in that film, Cuba Gooding Jr.

Our drama teacher asked us to play our favorite scene on the classroom TV as part of the presentation. I chose a scene featuring Gooding's character, Tre, speaking with Ice Cube's character, Doughboy. Doughboy's brother, who is also Tre's best friend, has just been killed, and Doughboy's comments project a bleak, pessimistic and sad future for the young men in the movie. Doughboy acknowledges the self-destruction in how he lives his life, saying: "Next thing you know somebody might try to smoke me. Don't matter, though. We all gotta go sometime, hm?"

At fourteen, I didn't know anyone who had been shot. I had seen a gun, but I'd never touched one. I had also never lost a close friend to gun violence. In the depths of the Dionysian trap, though, I really identified with Doughboy's view of the future. Being in the "hood" as portrayed in Hollywood movies was my mentality. I felt that I was destined to suffer in a world that didn't care about me. I simply didn't know any other way to exist.

3

Crisis of Distrust

■ ■ ■ ■ ▬▬▬▬▬▬▬▬▬▬▬▬▬▬▬▬▬▬▬▬▬▬

Growing up, I saw police officers as henchmen of the status quo seeking to keep me and people I cared about down. That's the feeling that every negative interaction with a police officer left me with. And this feeling was not unique to me. I saw it in the people around me, too.

My first contact with a cop occurred when I was eight. I was in the car with both of my parents and my younger sisters—a rare moment when we were all together. We were on our way back home from somewhere (I can't remember where), and we got into a minor car accident. The police arrived and walked my father to the side of the road. I couldn't hear them, but I could see them clearly from the backseat of the car. I remember the officers getting in his face. My father looked small standing in front of them. It looked like they were yelling at him. The officers then pointed to the curb, and my father sat down. It was shocking to see the man

I looked to as a primary authority figure controlled by police officers right in front of me. I can only imagine how humiliating it must have been for him to be treated that way in front of his kids.

One of the officers turned his attention to me. I was sitting in the back of the parked car, facing the outside, with my legs dangling out the open door. The officer clearly wasn't happy with the answers my father had given and asked me questions to see if my memory of the accident was the same. Although I was just a child, he was in my face, being aggressive. He told me that my father might go to jail. I was scared. I don't know what I said to him, but I wished he would leave me alone. I can recall his flashlight in my eyes, his intimidating dark uniform and his hat, which made it hard for me to see his face.

This entire incident could have involved people of any race. Racism might have had nothing to do with the officers' attitude. But this was the first time I believed I was witnessing racism in action. At this early point in my life, I was already associating aggressive policing with racism. Television footage of Los Angeles police officers beating up Rodney King stuck with me and influenced how I saw the world, as did the music I listened to, which passionately denounced the actions of the police. Another factor influencing my perception of the officers' behavior was that I saw any unfairness toward my father as racism. Growing up, I believed racism was the reason my father had no family. After his adoptive parents passed away and he was effectively re-orphaned at the age of fourteen, the aunts and uncles from his adoptive family did not embrace him. From what my father told me as a kid, he was rejected because he was a black African and his adoptive family of Ismaili Indians didn't see him as one of their own. I thought cops were motivated by the same bias.

I had more interactions with police officers and security guards as an adolescent—waiting for the bus, walking home from school and hanging out at the mall. Sometimes they stopped me to ask questions; other times they looked at me with suspicion or intimidation in their eyes. I attributed their behavior to racism. I saw whom they stopped and whom they didn't. The way I dressed—mostly in the baggy pants and hoodies associated with hip-hop—seemed to be one of the biggest factors separating me from other people.

It made me angry. Really angry. What started as fear for my father's safety grew into resentment. With every suspicious look cast or question asked, I became more and more resentful of the world around me. Everyone in uniform, even bus drivers, made me anxious and uncomfortable, as if they were part of some conspiracy to make me feel unaccepted in my own country.

Growing up this way—believing police authority is morally corrupt—isn't a problem just for me. It's a problem for my country, too. The international community considers credible law enforcement critical to a country's stability and economy and to the quality of life of its citizens. The World Bank lists "rule of law" and "control of corruption" as two of six indicators used to assess the quality of a nation's governance, which the bank defines as "the traditions and institutions by which authority in a country is exercised."[1] Western nations are considered the global standard for rule of law and control of corruption; they dominate the top twenty countries listed in the World Justice Project's annual Rule of Law Index, as well as Transparency International's yearly Corruption Perceptions Index.[2] These indices gloss over vastly different perceptions of and experiences with law enforcement in the West, though. Some communities in Europe and North America feel that there's not much distinction between the countries at the top of these lists and those at the bottom.

Consider my father's home country, Kenya, for instance. Kenya is ranked 100th out of 113 countries on the 2016 Rule of Law Index, and 139th out of 167 on the 2016 Corruption Perceptions Index.[3] On paper and in practice, Kenyan law enforcement is very different from that in Western countries. The way Kenyan police have responded to terrorism and violent crime illustrates this difference. Following attacks by the Somali terrorist organization Al-Shabaab—such as the killing of 67 people at the Westgate shopping mall in Nairobi on September 21, 2013, and the massacre of 148 people at Kenya's Garissa University College on April 2, 2015—Kenyan police have reportedly killed more than 500 terrorism suspects (emphasis on "suspects"), in addition to arresting and deporting thousands, most of whom are Somali.[4]

Despite these striking differences, profiling in minority communities in Kenya and the West similarly undermines police authority. Mohamed Ali Nur, the former Somali ambassador to Kenya, referred to local police practices as "profiling" and explained that Somalis in Kenya "get frustrated . . . every night and every day being stopped."[5] During his 2015 visit to Kenya, US president Barack Obama raised this issue with Kenyan president Uhuru Kenyatta. "If you paint any particular community with too broad a brush," Obama warned, "if in reaction to terrorism you are restricting legitimate organizations, reducing the scope of peaceful organization, then that can have the inadvertent effect of actually increasing the pool of recruits for terrorism and resentment in communities that feel marginalized."[6]

These comments could easily apply to communities in the

West that are frequent targets of police profiling. George Soros's Open Society Foundations report that since the 9/11 attacks on New York City, policing in Europe has been marked by "serious concerns about increased ethnic profiling in the exercise of police powers" and the "express assumption that organized crime groups are ethnically based."[7] Police profiling of Muslims similarly increased following more recent terrorist attacks in Europe.[8] Further, in London, the Metropolitan Police Service has been deemed "institutionally racist" by its own Metropolitan Black Police Association, which represents minority officers in the city.[9]

North American cities have also adopted practices widely criticized for unfairly targeting minorities, like stop-and-frisk in New York City and street checks, or carding, in Toronto—both of which potentially encourage officers to stop people whom they deem suspicious. In New York from 2003 to 2016, an average of 85 percent of those stopped and frisked were either black or Hispanic.[10] In Toronto, data collected from street checks between 2007 and 2013 indicated that between 23 and 28 percent of those stopped were black, which is more than three times the proportion of the city's black population.[11]

My own experience of profiling made me feel disrespected, so I wanted to disrespect cops in return. I had a confrontational attitude toward police officers, as I did toward all other authority figures. I'd roll my eyes when they tried to talk to me, speak disrespectfully and generally convey hostility with my body language by crossing my arms or refusing to make eye contact. *You don't care about me? I don't care about you, either.*

I was particularly unpleasant to one young would-be police officer who seemed like he was trying to be a good guy. He was a white security guard in his midtwenties at the Square One Bus Terminal in Mississauga. I passed through that bus terminal daily and would see him a few times a week. He tried to befriend me and my classmates, and told us about his plans to become a cop. He had completed the training, he said, and was waiting to be hired by one of the local departments. Some of my friends took a liking to him and would chat with him when we passed through the bus terminal. I refused. I looked at him like he was an enemy. When he made jokes, I didn't laugh. When he said hello, I looked in the other direction. When he tried to make conversation, I asked him if he had a problem.

I wonder if he ever did become a cop. And if he did, I wonder if the way I treated him when he was a security guard made him less likely to be a nice guy as an officer.

Years later, I asked Steve, a Toronto police officer who is a few years older than I am, about how these kinds of interactions made him feel when he was starting out on the job. Steve's law enforcement career began in low-income neighborhoods, and he and his fellow officers encountered a lot of resentment. He didn't grow up seeing negative police interactions, so when he ran into kids who felt the way I felt, it was an eye-opening experience. He said people in those neighborhoods saw police as "some entity that exists different from them," and they believed "[cops] operate for our own reasons and we don't care about them."

I also asked Steve what he wished those kids could understand about a young officer like him. He replied, "We're just people at the end of the day. We're people just like everybody else, doing a particular job that can be difficult, and you probably only encounter us in difficult situations. Like, why bother? If we hate each other, it's just going to be worse for everybody." As Steve's comments show, the negativity takes its toll on young men wearing badges, too.

The incident that has focused a lot of negative attention on police in North America since 2014—the killing of eighteen-year-old Michael Brown in Ferguson, Missouri—also shows the two sides to this problem. Ferguson police officer Darren Wilson, who was twenty-eight on the day he shot Brown, described the neighborhood where he and Brown crossed paths as a "hostile environment" in his grand jury testimony about the killing. Wilson also went on to say that the neighborhood "is just not a very well-liked community," that the "community doesn't like the police" and that it's "not an area where you can take anything really lightly."[12]

Evidently, Wilson didn't see himself as part of the community he served. He approached young men like Brown as if they were enemies, just as my friends and I had approached police officers as enemies. Of course, Wilson was being paid to work through those differences. He also carried a gun while he addressed his own discomfort and frustrations, which might have contributed to Brown's death.

Both sides of these interactions illustrate the perils of ineffective law enforcement. Where there is immense distrust and an inability to communicate, cops aren't going to have the credibility they need to solve or deter crimes. These are exactly the conditions necessary for criminal groups to thrive. I was a young person who needed good police officers in my life, to give me a sense of order and help me avoid criminal influences. Tragically, communities full of young men who most need the positive influence of cops are also those that attract the most negative attention.

Reading this might cause you to wonder how I reconciled my

impression of police as unfair to me and my friends with the reality that we glorified criminals. We wanted to be gangsters, yet we were mad at the police for treating us like gangsters. Many of the times I was stopped by police or looked at suspiciously, I was on my way to or from hanging out with people the police should have been paying attention to. Maybe they should have been paying attention to me, too. This might seem hypocritical, but even when we did things that were wrong, we still regarded the police as corrupt. We thought the police were scapegoating us while turning their attention away from bigger criminals.

There's a scene in the movie *New Jack City* that shows how the police can seem as immoral as or more immoral than criminals. Wesley Snipes's character, Nino Brown, a Harlem drug kingpin, is on the witness stand in a trial. With a certain righteous indignation, he explains that he is just a small player in a bigger, more corrupt system. "Let's kick the ballistics here," he says. "Ain't no Uzis made in Harlem. Not one of us in here owns a poppy field. This thing is bigger than Nino Brown. This is big business. This is the American way."

There are also many people in high-crime areas who don't stand in solidarity with criminals or look at them as role models but still resent the police. They don't like those who are creating chaos in their communities and perpetuating harmful stereotypes, but if a crime occurs, they aren't necessarily cooperative with law enforcement, either.

Harlem rapper Immortal Technique discussed the relative moral standing of police when he was asked about the Stop Snitching movement, an effort to pressure black and Hispanic Americans to refrain from cooperating with authorities when they have information about crimes. "I hear a lot of criticism about it; [that] it destroys the community, that it creates distrust and prevents crimes from being solved. People lead by example, though. . . . We should start a 'Start Snitching' campaign for the government to come to terms with what they've done to us before we point the finger at another brother."[13] Others, less deliberate than Technique, simply don't want to talk to the police because they don't trust what officers will do with the information, or they fear that cooperating will put them in harm's way.

The tension I experienced with police officers was oddly reassuring to me. Seeing my father's humiliation and learning about the treatment of black men by officers in other cities made being racially profiled feel like a disturbing rite of passage. A man is supposed to be hated by the police and vice versa, I thought. It meant I was growing up the way I was supposed to.

In 2014, I was part of a team that made a documentary film, *Crisis of Distrust*, about police–community interactions in Toronto. In the process of making this film, we met dozens of people who believed they or their loved ones had been profiled by Toronto police. These conversations further educated me on the ways negative police interactions can be a rite of passage into manhood. At some point, it became clear to me that these stories about police profiling were also coming-of-age stories.

One of the young men interviewed—we called him Matt in the film—did an excellent job of showing how profiling can influence a young man's perceptions of himself and the world. He gave us an account of being stopped by police on his way home from playing basketball. "Now here we are, gettin' harassed again," he recalled. "Cops are behind us, driving slow. Now they pull up to the side of us. Hop out the car. 'Where are you guys going? Where you guys from?' 'I live here. This is where I live.' Apparently, something [had] happened ten minutes' drive away and we fit the profile, so now where are we from? Where are we going? Who are we? And it should be disturbing. In the eyes of somebody watching on the outside, it's disturbing. 'Look at how the police treat these guys. Look what they go through, and I can't believe they're living like this.' But in our eyes, it's normal."

"Normal" is the key word. When you see tension with law enforcement as normal, you internalize it as part of who you are and who you expect to be.

Later on in his interview, Matt articulated the kind of self-defeating attitude that can take hold when you think your country is designed to work against you. "This is how life is. This is how it's supposed to be. Why? I don't know. Just the way life is. This is the mind-set of a person growing up having to deal with police harassment, police brutality, and used to having their rights abused."

It was weird to hear this kind of passivity and fatalism from Matt. We had met him in a program for youth involved in the criminal justice system. I don't know his background, but the program he was in seeks to prevent youth violence and typically recruits kids who have been involved with street gangs. He was in that program to change his life, and he exhibited a certain confidence and determination to better himself by going to school and starting a career. But the optimism he showed in parts of our conversation went away altogether when he started talking about the police. He sounded less sure that he could make the changes he wanted to make.

Matt had competing voices in his head. His faith that his efforts in school and work would reap benefits was still fragile and sometimes gave way to his belief that his country was designed to keep him down.

W. E. B. Du Bois, the twentieth-century US civil rights icon, described the competing voices in his head as creating a "double consciousness." He felt both American and un-American, torn between his nationality and experiences that made him feel rejected by his country. Du Bois, who lived for nearly a century, from 1868 to 1963, associated his rejection with his race. He described himself as "an American, a Negro; two souls, two thoughts, two unreconciled strivings; two warring ideals in one dark body."[14]

Du Bois was successful by any measure: the first black person to earn a doctorate from Harvard University, a celebrated author and the co-founder of the NAACP. Yet he still felt he was being alienated from the only country he knew because of the negativity that ate away at his identity. He felt as though the world looked at him with "contempt and pity"—and as un-American—because of his race.[15]

Like most of the experiences discussed in this book up to this point, the double consciousness that Du Bois wrote about isn't limited to any individual racial or religious group. People's perceptions about their acceptance by both authority figures and ordinary citizens influence how they will participate in their own country. How they respond to those perceptions also matters.

Yale Law School professor Tom R. Tyler has conducted extensive research on how negative perceptions of law enforcement can influence a person's participation in wider society. "Research on this broader engagement suggests that people in minority groups are more willing to engage in groups when they experience those groups and their authorities as acting using fair procedures," Tyler noted. "Hence, more broadly, organizations that are characterized by procedural fairness are better able to encourage the engagement of minority group members in themselves."[16] In other words, a lack of fairness in policing can significantly influence how a person sees fairness elsewhere in his society, including in school or at work.

Harvard University economist Roland G. Fryer Jr. has also made some important observations about the influence of negative police interactions. Following a series of high-profile police shootings of black men, Fryer conducted a study on the use of force in Texas, Florida and California. The main finding of the study, which Fryer described as "the most surprising result of [his] career," was that police shootings were not influenced by racial bias, but racial bias was evident in non-lethal uses of force, such as touching, handcuffing, pushing and pepper-spraying. Drawing from these data, Fryer described the broader view of a corrupt world that begins with negative police interactions. "It is hard to believe that the world is your oyster if the police can rough you up without punishment," he told the *New York Times*. "And when I talked to minority youth, almost every single one of them mentions lower-level uses of force as the reason why they believe the world is corrupt."[17]

These observations are focused on minority communities, but cynicism about police authority is far more widespread because of the public attention given to police-involved controversies. Videos of police shootings or other uses of force routinely go viral and become lightning rods for people who are frustrated with cops. Every social media sharing of perceived police misconduct helps members of the public see officers as a reflection of a moral rot in government that can afflict us all.

4

Capacity to Aspire

■ ■ ■ ■ ▬▬▬▬▬▬▬▬▬▬▬▬▬▬▬▬▬

My hopes and dreams weren't captured by the institutions that were supposed to guide me to a positive life. And I was desperate to find an alternative way to live. Every hour that I was supposed to spend doing homework and studying for tests was instead going toward finding a way out of the rigged system I was born into.

The moment I was deemed "illiterate" in tenth grade for failing a literacy test best represents the rejection I felt as a kid. Those test results reflected how little I cared about school. I gave zero effort to anything that happened in the classroom. But I did care when I was singled out among my peers for not being able to read and write. It was painful. English was the only language I knew. Being told I couldn't read or write in the language I relied on to think, dream, hope and pray made me feel like garbage.

I had to take the test again the following year; I contemplated dropping out of school altogether, just to avoid the embarrassment of exposing myself as somebody who was illiterate. But my mom, with tears in her eyes, pleaded with me to finish high school. It was hard for me to say no to her. I promised her I would get my diploma, hoping that eventually I'd find my way to a place where school didn't matter. Unfortunately for me, I needed to pass that literacy test in order to graduate. I did pass the test the second time. And could, in fact, read the letter stating as much. But the painful feeling of being labeled as illiterate stuck with me.

In response to feeling rejected by my school, I rejected the world around me. I gave up on learning, having a peaceful family life or feeling like I would ever belong in my own country. My moral compass was skewed by antisocial influences. I identified with the young men my country pointed fingers at: the gangsters, criminals, bad guys and outlaws. They were rejects like me. We were part of the same tribe.

Seeing my friend Lucas's name in a local Crime Stoppers press release was the first time I remember being conscious of how far I had strayed from mainstream values. It was 2007. I was nineteen years old and Lucas was a few years older. The press release asked for witnesses and potential victims to come forward. The way Lucas was described was jarring. I remember words like "violent" and "dangerous." And I remember feeling concerned that my friend was being presented to the world as an animal.

Lucas's problems with the justice system weren't new. I'd known him for four years, and in that time he had done several short stints in jail for fights or other troubles. Like me, Lucas grew up in the Toronto area. His parents were West African, but he and

I were both immersed in that Hollywood gangster subculture. I considered him the realest dude I knew, because he was living the kind of life that I fantasized about when listening to rap music or watching gangster movies. He was free, I thought, because he did what he wanted to do and didn't seem to care about the consequences.

I looked up to him, and I never thought of him as doing anything wrong. Lucas's family and girlfriends were often angry with him when he got into trouble, but I viewed him only as a loyal friend who offered me a place to stay when I needed one or gave me a few bucks here and there when I was short on cash. He was kind and caring to me and many others in his life. Lucas was also a very hard worker and refused to take a handout from anybody, even when it would have been easy to collect a welfare check he didn't need. The Crime Stoppers press release was the first time I realized how people who weren't one of "us" might see him.

I met Lucas in the summer before I started high school. He briefly worked with my father at a restaurant downtown, and my father had introduced us in what felt like an attempt to pass me on to Lucas so I had somebody looking out for me in my father's absence. The age difference between us meant that Lucas was more like a big brother than a friend. Throughout high school, I would frequently take the subway to visit him on the east side of Toronto or downtown. He'd tell me stories about what was going on in his life: fighting, getting girls, making money, being fearless. The hip-hop head in me loved hearing a good story.

One trip to the Eaton Centre shopping mall stands out as the day I became convinced that Lucas was the coolest guy I knew. I was fifteen or sixteen at the time. We took the subway to the mall, as we often did. Lucas had a wad of cash on him that day, and he could have bought nearly anything in the mall. He dressed like Allen Iverson—clothes two sizes too big and a do-rag under his fitted baseball cap. He approached the best-looking women at the mall to ask for their phone numbers with absolute confidence. At one point, two much bigger guys bumped into us while walking by, as if to signal that we were in *their* mall. (The Eaton Centre area was home to many such incidents—including a fatal shooting in 2005—partly because the mall is situated between Alexandra Park and Regent Park, two neighborhoods known at the time for gang activity.) Lucas turned around and got in the guys' faces, asking, "You have a problem?" He offered to fight them both right there, right then. The two backed away yelling, trying to appear tough while declining Lucas's offer to trade punches.

In the years that preceded the Crime Stoppers alert about Lucas, my life had started to change, which is why the press release was so unsettling. Toward the end of eleventh grade, two years earlier, I began to think about high school coming to an end. A sense of urgency overcame me, and I was determined to embark on the criminal lifestyle I had long fantasized about. I was worried that my bluff would be called if I graduated with no plan to back up all my tough talk and lofty ambitions. Buying a gun seemed like a good way to show my friends how committed I was to doing the things we had been talking about for years. Maybe that would motivate them to feel the same sense of urgency I had.

I went to one of my closest friends at school and asked him to locate a gun for me. A few days later he confirmed he could get one, quoted me a price and told me that I'd need to make sure I was serious, since it would take some work from his friends to get it. I told him that I'd get back to him. That day, I went home from school and cried.

I'm not sure why I cried (although crying wasn't rare for me in those days). But I was scared. I knew I was about to cross a line that would be very difficult to return from. I was close to trapping myself in a life that would make owning a gun normal. It was a decision that would have justified the way the police already treated me and people who looked like me. It would also have betrayed my mom's trust. It might have caused her to lose faith in me altogether, and she was the only good thing in my life.

The gun never came up in conversation with my friend again. I assume he forgot about it. Maybe he didn't really want to help me get one in the first place. Or possibly he knew how bad a decision it would be for me to cross that line and was relieved I never asked him about it a second time.

At that point, I abruptly stopped talking to most of my friends. I couldn't face them because I felt that I had exposed myself as a fake, a wannabe. I also just wasn't sure what to do with myself anymore; I was a person without a purpose.

School was the only thing I had left, so I put my energy into my classes for the first time. To graduate on schedule, I needed to take day and night school classes. I was also working as a dishwasher part-time. It was difficult managing all these responsibilities, but I did it, and I made plans to attend community college the following year, taking part in a transition program for students who wanted to qualify for a bachelor's degree program but didn't have the grades or the requisite classes.

Lucas was the only person I stayed in touch with that year. He didn't judge me and instead encouraged me to finish school. I think he genuinely wanted me to have a positive life, which included having a career. We talked a lot throughout my single year of community college and continued talking when I later transitioned to a university to pursue a bachelor's degree as well. I even stayed at his apartment for a big part of that time.

I was studying for final exams at the end of my freshman year in university when Lucas called me from jail to tell me he was facing serious charges. Initially, this situation didn't strike me as any different from his previous arrests. Then I read the Crime Stoppers press release.

Lucas spent about six weeks in jail before the charges against him were ultimately dropped. He called me a few times a week while he was inside. Our conversations got a bit tense when I tried to talk to him about changing his life and going to school like I was, or at least trying to get a stable job. To me, I was returning the positive encouragement he'd given me when I needed it. To him, I just didn't understand the situation. He was convinced there was some conspiracy against him. Prosecutors, witnesses, police officers and judges all wanted to get him. Being in jail wasn't his fault. I held my tongue and didn't argue with him, but I thought I would need to say something forceful when he got out if I was going to be helpful.

When Lucas was released, I held nothing back. He grew more furious with my every attempt to tell him that he needed to think about his own responsibility in creating the situation he was in. He threatened me, accused me of believing the government's lies about him and cussed a lot. We had the kind of no-holds-barred conversation that is hard to come back from. We never spoke again.

Lucas didn't like being told what to do, or being spoken to in an authoritative manner, and I hadn't expected him to receive my comments well. But I think he reacted the way he did because he could see that my moral compass had changed. I was no longer enamored of the Hollywood gangster subculture that we both grew up admiring. I had escaped the Dionysian trap. He felt judged and betrayed, as if I had sided with the law over him.

Following our blowout—my last conversation with Lucas—I struggled to figure out why my life was changing for the better and his wasn't. I wanted to understand why I was making the choices I was making, and why Lucas was making different choices. I didn't have a lot of tools to help me think about this, but in my freshman year of university I had come across one idea that made a world of difference: the capacity to aspire.

As articulated by New York University anthropologist Arjun Appadurai, the capacity to aspire is the ability to navigate and engage with the world around you.[1] Some people—often those with more resources at their disposal—have a greater capacity to aspire because they possess the knowledge and experience needed to achieve their goals, and thus they have more reasons to be optimistic about their chances of being successful. Other people—often those with fewer resources—possess less knowledge and experience, and thus have fewer reasons to be optimistic about their chances of being successful.

Appadurai uses the terms "wishful thinking" and "thoughtful wishing" when describing the capacity to aspire. You're a wishful thinker when you want a better life but don't know how to plan for it. Wishing is about all you've got. But you're a thoughtful wisher when you know the specific, attainable steps you need to take to get to the better life you're looking for.

The concept of the capacity to aspire stuck with me because it helped me better understand Lucas's life. Lucas desperately wanted to be admired by women and respected by men. He thought that meant he needed to be rich and tough, or at least appear that way. To achieve this kind of life for himself, he had very few paths in front of him. He was a school dropout with limited employment opportunities and few, if any, positive role models. The easiest path was a life of petty crime. He was fortunate that he didn't have many more destructive paths in front of him—he wasn't, for example, surrounded by sophisticated street gangs capable of recruiting him at a young age. Unfortunately, he didn't have many less destructive paths in front of him, either. He had no clear sense of how to start a career and pick up the skills needed to make money. He had no one to show him how to move away from petty crime toward a life where admiration and respect were attainable through positive behaviors.

Facing the reality that I wasn't cut out to be a gangster gave me the chance to pivot to a new direction and invest my time in the path available to me: postsecondary education. My capacity to aspire grew, and I was able to move my life in a different, more positive direction. I transitioned from "wishful thinking" to "thoughtful wishing" because I was learning how the world works. School and work were real options that became clearer each day.

Barack Obama has echoed this idea of looking at the paths available to young men. In a preface to *Dreams from My Father*, he wrote, "I know, I have seen, the desperation and disorder of the powerless: how it twists the lives of children on the streets of Jakarta or Nairobi in much the same way as it does the lives of children on Chicago's South Side, how narrow the path is for them between humiliation and untrammeled fury, how easily they slip into violence and despair."[2] The narrow path to which he refers is another way of thinking about the capacity to aspire. The more limited your capacity, the easier it is to "slip" and fall into a path of destruction.

President Obama's critics have accused him of attributing the destruction caused by young men to poverty and downplaying the importance of morals. One prominent Obama critic, conservative commentator Ben Shapiro, argued, "Terrorists in Indonesia aren't just angry because they're poor. Neither are kids in Chicago. Poverty and violence do not correlate. But poverty of ideology and violence *do* correlate."[3] Former Hoover Institution media fellow Paul Sperry has also challenged what he perceives as President Obama's emphasis on poverty, pointing to Jihadi John (Mohammed Emwazi), the infamous British member of the Islamic State in Iraq and Syria (ISIS), as an example of someone who doesn't fit into most people's image of the poor. Jihadi John traveled to Syria to join ISIS, but, Sperry says, he "grew up in middle-class London," "wasn't poor" and "received a degree in computer programming from the University of Westminster."[4]

Shapiro and Sperry are correct to point out the limits of relying on a single explanation for why young people turn to violence and crime—if that is what President Obama intended to do. But if we imagine that people's choices are determined by a broad range of factors, with poverty being just one of several, then I think President Obama's suggestion that we look at the paths in front of young people has merit. Those paths are inextricably linked to the morals that will guide a young man's behavior.

Psychologists Clark McCauley and Sophia Moskalenko, in their research on political radicalization and violence, explore the link between the paths available to young men and the development of their moral compasses. McCauley and Moskalenko identify "status seeking" (that is, pursuing respect and admiration) among peers as a key motivator for people who turn to violence. Young men are especially vulnerable to this way of thinking because testosterone levels appear to be an "important driver of status seeking."[5] McCauley and Moskalenko note that if a young man can achieve status through mainstream means, such as school or work, he is less likely to turn to violence. By contrast, if a young man is not able to achieve status through mainstream means, he is more likely to seek that status through violence or other negative behaviors. Of course, what qualifies as status can vary between individuals and communities. What warrants respect and admiration from the people around you helps determine the specific status you might pursue and how.

Lucas's connections to mainstream society were mostly limited to part-time jobs and the criminal justice system. For most of our friendship, my connection to mainstream society was primarily a school system that I resented. Our shared detachment made it easy for us to dismiss the morals of our country, as encoded in law, and gravitate to an alternative moral realm. But when I began developing connections to mainstream society through school, I was in the early stages of a long process of becoming more attached to my country. My morals started to change and Lucas's didn't. And our friendship couldn't survive that difference.

5

Competing for the Future: Part I

■ ■ ■ ■ ▬▬▬▬▬▬▬▬▬▬▬▬▬▬▬▬

I was first invited to join a clash of civilizations when I was in community college in 2005.

Samuel P. Huntington, a former chair of the Harvard Academy for International and Area Studies, popularized the term "clash of civilizations" to describe what he saw as the leading form of conflict in the modern world. "The great divisions among humankind and the dominating source of conflict will be cultural," Huntington predicted in 1993. "People have levels of identity: a resident of Rome may define himself with varying degrees of intensity as a Roman, an Italian, a Catholic, a Christian, a European, a Westerner. The civilization to which he belongs is the broadest level of identification with which he intensely identifies."[1]

The West versus Islam is one key conflict Huntington used to support his theory. He attributed this conflict to the growth of political Islam, also known as Islamism, in majority-Muslim countries. As the *Economist* defines it, political Islam involves "the mixing of religion with politics [that] implicitly involves the right to interpret and to impose the will of God."[2] Movements that fall into this category often promote anti-Western sentiments because the influence of the West competes with political movements seeking to impose Islamic law (known as Sharia) on public life or dissolve the separation between religious and state authorities.

In Europe and North America, belief in this clash of civilizations motivates a significant amount of activism. Groups opposed to Muslim immigration fuel their agenda by encouraging people to see a conflict between the West and Islam playing out within their own borders. Groups promoting anti-Western sentiment claim the authority of Islam and offer Westerners who feel like they don't belong in their own countries an alternative civilization to align with. Amarnath Amarasingam and Jacob Davey, of the London-based Institute for Strategic Dialogue, have argued that extremists on both sides embolden one another. "The ideologies of these movements are symbiotic, with both sides playing off a fear of the other to tailor their messages to attract new audiences. Left unchecked, competing outrages and persecution narratives could lead to a cascade of radicalization, in which extremists on each side feed the other's growth."[3]

My first friend in community college, Brandon, was in the middle of this conflict. A Canadian of Caribbean heritage, he was four or five years older than me. As two of only three black men in our transition-year program, we both felt out of place, so we gravitated to each other pretty quickly. We also discovered a common interest in the racial politics of the twentieth century. Brandon was the first person I'd met in real life whom I could talk to about the ideas I had read online. It was fun to finally be around someone who could quote W. E. B. Du Bois and knew more about Martin Luther King Jr. than simply that he'd had a dream.

Brandon wasn't just interested in racial politics intellectually. For him, reading about black nationalism and the American civil rights movement was a way to deal with feeling like an outsider. To counter his preoccupation with the negative stereotyping of and discrimination against black people (he thought about those things *a lot*), Brandon wanted to find a positive and powerful identity as a black man. He was frustrated by the limits of his own capacity to aspire; the paths in front of him offered by Hollywood gangsters or criminals were as offensive to him as the way police officers treated him.

Brandon and I discovered that we shared a common inspiration in Malcolm X. We both had recently read *The Autobiography of Malcolm X* and found it to be a life-changing story of a man who traveled from the bottom of society to the top, motivated not by money but by a love for his community. Malcolm was a symbol of the problems we saw in our own communities, but also a symbol of change.

Growing up in Michigan in the 1930s, Malcolm came of age at a time when racism was viscerally prevalent throughout American society. His capacity to aspire was limited at a young age, so much so that his schoolteacher discouraged him from imagining a future as a lawyer or pursuing similar professions. Malcolm also fell into a life of petty crime. After he dropped out of school in eighth grade, his efforts to fit in with his friends led to a six-year stint in prison for burglary. There, he found a path to redemption in Islam, but not traditional Islamic denominations. Rather, he was drawn to the Nation of Islam (NOI), a group that fused Islamic beliefs with the black nationalist politics of the twentieth century. The NOI was founded in 1930 in Detroit, Michigan, by Wallace Fard Muhammad, who was said to have traveled to the United States from Saudi Arabia to reveal Islam to black Americans. The NOI's leader at the time Malcolm joined was Elijah Muhammad.

Malcolm's journey was propelled by his love for reading in prison and his commitment to learning after he was released. To Brandon and me, young men in community college trying to make something of ourselves, Malcolm's journey was a testament to the value of an education and an example of how we might use ours to serve as a voice for our communities. Brandon and I both lacked role models who'd pursued higher education, so Malcolm was an encouraging person for us to keep in mind when we ran into adversity as students or felt disconnected from our social circles because we spent time on schoolwork.

Brandon wanted to be like Malcolm, so he followed his lead and joined the NOI, which was at that time under the leadership of Louis Farrakhan and headquartered in Chicago. In 2007, the *New York Times* estimated that the group had between 20,000 and 50,000 members, although this number is widely disputed.[4]

Before I met him, Brandon had been attending Friday evening services and study groups at the NOI's Toronto mosque for over a year. You could tell when he was going to the mosque, because on those days he wore a suit and bow tie. Even when he didn't plan to visit the mosque, Brandon always carried a copy of some NOI book with him and would want to share with me what he'd learned. I was familiar with some NOI doctrine because of my interest in a spinoff group called the Five Percenters. The NOI itself was not an option for me because I didn't like many of their ideas, and I blamed Elijah Muhammad and his followers for encouraging violence against Malcolm, likely contributing to his assassination. Still, Brandon and I could have fun, informative debates about what he learned at the mosque.

Some of the NOI beliefs that Brandon and I discussed are the basis of the group's Muslim Program, which consists of two ten-point lists: "What the Muslims Want" and "What the Muslims Believe." NOI Muslims want freedom, justice and equality for black Americans; a separate and independent territory for black Americans; the release of all Muslims from federal prisons; the end of police brutality; employment equality in America; exemption from taxation for Muslim Americans; equal but segregated schools; and a ban on interracial marriage for blacks and whites. What they believe is that the Quran is God's truth; the Bible is true but tainted; black Americans can change their ways; Judgment Day will happen in America; segregation is superior to integration; Muslims should not participate in wars (which is why Muhammad Ali, a onetime NOI member, wound up in prison after being drafted to Vietnam); women should be protected and respected; and the founder of the NOI, Wallace Fard Muhammad, is the prophet both Muslims and Christians have been waiting for.

A key feature of the NOI is its preaching of conflict between the West and Islam. The NOI hopes this conflict will lead to the death and destruction of America for its sins against black Americans and Muslims. But there are few examples of NOI teachings being directly linked to violent crime. University of Windsor political science professor Martha F. Lee, in examining violence and religious movements, described the NOI as "a case study of why and how a religious movement with a radical belief system [does] not engage in violence related to its doctrine." According to Lee, "The most notable act of violence in its history—the assassination of Malcolm X—appears to be linked to the very secular and common problem of political jealousy, perhaps fostered by government agents."[5] Indeed, one of the acts that led to Malcolm's split from the NOI and his eventual assassination was his defense of the killing of President John F. Kennedy—a defense that Elijah Muhammad deemed misconduct worthy of silencing.

The Centre for the Prevention of Radicalization Leading to Violence (CPRLV) in Montreal has developed some helpful tools to distinguish between radicalization and radicalization that leads to violence. According to the CPRLV, those who are indoctrinated with destructive ideas by radical groups have different ways of engaging with those groups: self-sacrifice, participation and active support. On this spectrum, participation and active support for radical groups do not always lead to violent acts.[6]

After a few weeks of attending classes together, Brandon and I were close enough that he invited me to a Friday evening service at the mosque. I was hesitant to go at first, but I took the invitation as a sign of trust between us and an indication that he felt comfortable sharing that world with me. I wanted to go to support my friend. It's a big step to invite someone into a radical world such as that one, because believers often face ridicule and contempt, even from people they trust. In Brandon's case, his Christian family and friends were unhappy he'd converted to Islam, and the Muslims he knew outside of the NOI called him a fake because he wasn't part of a traditional Islamic denomination. I decided to go, and over the course of the year we went to school together, I attended the NOI mosque with him between ten and twenty times.

The mosque in Toronto was in the second-floor unit of a mixed residential and retail building west of the St. Clair West subway station. The area is near the Little Jamaica neighborhood, which was contending with violent crime and related stigma at the time, and also close to some of the most prosperous parts of the city. Next door to the mosque was a Starbucks with a very different clientele, which made for a striking visual when going from one to the other.

The unit housing the mosque was aged but well taken care of. At the top of the stairs was a reception area with a library of books written or endorsed by the NOI. The main meeting area featured a slightly raised stage with a podium. Toward the side of the stage was a television screen that was used to broadcast telecasts from Farrakhan and others at the organization's national office in Chicago. There were pictures of the NOI's first two leaders, Elijah Muhammad and Wallace Fard Muhammad, prominently displayed on the walls.

The Toronto mosque was led by Brother Jeremy, a former musician from a mixed-race family. He was in his late twenties or early thirties when I met him. Brother Jeremy's youthfulness was representative of the Toronto NOI community, which was made up of mostly young men of various Caribbean and African ethnic backgrounds. Occasionally there were also women at the mosque, but typically I saw only men there. The men were always dressed in suits and bow ties, and the women in skirts and headscarves. Each time I was there, I saw a core group of fifteen to twenty regular members, mixed with people who attended irregularly and newcomers who had usually been invited by a friend or family member.

During most Friday evening services, which were the only mosque activities open to the general public (so they were the only activities I witnessed), Brother Jeremy would deliver fiery sermons in line with the NOI's rhetorical tradition. Occasionally, he would forgo his sermon and instead play video of a lecture delivered by Farrakhan. Brother Jeremy encouraged those in the room to give donations, as is common at other religious services. He also encouraged us to buy NOI books, DVDs and newspapers. Members of the mosque even sold bean pies and soups that adhered to the group's dietary restrictions.

The lectures and conversations at the NOI mosque were less theological or dogmatic than most I've heard at other religious services. Brother Jeremy would make references to the Quran and the Bible, but scripture wasn't his focus. He instead offered a core message that resonated deeply with the mostly young and male audience around me: *This world around us isn't made for you. You don't belong here.*

Like Farrakhan, Brother Jeremy attributed every inequality in black communities to the inherent corruption of Western society, which the NOI often referred to as "the white man's" or "the devil's" civilization. NOI doctrine dictates that the Western world is, at its core, aligned against blacks and Muslims. There was, unfortunately, no shortage of news stories for Brother Jeremy to use to tell this narrative because of the many inequalities that plague black communities, from incarceration rates to police brutality to school dropout rates to poverty. He used these data points to argue that North America and Europe would never accept minority communities, and that efforts to make a home in these parts of the world were naive and ill-fated. Even when Brother Jeremy referred to signs of progress, such as the American civil rights movement or successful black business leaders, he would describe them as proof of a corrupt civilization trying to trick us into thinking we had a fair chance.

During my visits to the mosque, I could see the influence that this story had on the young men in attendance. The corrupt world around them became an explanation for their own personal dissatisfaction. If you experienced unfairness, it was because society at large was at fault. If you were unhappy with your school or your job, it was because you were not meant to be successful in the first place. If you didn't have a girlfriend, it was because the women you met had been conditioned to find the wrong things attractive. Experiences that many young people go through—identity confusion, lack of personal and professional direction, feelings of not fitting in—become associated with what the NOI sees as the evils of Western civilization.

There's little room for personal agency in this worldview. Everything an individual does wrong becomes the fault of the West. Brother Jeremy attributed the problems he observed in black communities—like inner-city violence, the Hollywood gangster subculture or fatherless families—to people who'd strayed from their true Muslim nature and lost a "knowledge of themselves." When black people did something wrong, he'd say it was because Western civilization had turned them into flawed or damaged people through racism, slavery and colonialism.

Indeed, it appeared to me that for many NOI mosque attendees, Brandon included, being against the West was more important than learning about Islam. Islam was mostly incidental to how the mosque in Toronto operated. Brother Jeremy talked more about the

Bible than the Quran, claiming that's what black people in North America were familiar with. Even as Brandon became more immersed in the NOI, he appeared to gain no familiarity with traditional Muslim authorities and scholars. In conversations with me, he dismissed most denominations of Islam as corrupted by Western influences. However, both he and the NOI needed Islam as a political identity. Without that association, they were part of a relatively small movement pushing a form of black nationalism rejected by the clear majority of black people. With their association with Islam, they were connected to more than one billion people across the world, including countries at odds with American foreign policy. Brandon didn't agree with every attack against the West that appeared on the news, but he often spoke of those espousing anti-Western sentiments as allies against imperialism.

The NOI gave the young men who walked through its doors a role to play in an epic, Hollywood-esque clash of civilizations. Brandon's role was to build a nation for black Muslims, which in the absence of physical territory would be an ideological nation with physical dimensions, like mosques to worship in and street corners to preach on. He raised money for this nation by selling copies of the NOI's *Final Call* newspaper in busy pedestrian areas. He also changed his name as part of a pledge of allegiance. Brandon formally requested and received his X from Louis Farrakhan so he could replace his family name, which he denounced as a "slave name." He also changed his first name from Brandon to Sharif, the Muslim name he was given by Farrakhan. As Sharif X, Brandon attended the mosque three or four times a week, and even took part in combat training with the Fruit of Islam, the NOI's security group, which was charged with protecting NOI leaders and others.

Brandon desperately wanted to receive this combat training because, as a young man in the West, he believed he lived in the belly of the beast, where he might need to defend the NOI and his community from potential enemies.

Brandon frequently suggested that I read some of his NOI material, but I usually refused because I just wasn't interested. His favorite book, however, *Message to the Blackman in America* by Elijah Muhammad, caught my eye. Published in 1965, the year Malcolm X was killed, the book summarizes some of the NOI's ideas about race, history, politics, economics, religion and prophecy. As its title suggests, the book was written to communicate these ideas to black men, to teach them who they are and what they should aspire to be. The preface promises that the book will provide black men with "enough light on our path in search for that Supreme Wisdom to keep us from stumbling and falling."[7] That light was the "wisdom of Allah," which is how members refer to the NOI doctrine. I thought *Message to the Blackman in America* might answer some of the questions I had about masculinity. After all, it seemed to have been helpful to Brandon. I asked him if I could borrow his copy, and he obliged.

A few weeks later, when I'd read the book and was ready to return it to Brandon, I realized it was missing. All the school papers I had left it with were still on the kitchen table, but I couldn't find the book anywhere. It looked as if the area had been recently cleaned, so I asked my mom if she had seen it. She stammered and looked away when she said no. I asked her if she was sure. She stammered yes and looked away again.

We both knew she had removed it because she didn't want me to have it. Neither of us actually wanted to talk about the book, though. I didn't want to have to explain to her why I had it or why I went to the NOI mosque. And Mom didn't want to have to explain why she'd moved it. She, a white woman, was probably uncomfortable when taking a book addressed to black men away from her son. So I dropped it and gave Brandon twenty bucks to replace the book.

Since that day, I have often wondered what my mom saw in the book that made her want to keep it from me. Maybe it was Muhammad's science fiction theory that white people had been created on an island by an evil scientist. Or maybe she just didn't like the book's criticisms of Christianity and its claims that Islam is the only true religion for black people—something that I'm sure offended her, a Protestant.

I wish I could have told her that I had the book because I was desperate for some direction in my life, for some sense of what kind of man I was supposed to be. This was the same reason I listened to Jay-Z all day, spent so much time on the internet and sought out friends older than me. All the ideas I was drawn to were ones that held the promise of filling the voids in my life. These voids weren't being filled in school, where I never once had the chance to talk about masculinity, aside from basic sex education in health class.

I was never close to joining the NOI, so my mom didn't need to worry about that. She should have been more concerned about what I was reading online. While Brandon was part of a community with a physical meeting place and sought answers to his questions in printed books, I was seeking answers online, by myself, in virtual communities that offered conspiracy theories and NOI-inspired civilizational clashes. The kind of male networks I wished for in my family, at school or in my neighborhood I found instead through blogs, websites, message boards, AOL Instant Messenger and MSN Chat.

At first, I primarily frequented hip-hop websites, where mostly male voices would have far-reaching conversations about life in the neighborhoods where rappers and their fans came from. Then the 9/11 attacks on New York City happened, and I became increasingly interested in politics. I was less than two weeks into high school when the twin towers fell at the hands of al-Qaeda terrorists. Prior to 9/11, I'd never paid attention to politics or even watched a speech by a politician. But I tuned in that day to CNN to see what was going on, and I remember watching a lot of speeches by George W. Bush and profiles of Osama bin Laden. September 11 also temporarily changed the shows I regularly watched, like BET's *106 & Park*, which became very serious very quickly. Nobody could go without talking about what had happened.

Canadian journalist Michelle Shephard has dubbed people my age, born between the late 1980s and late 1990s, "Generation 9/11" because of the impact that attack had on us growing up. As Shephard explains, people in this group have "grown up with the world at their fingertips—making them more aware of world events, even superficially, than generations before." We've also grown up with the aftershocks of 9/11—with "Muslims being regarded with suspicion and with free speech and privacy under threat."[8]

Regrettably, I gravitated to conspiracy theories online. There were articles and stories about President George W. Bush's grudge against Saddam Hussein because of the First Gulf War, the use of false flag operations to manipulate the public and the influence of Saudi Arabia and Israel on US foreign policy. I found pictures and videos of how the twin towers fell and read arguments about whether airplane impacts could cause buildings to fall in this way. The Bush administration's search for weapons of mass destruction in Iraq lent itself to conspiracy theories because of the inaccuracies that led to the 2003 invasion of Iraq.

Conspiracy theories weren't new to me: the rap music I listened to was full of them. Dead Prez rapped on the album *Let's Get Free* about all the "white man lies" schools teach to black children, while Prodigy from Mobb Deep insisted that secret societies like the Illuminati were after him. And rappers and fans alike constantly questioned the official explanation of how and why Tupac was killed. Rap music and the internet complemented each other perfectly. You could learn about a conspiracy in one medium and find support for it in the other.

By 2004, rappers were actively pushing 9/11 conspiracy theories to their audiences. That year, Jadakiss, a rapper from Yonkers, New York, had a hit song called "Why?" in which he asks why George W. Bush "knocked down" the twin towers. A year later, Immortal Technique sampled Jadakiss's song as the chorus for a single he made with Mos Def, whose part mostly consists of blaming Bush for 9/11 and declaring Osama bin Laden innocent.

Caught in this whirlwind of information and misinformation, I found it impossible to distinguish a conspiracy theory from an accurate and well-researched report. I just didn't have the tools or the ability to vet information, so I believed anything that resonated with me. I was angry at the world for failing to give me what I needed to make my life better, and I accepted at face value any stories that validated my anger and helped prove that the world around me was full of lies. By default, online news outlets, rap music and other media that offered critical or alternative views had a certain kind of credibility with me. Challenging the powers that be was inherently a good thing, in my view, and anyone who did so seemed more trustworthy.

My online research eventually led me to the Five Percenters, also known as the Five Percent Nation of Islam and the Nation of Gods and Earths. I discovered this group on hip-hop websites via references made by the Wu-Tang Clan, Poor Righteous Teachers and Nas. Many rappers from the 1980s and 1990s identified as Five Percenters or referred to their ideas. The virtual community I found in the mid-2000s was a small network of Five Percenters, mostly black American men, who supported one another's worldview by sharing news articles and rap songs and by debating interpretations of NOI doctrine. I spent hours after school consuming conspiracy theories and propaganda about the evils of Western civilization, which meshed well with the cynicism about Western governments and news media I'd developed when reading about 9/11.

The Five Percenters are a spin-off group of the NOI led by several men who left the Harlem mosque in 1964, shortly after Malcolm X's public departure from the organization. They share much of the NOI's doctrine emphasizing the corrupt nature of Western civilization, yet there are big differences between the two groups. The Five Percenters are atheists who don't identify as Muslims or view the Quran or the Bible as holy books. They grew into a separate organization because they brought the NOI's black nationalist ideas outside of the mosque and catered to young people involved in Harlem's criminal underworld, offering an accessible and youth-friendly version of NOI doctrine that placed less emphasis on rules and rituals.

The name Five Percenters is drawn from the NOI belief that

the human population can be divided into three groups: 85 percent are the masses of people controlled by the elite 10 percent, the rich bourgeoisie; the remaining 5 percent are the "poor righteous teachers" who seek to liberate the 85 percent from the 10 percent. Many Five Percenters believe the elite 10 percent is made up of white people and the leaders of Western civilization, and the 5 percent includes members of the NOI and others who know the truth about the corrupt nature of Western civilization.

The Five Percenters aspire to build a nation through ideas and culture, not necessarily with physical land and borders. Like the NOI, the Five Percenters don't have a history of encouraging their members to engage in violence related to their ideas. Unlike the NOI, the Five Percenters are open to anyone who wants to learn about their ideas—to join, you don't need to sign up, pay a membership fee, ask Farrakhan for a name change or sell newspapers. Membership involves studying their doctrine and memorizing it so you can teach it to others.

The Five Percenter virtual community was attractive to me because it provided a network of men I could talk with and learn from. With anti-Western rhetoric softened by New York City hip-hop slang, the Five Percenters offered quick and easy answers to the questions I was asking about my life: it feels as if people are lying to you because they are; the world around you is unfair because it's inherently corrupt; you can escape from this evil by joining a movement to resist and defeat Western elites.

Identifying with this movement gave me a renewed purpose in my life. I felt that I was in the middle of a power struggle for the future of humanity, in which somebody like me, with all my flaws and frustrations, could make a difference to who won or lost.

6

Competing for the Future: Part II

■ ■ ■ ■ ▬▬▬▬▬▬▬▬▬▬▬▬▬▬▬▬▬▬▬

Brandon and I both started community college in the same place, unsure of how we would fit into an academic environment. We had track records that made us doubt our ability to perform as students. At the end of our transition year, however, I was ready to start a bachelor's degree program and he wasn't. We finished that year in completely different places, as students and as people. Perhaps the biggest difference was that school had become my outlet to explore ideas I had previously engaged with only through music or online. For the first time in my life, school was a place where I could learn and grow. Brandon never felt quite the same way. For him, the NOI mosque was where he would learn and grow.

One of the classes Brandon and I took together taught academic writing skills. It mostly covered material I should have learned in high school but didn't (because I didn't try to). In high school, we'd had little choice in what we could write about, but our professor let us pick any subject we wanted as long as we could show we understood the writing skills we'd learned in class. I picked a topic that was personally relevant to me: media coverage of the D.C. sniper attacks.

John Allen Muhammad and Lee Boyd Malvo captured the world's attention in 2002 by killing ten people and injuring three in the Washington, D.C., area. News reports drew links between the murders and the Nation of Islam because the sniper left messages containing slang popularized by rappers influenced by the NOI and Muhammad had been an NOI member in the 1980s. I enjoyed writing about this topic because it was relevant to things I was thinking about on my own time, such as the goings-on at the NOI mosque. Brandon, however, wasn't excited by the idea of making an essay assignment relevant to subjects he liked reading and talking about. I remember him scrambling in the library to finish it on time. He just wasn't that engaged in school and instead sought out opportunities to learn at the NOI mosque.

The mosque gave Brandon something that school didn't: a place to belong. The NOI knew how to deal with his need to feel empowered and positive about himself. Our school was designed for people looking for employable skills that would lead to a job, and Brandon was just another guy paying tuition in hopes that life might get better. Members of the NOI mosque treated him like they needed him—specifically *him*—because they did.

Brandon was a completely different person at the mosque than he was in school. I could see it in his face and his behavior. At the mosque, he was confident, eager to ask questions and willing to put himself out there to meet new people. At school, he was quiet and aloof. Brandon was more excited to read NOI materials than anything he was assigned to read for the courses he was enrolled in. He was also more eager to invest in the relationships he made through the mosque than in the relationships with his classmates and professors.

After I graduated from community college, I stopped going to the NOI mosque with Brandon. By that point, he was so into it that I'm not sure he really liked having me around anyway. What had once been debates became heated arguments in which he took personally my attempts to point out flaws in the NOI's rhetoric. We still saw each other once a week or so, when he was out selling NOI newspapers. We'd catch up about school and family, but I avoided bringing up the NOI as much as possible.

In 2007, Brandon asked me to join him at the NOI's annual celebration, called Saviours' Day. That year it was to be held in Detroit, where the organization was founded; members believed it would be Louis Farrakhan's last Saviours' Day speech because he was having health complications. Brandon said he wanted me to come along because it was his first Saviours' Day as a full member and he needed the support. I agreed to go.

We traveled to Detroit in a minivan with a handful of NOI members and supporters—all black men under the age of forty. I spent most of the four-and-a-half-hour ride either sleeping or explaining myself. The others wanted to know why I refused to join the NOI, and when I tried to share my many points of disagreement with the ideas of the organization, they would criticize me and ask even more questions. I didn't want to get into these debates about the group's ideology and my objections to it, but they kept asking me. Our conversation was uncomfortable at times because of how personally some of the guys took my comments.

Almost everyone in the minivan had once attended a Christian church, but all came to see the church as part of the same world that they thought black people and Muslims should reject. The NOI presented an opportunity to escape that world, but it also offered a relatively soft landing. You could reject the corruption of the West to side with more than a billion other Muslims and the many Muslim-majority nations across the globe. Not only were they on the right side of history, but they were not alone on that side.

When we got to Detroit, I saw tens of thousands of men and women in NOI attire: suits and bow ties or long skirts and headscarves. It looked as if the NOI had taken over the entire city. We found our way to Ford Field, where the festivities were taking place, and took our seats to hear Farrakhan's speech, which reinforced many of the observations I had made that day about why being a Muslim appealed to this group of black nationalists.

Farrakhan spent a significant amount of time in his speech positioning the NOI as an ally of Iraq's Saddam Hussein, Iran's Mahmoud Ahmadinejad, Lebanon's Hassan Nasrallah and Venezuela's Hugo Chávez because they shared a common enemy: the United States. He also characterized Iraq under the leadership of Saddam Hussein as a wonderful place sabotaged by American intervention. "Shia and Sunni live together, Christian and Jews live together in Iraq," he said. "You didn't hear none of this stuff [about terrorism] before America came in. . . . But it's happening now. You don't need to look at Shia and Sunni—you need to look at those who came in." Farrakhan then provided an inflammatory explanation of these aggressions of the United States as a clash of civilizations between Islam and "so-called Jews and Christians," whom he accused of being afraid of those who want an "Islamic way of life."[1]

The tens of thousands of people around me applauded with enthusiasm at everything Farrakhan said. The place shook as if the Detroit Lions had just won the Super Bowl. Following Farrakhan's speech, a sea of people in bow ties and headscarves made their way out of the stadium and headed home.

If I thought I'd had it tough on the car ride to Detroit, it was nothing compared to what was in store for me on the ride back. My travel companions were returning home even more convinced that there was indeed a clash of civilizations and they were on the right side. This time I couldn't even sleep in the car because of how noisy everyone was with praise for Farrakhan and his vision for black people.

What Brandon and I had heard in Detroit that day might have been life-changing for both of us. Brandon immediately doubled down on his commitment to the NOI. I looked into his eyes and saw a man who was empowered in a way that I'd never seen in him before. Farrakhan had spoken directly to him, it seemed.

I considered Farrakhan's comments to be immoral, and his speech showed me how immoral your views can become when you have a conflict-oriented view of the world. He was praising dictators, terrorists and extremists because of a rigid worldview that required the West to be evil and its opponents to be heroes. Seeing Farrakhan share such an immoral message with tens of thousands of people in Detroit was a wake-up call for me. I told Brandon I couldn't join him in any more NOI activities, even if it was just to support a friend.

I was compelled to draw a line between me and the likes of Farrakhan largely due to the positive influence of the university community I had recently joined, as well as my departure from the Five Percenter virtual community I had once looked to for role models. In the months before visiting Detroit, I had started to attend Five Percenter meetings offline, in physical meeting places in the Toronto area. I went to my first gathering after I found a contact number online for a Five Percenter near Toronto and gave him a call. He invited me to a meeting that was a two-hour train ride outside of the city, and I went. There were another ten or fifteen young men there, from a variety of ethnic and cultural backgrounds, including Caribbean, white, Afghan, Filipino, Chinese and African. All of them were at different stages of learning about NOI doctrine. At least half of the men were involved in the Toronto hip-hop scene as rappers or DJs. Many wore shirts or jewelry displaying the Five Percenter symbol (called the universal flag) or the Wu-Tang Clan logo.

These local Five Percenters welcomed me warmly and told me how their monthly meetings were structured. They offered to put me on a plan to learn about their ideas—or "study the lessons," as they said. Over several months, I attended half a dozen of these meetings and met people in the Five Percenter network from other cities, like Milwaukee and New York. I started to memorize parts of their doctrine, and they would quiz me on it. "Who is the original man?" was the first question I needed to answer. When I got that one right, we moved on to "Who is the colored man?"

We never really got past this second question because the answer I was supposed to memorize described white communities in the West as the "devil" and "skunk of the planet earth." I couldn't accept this as truth. When I voiced my disagreement, I was dismissively told I was being a "half-white" man and I would need more time to understand the lessons. I wasn't motivated to learn about their ideas once I knew that accepting certain views about white people was necessary, so I gradually stopped participating. There is diversity of opinion on these issues in the Five Percenter community, but I encountered only a dogmatic, Farrakhan-like need to view everything as a conflict between races.

My inquisitive nature conflicted with the rigid confines of NOI doctrine. I was trying to keep an open mind regarding what I learned in school, while the Five Percenters were trying to fit everything into a conflict-oriented view of the world: West versus anti-West, black versus white and rich versus poor. The diverse communities I was exposed to on a university campus made it difficult to see life so simplistically. This was the second time in as many years that I was sure some of the people I considered friends would consider me a fake, a wannabe. I didn't fit into the Five Percenter community that existed offline, and I stopped fitting in online as well.

Professor Andrea Davis at York University helped me build a moral compass that steered me away from the NOI and the Five Percenters for good. I took Professor Davis's first-year Cultures of Resistance class, which was about black history in the Americas. Course readings, class discussions and writing assignments all addressed the same subjects being debated by Five Percenters and NOI members, including broken families, police profiling, inadequate schools, inequitable criminal justice systems, ineffective political systems and poverty. Professor Davis regularly challenged the ideas I brought to the classroom, encouraging me to be more intellectually curious. She created an inspiring environment that allowed me to connect my life on campus with the world I lived in outside of school. I could even email her articles about or by Five Percenters and NOI members, and she would include them in class discussions.

Professor Davis's support was a big part of why I excelled as a student at York and ultimately made it to Yale. I learned how to genuinely care about school because she helped me find role models in the pages of the readings she assigned. Under her guidance, I immersed myself in the writings and speeches of W. E. B. Du Bois, Marcus Garvey, Booker T. Washington, Martin Luther King Jr., Malcolm X, Manning Marable, Frantz Fanon, Walter Rodney and many more. Most important, Professor Davis gave me the skills I needed to think critically about which examples I might want to follow and which ones I didn't.

The various influences in my life at this time inevitably collided, and I reached a moment of clarity.

In 2007, toward the end of my freshman year at York, I heard about a protest at the provincial legislature in downtown Toronto. The protest had been organized by a group I didn't recognize to demand the province stop its plan to build a new "superjail" near one of the neighborhoods I grew up in. Some people I knew from the Five Percenter community and the NOI mosque wanted to participate, so I went downtown to meet them there. Twenty to thirty people had gathered for the protest, many carrying signs decrying racism to signal their concern that this "superjail" would lead to the incarceration of more black people.

The protest was partially motivated by conspiracy theories regarding the Canadian government's intentions to imprison black people en masse. But there was good policy thinking involved, too. Like most North American cities, Toronto was at the time enjoying declining crime rates—which suggested there could be better ways to use public resources, such as improving schools and supporting low-income families. Additionally, black Canadians were already being incarcerated at a highly disproportionate rate, so any increase in incarceration, as was likely to happen if the proposed jail was built, would probably put more black people behind bars.

The protest organizers were handing out signs and gave me one. I don't remember what was on it, but I do remember taking it without thinking. I felt uncomfortable about the whole situation. Specifically, I felt that the worldview the protesters were encouraging was coming into conflict with the new worldview I was developing as a university student. People at this protest were delivering the same "me against the world" message that had made it easy for me to retreat from mainstream society and give up when I was a high school student. All the talk about how corrupt our country was, how elites were out to get us and how sinister were the intentions of authority figures was bringing me back to that place where I'd struggled to find the motivation to try in school.

The protest amplified some of the worst voices in my head—voices that had been encouraged by groups like the NOI and the Five Percenters, but could also be traced back to the Hollywood gangster subculture I was drawn to as a child. I had been fighting these voices ever since I entered community college because I was changing course after years of pessimism and thinking of myself as a victim. I had to fight against every urge I had to give up. Even when I was getting good grades, I came close to dropping out because I thought I was living in a rigged system that wouldn't offer me anything helpful in exchange for my efforts. I would have dropped out if not for Professor Davis and others, who went out of their way to tell me with conviction that I had a positive future waiting for me if I kept going.

Heading back home from the protest, I realized that the diverse influences in my life were competing for my future. I had to take some control by choosing the right influences, but the right influences also needed to choose me.

I'm lucky that education won in the power struggle for my future. It wasn't an easy fight. There were plenty of times I could have gone all in with my friend in the Nation of Islam mosque or my friend in the streets. There were times I was tempted to follow my father's footsteps into the restaurant industry instead of attending classes, but my anger toward him steered me away from that. The online radicals I met also offered a community that was welcoming and traditions to be part of, but I couldn't get comfortable with their ideas.

Going to school gave me opportunities to write about all of the above. For a kid who once felt the shame and sadness of being labeled illiterate, a pen and paper (or a keyboard and monitor) opened up a new world of expression. And it was also therapeutic knowing that with every word I wrote, I was climbing out of the hole I had helped dig for myself in high school. Finally—with the help of mentors and professors who believed in me—I had the tools to fight new battles with myself and the rest of the world.

7

Social (Im)mobility

Pursuing a bachelor's degree initially felt like walking around in the dark. Unsure of how exactly to succeed, I accepted help where I could get it and kept moving forward in hopes of finding a way out. After two years, doing well academically became less of a struggle and more of a routine. I worked part-time or full-time hours in kitchens and warehouses, used my mornings to read for classes and took time off from work leading up to exams or final papers so I could give them my best shot. My life was uneventful, but the routine was working. Getting A's in school became normal.

Routine can be a double-edged sword, offering the stability needed to succeed but also becoming a barrier to making helpful changes. For instance, I chose which community college and university to attend because of routine. Both schools were located on the same street, Steeles Avenue West, which serves as Toronto's northern border. That street also goes into the Brampton neighborhood I grew up in. I already rode the buses that would take me to both schools. They were in familiar territory. I'd need to interrupt my routines if I wanted to do anything new.

Thinking about my future away from Steeles Avenue West required a mix of personal initiative and luck. A couple of years in university taught me that people who study liberal arts at less well-known schools don't necessarily get jobs in their chosen field, regardless of how good their grades are. A number of graduating students had shared their bleak job prospects with me. And after losing all of my friends and changing my life abruptly so I could focus on school, I had no intention of graduating without new job prospects.

The career options I was looking for seemed best offered by two possible next steps: law school and business school. My reading and writing skills had improved enough that I'd make for a decent lawyer or businessman, I thought. A master's degree in another liberal arts field wouldn't give me the kind of practical education that I thought would lead to job offers. By chance, I took the Law School Admissions Test (LSAT) required to apply to law school before taking the test required to apply to business school. I borrowed money so I could enroll in a test prep class and treated studying for the LSAT like another job for two months. Thankfully, the LSAT was the first standardized test I did well on, far different from my experience with the high school literacy test a few years earlier. I chose to not take the business school test at all. I didn't want to try my luck too many times.

Steeles Avenue West did have a law school on it. I would have applied there and, if I'd been fortunate enough to be admitted, would have attended. However, a chance meeting with an American history professor would take me far away from Toronto.

On the Labor Day before my senior year of university—just a couple of months before applying to law school—I was invited to a black history conference to present research I had conducted about the influence of Jamaican-born activist Marcus Garvey, whose work inspired the Nation of Islam and many other black nationalists around the world. The conference was held in North Buxton, Ontario, which is a town founded by black American families who came to Canada via the Underground Railroad. David Blight, a history professor at Yale University, delivered the keynote address at the conference, and fortunately for me, he arrived early enough to see my presentation. I was intimidated by him, thinking he must possess some incredible genius to teach at a school that I had only ever heard of on television or in the movies. I told Professor Blight I achieved a high score on the LSAT and intended to apply to law school later that year. "You should apply to Yale," he said. I was surprised and asked if he thought I had a chance to be accepted. He said I was talented enough to be a competitive applicant.

Professor Blight's encouragement planted a seed of ambition in my mind. I didn't think I would get into Yale, but I also didn't think it would be ridiculous to apply if someone as smart as him thought it would be worthwhile. So a few months later I submitted my application with no expectations. Not only was I accepted, but the school's generous financial aid policies meant that I could actually afford to attend. I felt like I had won the lottery.

In retrospect, I might have benefited from taking time away from school between undergrad and law school. My life was changing far too quickly for me to keep up with and I was overwhelmed.

Still, I wasn't sure if Yale would want me if I waited any longer (I'd later learn that deferring enrollment is totally normal and I was worried for no reason, but at the time I didn't know any better). I also wasn't sure if I'd lose the positive momentum I'd gained as a student. After all, I had only been a good student for four years and had a much longer track record of academic failure. Impatiently, three months after receiving my bachelor's degree, I moved more than five hundred miles away from Steeles Avenue West to New Haven, Connecticut.

The student community I was part of at Yale from 2010 to 2013 was—unsurprisingly—very different from any group I'd joined before. Yale students were, on average, much wealthier and much better educated than I was. Unlike the people I'd spent most of my life with, Yale students weren't in danger of losing their connections to their country. In part because of their impressive abilities, they were the heirs apparent to the mainstream institutions my friends and I had been so detached from growing up. Even the majority of students who grew up in less privileged circumstances had performed well in school for most of their lives, had benefited from having parents and older siblings as positive role models and had never seen the ugly side of law enforcement or the criminal justice system.

What I observed at Yale was captured effectively in a book written by two of my professors, husband-and-wife team Amy Chua and Jed Rubenfeld. *The Triple Package: How Three Unlikely Traits Explain the Rise and Fall of Cultural Groups in America* sets out to explain the economic and educational success of groups as diverse as Cubans and Nigerians, Mormons and Jews. In my first year of law school, I studied contracts with Chua and criminal law with Rubenfeld, so I got to know them and watched them develop some of their ideas firsthand. One of their book's main points is that your ability to earn money or perform well in school can be affected by what people think of you and how you react to what they think. Simply put, people who seek the approval of others or compare themselves to others because of some insecurity are especially motivated to make more money or get higher test scores.

Ever since *The Triple Package* was published, in 2014, critics have challenged Chua and Rubenfeld's ideas on the grounds that they're largely based on anecdotal observations, many of which are from their time at Yale. Nonetheless, the role of external expectations in economic and educational achievement appears to withstand some scrutiny—at least as an explanation for individual success, if not necessarily group success. Psychologists Joshua Hart and Christopher F. Chabris tested the triple-package theory through a series of surveys of American adults. The surveys were designed to see which cultural traits correlate with economic or educational attainment. The results supported the idea that external expectations are relevant to individual success. Hart and Chabris concluded that "basing one's self-worth on external sources probably reflects a type of insecurity . . . and seems compatible with the [triple-package] view that success is motivated by external expectations, so perhaps here Chua and Rubenfeld were onto something."[1]

Chua and Rubenfeld's theory and Hart and Chabris's survey results spotlight a certain kind of relationship with external expectations common to many successful people, including my classmates at Yale. They look to parents, teachers, mentors and peers for a measuring stick showing them how to live. Successful people feel affirmed—maybe even empowered—when that measuring stick indicates they're doing reasonably well. Ergo, they put effort into school and work so they'll feel better about themselves.

This relationship with external expectations was new to me when I arrived at Yale. I was used to seeing people fight with how authority figures and institutions perceived them, not working hard to satisfy their expectations. When you grow up fighting against stigma and negative stereotypes, as I did, the world offers only a harmful way to measure yourself. It's hard to be motivated to impress authority figures or mirror the values of mainstream institutions when their expectations drag your self-esteem down instead of lifting it up.

A 2004 article published in the *Personality and Social Psychology Bulletin* looks at how the perceptions of others can harm a person's sense of self. The article uses a hypothetical example of a young woman working through body image issues. "It is likely that this woman will look to others to determine whether she is meeting certain criteria such as cultural standards of beauty and thinness," the authors wrote. "When this woman is made aware of these cultural standards—perhaps by looking through a fashion magazine or watching a television program with thin, attractive women—her feelings of self-worth are likely to plummet."[2] This same process of learning about how people see you, or might see you, also applies to economic and educational success. Those fighting stigma and negative stereotypes are conditioned to think they can't meet cultural standards for success. Yale, by comparison, was full of people who spent most of their lives enthusiastically meeting and exceeding those standards.

Off campus, there were many people who experienced life

more like I did, but often more intensely because of the wide disparities between the university and some of the surrounding neighborhoods in New Haven. The dynamic between Yale and the rest of the city brought to life some of the dystopian images I'd seen in the movies. At the center of New Haven lies one of the most opulent universities in the world, and thousands of students, staff and faculty who share in that opulence. But many of the residential areas around the university are home to lower-middle-class or low-income families who have no connection to Yale. The center is mostly white, Asian and cosmopolitan, while many of the surrounding areas are mostly black and Hispanic.

To get a sense of what the Yale–New Haven dynamic looks like in numbers, consider that the university's financial endowment was $25.4 billion in 2016.[3] In 2017, law school tuition was approaching $60,000 per year and the undergraduate college's tuition was approaching $70,000. In 2014, the *Yale Daily News* reported that high-level administrators were earning as much as $864,319 a year, and the average faculty salary was just shy of $200,000.[4]

To compare, New Haven County's poverty rate in 2015 was 26.6 percent, and almost half of the county's residents were considered low-income. The county also experienced higher rates of housing, food and transportation insecurity than the statewide average.[5] Moreover, from 2001 to 2014, New Haven's crime rate was consistently higher than the national average, and the city had two to three times more murders per 100,000 people.[6] These numbers have been trending down in recent years, but New Haven's crime rates are still higher per capita than the country's average.[7]

The Yale–New Haven dynamic became a significant part of my experience as a student there. Campus security often treated me like an out-of-place New Haven resident, which I attribute to the clothes I wore. At Yale, I dressed the way I always had: baggy jeans, hoodies, fitted baseball caps and Timberland boots. This wasn't Yale attire, in the eyes of campus security, and I was often asked to show my student ID. Even when I lived on campus, I was frequently stopped outside my apartment or eyed suspiciously by passing security.

I even complained once about how I was treated when two security guards interrupted a phone call I was having. I was outside the building I lived in because of the poor cell reception indoors. I explained to the guards that I was a student and lived in the building right behind me. I even had a key with me as proof. But they refused to let me continue with my call or go inside without proving that I belonged there. I didn't have my student ID with me, so I had to wait with the guards while they called their dispatch officer to confirm that the ID number I'd given them was legitimate.

My student ID didn't just give me access to the library or a discount at the bookstore. My ID card was my way of proving that I belonged on campus and wasn't a "local."

I felt more comfortable and at home in New Haven itself, and I gravitated to opportunities that would take me off campus and into the surrounding neighborhoods. One such opportunity was the Marshall-Brennan Constitutional Literacy Project, which places law students into local high schools to teach constitutional law. I would teach a class one, two or three times per week, giving me the chance to work with mostly black and Latino students from low-income neighborhoods. Some students were very strong academically, while others needed a lot of help. The best part of the initiative was organizing moot court competitions for students and accompanying them to Philadelphia or Washington, D.C., to participate in national competitions with students from around the country. A couple of us teachers even helped our students advocate for New Haven's board of alders to endorse a proposal to lower Connecticut's voting age to sixteen.

Marshall-Brennan was the first time I saw myself involved in activism and community organizing from a position of advantage, focused on the needs of others rather than me and my friends. Part of why I wanted to escape Yale's campus so often is that I didn't know what to do with the opportunities I was being gifted. I now had resources, networks and skills around me that could be used to help other young men. I didn't want to just attend classes, befriend rich people and suck up to professors. Now that I was part of this elite group, I had to share what I'd gained with others. I impatiently saw my role as someone who could chip away at the barriers between Yale and its neighbors, even just a little bit, and considered my own academic learning to be less of a priority.

Marshall-Brennan connected me with youth who educated me on what it was like to grow up as a neighbor to wealth, while still being excluded from it. Kevin was one of the students I had the privilege of teaching, and he was a particularly powerful voice for his community. When I met him, Kevin was an eleventh-grade student at New Haven's Cooperative Arts and Humanities High School. We have stayed in touch since he graduated, and I asked him to tell me what his teenage years were like. He described being in an army recruitment class at around the same time he was in my constitutional law class and watching the instructor offer a warning to people unfamiliar with the city. "A guy got in front of the class and told us, 'Don't go past these streets to your left and

these streets to your right.'" Kevin grew up in the areas the instructor was telling people not to go to. He shared with me what
he wished he could have said to the instructor at the time: "You
shouldn't tell people to not experience the neighborhoods and only
give them certain areas, like New Haven is just one small place
downtown."

Kevin also told me what it was like seeing university-affiliated
people in the city. "We have Yale people living in our neighborhoods," he said. "They don't look like us or talk like us. When you
have programs where they want to help us, they're weird or they
try too hard to fit in. When there are programs at Yale we want to
go to, they're too expensive. The only time you see us there is when
they want to hire black kids."

Growing up with Yale as his neighbor was for Kevin at times
more harmful than good. Kids who grow up in this kind of environment can easily feel as if the world is excluding them by design.
Every day, these kids walk past a wealthy university with one of
the smartest student bodies in the world. Is it any surprise that a
young person would think the university was simply refusing to do
what was needed to make his life better?

A common response to this kind of exclusion is to try to hide
or change the markers you think are causing people to keep you
out. Kevin, for instance, has lived in several different places around
New Haven, and he noticed that he had more success applying for
jobs when he gave some addresses rather than others. The last time
I spoke to him, he'd moved back to one of the supposedly bad areas, but he continued to use an old address from a nicer area on his
job applications. He believed that employers stereotype young

people from these supposedly bad areas, and he didn't want to lose an opportunity because of it.

Kevin's decision to change details in his background is far more common than you might think. A University of Toronto study found that 40 percent of job seekers from ethnic minority communities across North America "whiten" their resumes by "adopting Anglicized names and downplaying experience with racial groups to bypass biased screeners and just get their foot in the door."[8]

Communities with high numbers of people in the criminal justice system, like the New Haven neighborhoods around Yale, also have the highest rates of exclusion from the workforce. Economist Nicholas Eberstadt, in his study of unemployment among American men, found that those with criminal records were most likely to be excluded from the workforce. "Men with at least one spell in prison always have the lowest employment rates and the highest rates of absence from the workforce," he observed. "Next come men who have at least one arrest in their past."[9] This situation occurs in Europe and Canada, too.[10]

Government job programs sometimes support people's perceptions of unemployment as an active form of exclusion. When job opportunities can magically be created by government funding, there is an accompanying assumption that job creation is a choice that could have been made beforehand but purposely wasn't. The message sent is that the only reason people didn't have jobs before is that those who write the checks didn't care.

I asked Jack Paulishen, one of the public school teachers who mentored me while I was in New Haven, why he thought the proximity to Yale wasn't more empowering to kids like Kevin. Paulishen is a real estate appraiser turned schoolteacher who has taught at James Hillhouse High School for more than fifteen years. He shared two stories that stood out to him from his years of teaching.

The first story was about a kid who wanted to work at Yale. "I'm applying to one of the dining halls there. If I get in there, I'm going to be all set," this student told him. "In this kid's mind," Paulishen explained, "it was never that he could do something more than that. Some kids resign themselves [to the idea] that the best job they're going to get is in the university." Dining hall jobs are among the few positions that go to local New Haven youth, so the many other opportunities on campus are often seen as out of reach.

The second story was about a student who was so talented in the classroom that Paulishen thought he would make a great teacher. He asked that student, "Has anyone ever spoken to you about being a teacher?" The answer was no. "Being a teacher is a way he could have a nice life for himself," Paulishen noted. But the student, a player on the school's basketball team, hadn't thought about any careers aside from playing basketball. It's a common problem, according to Paulishen. "So many kids come in and we talk to them about what they want to do with their life. They want to be rappers, record producers, play in the NBA. Those seem to be the influences that they have. They aspire for this really high, almost unattainable success. They overlook the middle class. How about a job in law enforcement or [as] a firefighter or a teacher?"

Paulishen's observations highlight what he sees as a lack of role models for kids who need support in order to imagine diverse outcomes in their lives. Many high school students are uncertain about their futures, but Paulishen found that his students needed a degree of certainty to stay engaged in the classroom. If it seems more feasible to become the next Jay-Z or LeBron James than it does to be the next Jack Paulishen, students may be less likely to take the courses needed to get into university or even complete high school. Moreover, students facing poverty and other hardships may need to be clearer about their ambitions earlier than their classmates, since they might have only one chance to take advantage of the opportunities in front of them before the need to earn short-term money becomes overwhelming.

Yale classroom discussions were lacking some of these grassroots insights into America's biggest problems. All attention was directed to the role of judges, senators and lawyers in creating or eliminating inequalities. The agency of individuals, families and communities to improve their own lives was barely if ever acknowledged. This perspective was so prevalent at Yale that I vividly remember every time it was challenged in front of me. The moment that sticks out most is when U.S. Supreme Court Justice Clarence Thomas visited Yale in 2011. It was his first time returning to the law school since graduating, and I was asked to organize his meeting with the Black Law Students Association. Justice Thomas's visit was criticized by many of my classmates, and the legal news website Above the Law even covered the controversy. Some of the students who most passionately despised Justice Thomas and his legal opinions were black law students at our meeting. But the conversation was far less confrontational than I expected, in part because Justice Thomas surprised us with his comments. Instead of limiting his remarks to politically conservative talking points, Justice Thomas talked about seeing communities themselves as where the fight against inequality must begin, not courts. He talked about the activism of black self-empowerment that he had observed as a young man in the mid-twentieth century, including the work of the Nation of Islam, and lamented its disappearance in favor of government-dependent thinking. I didn't agree with all of what he said, but I appreciated him bringing a perspective on tackling inequality that is more common in the outside world than within the walls of Yale.

New Haven's social immobility problem is widespread across the United States. In 2017, the Equality of Opportunity Project published a research paper assessing American social mobility since 1940. The paper showed that only 50 percent of Americans entering the labor market today are earning more than their parents, compared to 90 percent in 1940. The primary reason for this change in social mobility is the unequal distribution of economic growth today compared to the 1940s and 1950s.[11]

A 2017 report published by the American Enterprise Institute showed that labor force participation rates in America had "declined precipitously from 96 percent in 1967 to only 88 percent in 2016 (and 83 percent among those with only a high school degree or less education)."[12] This decline has left 7 million or more working-age men out of the labor force. The report outlines issues that must be addressed to help these men enter or reenter the workforce. These include improving post-secondary education or training, reducing dependency on public benefit programs, fighting opioid addiction, developing job programs specifically for workers with criminal records, creating jobs generally and encouraging able-bodied men to work instead of collecting public benefits.[13]

This social immobility problem is made even more complicated by the sweeping economic changes affecting the West at large. The International Labour Organization (ILO) has documented that "in advanced economies, the standard employment model is less and less dominant." The ILO has also observed that "the incidence of wage and salaried employment has been on a downward trend, thus departing from historical patterns," and that "own-account work and other forms of employment outside the scope of the traditional employer-employee arrangement are on the rise."[14] The West's changing economic landscape can be attributed to a number of factors, such as a decline in manufacturing, an increase in automation, a growing gap between the skills people have and the jobs that are available and an increasingly unstable employment environment characterized by temporary and short-term work.

As universities prepare graduates who can lead their countries through economic turmoil, they ought to keep in mind the importance of creating opportunities for social mobility, especially for communities that haven't seen such opportunities in generations, if ever. Many schools, like Yale, have the chance to start by first focusing on the needs of their neighbors.

8

Reentry

■ ■ ■ ■ ▬▬▬▬▬▬▬▬▬▬▬▬▬▬▬▬▬▬▬▬

At 280,000 people, Newark, New Jersey, is the state's largest city—but a third of its residents live below the poverty line.[1] I first traveled there to interview for an internship at the end of my first year of law school and was struck by the city's challenges with poverty. Outside the main train station, Newark Penn Station, I encountered a crowd of struggling Newarkers drinking, smoking and asking for change. I crossed the city's Four Corners intersection, once the busiest intersection in the country, and headed from the train station to city hall. Four Corners was far from the bustling area it had once been. The sound of music filled the air as local rappers tried selling their CDs and pedestrians tried to avoid making eye contact. Most of the nearby businesses were small retailers and fast-food restaurants. There was lots of unused retail space, and many stores looked like they were in the process of closing. I've rarely seen a downtown so economically depressed.

I would later learn that the downtown was struggling partly because, unlike most other places, Newark had been unable to keep violent crime away from the center of the city. Gang violence (fueled by drug sales) was out of control, claiming hundreds of young men's lives each year. In 2011, the year I was there, the city was in the middle of an 11 percent increase in violent crime and was also letting go of one-sixth of its police force because of budget cuts—making it one of the ten most dangerous cities in the country.[2] On average, 13 percent of New Jersey's prisoners came from Newark, which has only 3 percent of the state's population.[3] Single mothers often shouldered the burden of taking care of families because so many men were incarcerated.

Newark's challenges are why I wanted to work there. New Haven introduced me to the plight of inner-city America, and Newark's mayor at the time, Cory Booker, was leading a government facing that plight head on. From news articles and online videos, I saw Mayor Booker as a potentially kindred spirit: a young, black Yale Law graduate who was using his education to create opportunities for others. Still, nothing I read about Booker would prepare me for seeing the city with my own eyes. I was overwhelmed and at times depressed by what I observed in Newark. It was an extreme version of the kind of destruction I had seen in only small pockets of Toronto or some of Yale's surrounding areas. I wanted to find some signs of progress—some hope that the destruction, which seemed out of control, could be contained. Father's Day offered me the hope I was looking for. It was the first time that holiday left me with a positive feeling.

As part of my internship with the city's Department of Economic and Housing Development, I attended a Father's Day barbecue hosted by the Newark Comprehensive Center for Fathers (NCCF). Held at a local playground, the barbecue was open to the public. I arrived to the sight of dozens of kids playing together while their fathers and mothers hung out and talked. Smoke from the grills and music filled the air. Everyone had huge smiles on their faces. That's how I'd always imagined Father's Day was supposed to be.

I went to the barbecue with colleagues from Newark's Office of Reentry, which offered programs to help people transition from incarceration to life back in their communities. Helping people make this transition included getting them access to training, education and employment opportunities, as well as helping them acquire identification documents and secure housing. NCCF was one of the Office of Reentry's community partners, because both groups worked with men who were making the transition from prison to family life.

NCCF was the first organization I'd ever heard of that explicitly focused on the challenges fathers must overcome to support their families and be good role models. I was excited to meet the organizers of the barbecue and pleased when they invited me to visit their office to learn more about what they do. I took them up on their offer and visited a few days later.

The office was humble and small. There was a reception desk, meeting rooms and workspaces for five or so employees. There was also a designated classroom for NCCF's cornerstone Fathers NOW program, which brought together two dozen or so men for eight weeks of structured sessions from 9:00 a.m. to 3:00 p.m., Monday to Friday.

During my visit, the Fathers NOW participants were applying

for jobs and creating resumes. Job placement was central to the program—and a big draw for participants—but Fathers NOW consisted of a lot more, including education and training opportunities, counseling, parenting skills development and community service, like volunteering in kids' schools.[4] The program also provided childcare and professional-looking clothes. The underlying belief that shaped the Fathers Now program was that "men who are in difficulty can be given a stake in society if they are better connected with their children[,] who may be living apart from them. Meanwhile, some of the huge problems which arise from children having no contact with their fathers can also be tackled."[5]

My tour guide at NCCF was King Pikeezy, a rapper and father of two who was born and raised in Newark. Pikeezy had graduated from the Fathers NOW program and was named father of the year by NCCF before being brought in to lead the organization's alumni efforts. Unlike most program participants, Pikeezy did not find NCCF after being incarcerated. Instead, the organization helped divert him from a path that likely would have led to prison.

Pikeezy had actually been on the right track. But he took a break from college and returned home to Newark. His mother passed away shortly thereafter. Back in his old neighborhood and without his mother's positive influence, he found himself spending time with peers who hadn't made it to college, including gang members and drug dealers. With these destructive influences around him, Pikeezy began heading down a path familiar to many in Newark.

Thankfully, two people in his life challenged the decisions he was making. A concerned friend told him he was worried about all the time Pikeezy was spending with gangsters—he even pointed out that Pikeezy's mother wouldn't have approved of this behavior if she were still around. Pikeezy's girlfriend was also concerned, and she asked him to go out and get a stable job. He listened to these protests and found within himself a desire to change. A friend who was in the Fathers NOW program told him, "Someone like you would really excel here. You would love them. You gotta come check it out." Like me, Pikeezy felt inspired by what he saw when he visited the group's office for the first time. He signed up that day. He said going there and seeing the familiar struggles of other men—many of whom were rival gang members he wouldn't otherwise have interacted with in a positive way—made him change his life for the better.

Pikeezy was not the only Fathers NOW success story. Hundreds of men graduated from the program. It had a reported 70 percent success rate in placing men into jobs, and only 3 percent of participants found themselves back in the criminal justice system.[6] Beyond these quantitative markers, I also observed qualitative signs of success. Graduates of the program remained engaged with NCCF staff and told me they felt like they were part of a brotherhood. This sense of brotherhood was obvious to me, even as an outsider, because of the commitment Fathers NOW got from the men who walked through its doors.

Abdul Muhammad, the lead instructor in the program, explained the significance of this commitment for men transitioning away from destructive influences. "Keeping the guys in tune for eight weeks without jobs [is] a challenge," he said, "but most stick it out. A lot of men are used to instant gratification. They've been in the streets. But they are learning about patience, that they have to let this process work out for itself."[7]

Pikeezy and others at Fathers NOW explained to me that a key part of the program was the talking circle, which gave participants an opportunity to speak openly with each other every morning and in the afternoon before the day was over. "You could talk about everything you did in the last twenty-four hours," Pikeezy said. "Everything good, bad. It was an eye-opener. We could see that we are going through the same issues. He may be Crip or Blood, Christian or Muslim, but we're going through the same issues."

Pikeezy spoke about the talking circle as an opportunity to remove the mask he'd learned to wear in order to survive in the streets. The mask was, at least in part, tied to his sense of masculinity, which was about being cool, tough and strong. Fathers NOW helped Pikeezy take that mask off and build the capacity to aspire without it. With masks on, men aren't open about how they feel and the challenges they face. With masks off, they can build a positive brotherhood.

Removing the mask was possible partly because of the all-male space Fathers NOW provided to its participants. If women were around, Pikeezy said, "guys would have [kept] their mask on, trying to holler at the women. Women would have brought other influences." In a profile of Fathers NOW for NJ.com, Chanta L. Jackson described Abdul Muhammad's reasons for creating a mostly male environment: "It's important and beneficial that the staff is almost all male because many of the participants have relationship problems with women. It's important that they don't have any distractions[,] and many times, men are more willing to take criticism from other men."[8]

And yet women were incredibly important to the success of Fathers NOW. The ability to form healthy and positive relationships with the women in their lives, including spouses, daughters and mothers, was a critical measure of success for the fathers in the program. Of course, these relationships couldn't be considered healthy and positive without the support of the women involved.

Facilitating positive relationships between men and within families is an important part of countering the influence of gangs, which are also heavily relationship-based. Gangs offer a brotherhood for members to belong to and misdirected guidance to young men looking for support. In neighborhoods where gangs are prevalent, joining a gang doesn't always feel like a conscious decision. Rather, the social networks in your neighborhood or at your school are also criminal networks. For these young men, the desire to make friends or fit in can alone lead you to gang activity. A local Chicago newspaper documented how relationships between younger and older men facilitate gang recruitment. "Young guys will do anything," said a former gang member living in an Illinois halfway house. "I make it seem like I'm his best friend . . . I make sure he's smooth, mature . . . I say I'll put you under my wing and I'm going to finesse [or manipulate] him."[9] Another former Chicago gang member told National Public Radio, "Most of the other people in the neighborhood were the pimps, drug dealers, dice shooters, ticket scalpers, some type of hustler, some type of, you know, shyster. So I looked up to those characters . . . coming from that dysfunction, all of those behaviors are learned. So a lot of these guys that are carrying out these shootings and acting up on the streets— it comes from a lot of times the uncles, other older males in the neighborhood. It's pretty much all of this stuff is learned."[10]

NCCF created Fathers NOW with an understanding that helping young men leave gangs requires disrupting their existing social networks and offering an alternative network for them to belong to. Researchers have found that gangs in Newark, like in other North American cities, are organized more like informal, decentralized social networks rather than traditional organizations, despite a lot of gang activity occurring under the banner of well-known criminal brands like Bloods and Crips. A couple of years before I worked in the city, the *Journal of Gang Research* published a 2007 study of Newark gangs that observed, "Many criminal enterprises act as loosely structured networks that, while having pockets of cohesive structure, tend to have opaque and dynamic boundaries . . . gangs are more like amoebas than hierarchical business structures."[11] In these structures, gang recruits typically have personal connections to gang members and then are gradually initiated, building trust through criminal acts, earning money and demonstrating a propensity for violence.

Personal connections are not necessary for gangs, though. Social media has emerged as a powerful recruiting tool for gangs seeking out young men who aren't already in their networks. Social media platforms allow gangsters to share images of money, guns, cars and sex that glorify criminal lifestyles. For example, in 2017, a twenty-year-old member of the Newark-area Ella Street Gang pled guilty to using Twitter as part of his gang activities: selling guns and recruiting young men who wanted to buy his guns to join his gang.[12] Young men drawn to crime through social media are more similar to me growing up in Toronto than to young men introduced to crime from their family or neighborhood friends. In place of the music videos that I was fascinated by, these young men have social media accounts to help them fantasize about a Hollywood gangster lifestyle. But unlike music and television gangsters,

gangsters on social media can build personal relationships with their followers, even asking them to participate in the gangster lifestyle they glorify online.

Furthermore, helping young men build positive relationships can disrupt the fear and vengeance that also fuels gang activity. A large percentage of North America's gang violence—in some cities, most of it—is considered retaliatory: one young man justifies becoming a killer because he believes a rival gang is responsible for killing his friend. Sometimes this retaliatory violence will claim the lives of innocent people with no gang affiliation at all. Yale sociologist Andrew V. Papachristos has likened the way gun violence travels through social networks to a blood-borne pathogen such as HIV.[13]

Gangs suffer from a climate of fear and vengeance when members are killed, but a climate of fear and vengeance also helps gangs recruit new members who want to protect themselves and their families or are looking for revenge. This focus on fear and vengeance highlights some of the ideology violent gangs are built upon. In addition to valuing money and status above human life, gangs also promote a worldview that embraces moral relativism. A gangster's actions are determined not by a sense of what's good and right but instead by the behavior of those around him: it's okay to earn money illegally because you're poor in this unfair world, and it's also okay to commit violence against others because they have or might commit violence against you and your friends.

As a law student, I received an education in morality insofar as legal and moral issues overlap. What was absent was any discussion of the grassroots moral decisions all people make. A top-down view of society, which law school offered, didn't care to explore the morals of young men like Newark's gangsters, whose skewed moral compasses weren't going to be fixed by a judge or senator. Interventions that intend to help young men leave or avoid criminal networks, but are born out of this top-down perspective of society, fail to see the moral components of violent groups.

NCCF and Fathers NOW offered an alternative moral code that encouraged young men to rise above their circumstances and be better than those around them. The Fathers NOW moral code, focused on family and responsibility, promoted morals that applied to everyone, regardless of how much money you make or how many friends you've lost. They engaged in a battle of moral universalism versus moral relativism.

NCCF ceased operations in 2015, when its parent organization, Newark NOW, ran out of money. The political landscape in Newark had changed when Cory Booker resigned as mayor to become a US senator for New Jersey. Neither Newark NOW nor NCCF could survive in the city's new environment.

I was sad when I heard about the closing of NCCF and learned that some members of the program felt their community had been abandoned or even betrayed. NCCF's closing left a void in people's lives for many different reasons—not least because it was one of the few groups in the city actively creating positive and affirmative dialogues about masculinity. Fathers NOW participants wrestled with the kinds of questions my mom and I should have been talking about when I was a kid: What expectations should men have of themselves? What should their families expect of them? How should men think about masculinity?

Men at NCCF were encouraged to talk about fatherhood and to be thoughtful about their role in their families and in wider society. Many of them learned to be humble enough to seek counseling and parenting advice, and engaged enough in their children's lives to show up at school and provide or find childcare when needed. They also thought about the risks that crime posed to their families, not just themselves.

What I saw in Fathers NOW was an organization taking some control in a city facing chaos. A small group of young men had come together to build a community based on the values they knew were lacking most in their neighborhoods. In building this community, they refused to retreat from the battleground where the fight for the future of young men in Newark was being waged.

9

Diversity: Part I

■ ■ ■ ■

I met Peter Sloly, the deputy chief of the Toronto Police Service, when I was in my second year of law school in 2012. He was well known in North American law enforcement communities as a progressive voice. He was also well known in Canada's black communities as a trailblazer.

His background is unique. Born in Jamaica, Sloly immigrated to Toronto at a young age and became a member of Canada's national soccer team. Once his soccer career ended, he became a cop. Sloly grew up witnessing firsthand the negative police interactions that are common in many minority communities across the West. He brought those experiences with him to the police force. His willingness to talk from personal experience about issues like racial profiling, while also wearing a badge himself, made him special. Sloly also served as part of the United Nations' international peace-keeping mission after the Kosovo War.

In his early forties, Sloly became the youngest deputy chief in the history of the Toronto Police Service and was tasked with overseeing the force's community engagement efforts.[1] He made his relative youth a strength by endorsing social media as a way both to communicate with the public and to gather information about criminal groups that were organizing and promoting their ideas online.

I had seen Sloly speak on television and had read his words in local newspapers. He struck me as the real deal—somebody who really wanted to lead the changes that were necessary for young people to experience law enforcement differently. I reached out to him with an email in the aftermath of the tragic Toronto police killing of Michael Eligon, a twenty-nine-year-old black man suffering from mental illness, in March 2012. Not expecting a response, I simply wanted to let somebody in the city's police force know how the killing had made my friends feel. Eligon's death had fueled their belief that our society was deeply racist and permitted—maybe even encouraged—the killing of black people by police officers. I thought Sloly was somebody who could do something to improve the situation.

To my surprise, he answered my email. He said he couldn't comment on the specifics of the Eligon case because it was under investigation at the time, but he invited me to meet with him in his office to learn more about his work. I was caught off guard. It was easy for me to write the email when I thought he wouldn't reply or would be dismissive of my concerns. Going to talk to him personally was a different matter altogether, and one I wasn't totally comfortable with. Still, he'd called my bluff, and I felt like I should step up to the challenge by accepting his offer.

We met the next time I was in town. Walking into police head-quarters was a surreal moment for me. I wondered what some of my friends would think if they could see me coming to meet with the police. Surely some would call me a sellout. But I was there to have a conversation that I thought needed to happen if we were going to make things better, so I checked in at reception and was escorted upstairs to the office of the deputy chief.

I walked in, looked Sloly in the eye and shook his hand. Our meeting was the first time I had greeted a police officer in my hometown as I would anyone else. At the time, Sloly was in his midforties and still looked like a soccer player. He wore a white uniform shirt covered with badges to signal his rank, which was a stark contrast to the dark shirts worn by most other Toronto cops, and it made it a bit easier to see him as an individual rather than an anonymous officer. I took a seat at his meeting table. Hanging on the walls were awards from various police and community organizations, in addition to his university degrees. He was obviously respected by people inside and outside of policing. Now was the time to see if the hype was deserved.

Most of our conversation centered on our respective observations of police–community relations in the city. He also told me about his admiration for Barack Obama, whom he mirrored in his own reconciliatory approach to talking about race and policing. Sloly described his experiences as a black person and an immigrant to Canada to share his understanding of negative police interactions. He also mentioned officers he had worked with who'd built positive relationships with the communities they served. As he spoke, I could see the body language of a cop trying not to come across as a cop. He carried himself like a soldier, in a very disciplined and rigid manner, but he tried to be warm and friendly, too. He was doing his best to be more open and accessible than he'd been taught to be. I could see the effort in his eyes.

Two things stood out to me in Sloly's vision for good and safe policing. First, he wanted to explicitly address bias. He explained that police officers, like all people, have biases, and that recognizing those biases needs to be a normal part of an officer's job. Training should attempt to counter biases, performance reviews should be mindful of patterns that illustrate biases and police culture should avoid incentivizing behaviors that are influenced by personally held biases (for example, stopping people based on racial profiling).

Second, Sloly wanted to focus on local community policing. Think of this as the neighborhood beat cop patrolling on foot and in a car. Beat cops would replace citywide officers who move around from one neighborhood to the next on every shift, building few trusting relationships along the way. Community policing would enable the kinds of relationships that garner the best information and reduce the influence of bias (because officers would know which individuals require police attention and which don't).

As we talked, I could see that we weren't speaking just as a citizen and a police officer. We were speaking as two activists. I hadn't been prepared to see Sloly this way because his uniform and badge didn't fit my image of an activist. His eyes told a familiar story of exhaustion and determination, though. The battles he had fought to bring about change inside the police force, however slowly, had taken their toll. There was a better world in his head, and he was working hard to make that better world visible to others. It's not an easy task for any activist, but as he shared his vision with me, I could see the better world he imagined. I could see the communities most in need of better law enforcement having positive interactions with those being paid to keep them safe. I could also see a world where people are less pessimistic about their society's prospects for equality and fairness.

I left police headquarters that day viewing Sloly as the activist he was: an institutional reformer, bridge builder, promoter of engagement and believer in constructive dialogue. I hoped that he could accomplish the goals he'd set—and not just in Toronto but across the Western world, where police profiling is a significant reason young men feel like outsiders in their own countries.

In 2013, a year after meeting Sloly, I graduated from law school and moved back to Toronto hoping to improve policing in the city. I was part of the Policing Literacy Initiative (PLI), a team of young activists trying to stop racial profiling in low-income neighborhoods. PLI's approach was to study issues with youth in heavily policed neighborhoods, generate ideas for how law enforcement could improve and advocate for reforms through dialogue with city leaders.

This work gave me the chance to interact with Sloly at least a dozen times. His efforts to build public support for the reforms he was championing brought him to the same neighborhoods I was working in. He invited people to join committees at their local police divisions, participate in meetings with officers, learn how to file complaints when necessary and provide feedback to him on the policy changes he was leading.

One example of Sloly's message to community groups can be found in an interview he did with *Toronto Life* magazine about the possibility of becoming chief of police one day. "I understand what it feels like to be followed by store security," he said, "to get pulled out of a line . . . to hear my brother tell me he was blocked in by two police cars. . . . Policing is an institution that is always a little bit behind the times. . . . We've done a much better job in the last 10 to 15 years, but there's still a long way to go."[2]

Some audiences greeted Sloly with hostility. He was often treated like a punching bag—a proxy for every officer with whom people had ever had a negative interaction. Other audiences reacted more positively to his message while still maintaining their skepticism. He soldiered through it all. Whatever people thought of the police generally or him personally, no one who really listened to his words could deny that he was genuinely committed to building bridges with young people who felt the police were targeting their communities unfairly. His goal was not just to reform the force but also to build public trust during the process of reform.

I saw Sloly inspire dozens of Toronto youth to become activists. Many of those involved with PLI only knew activism as yelling, marching and being angry, and they'd never been motivated to participate in such efforts. When we met with Sloly in 2013 and 2014, most of us were far along in our journey to leading healthy and positive lives. Along the way, some of us had lost siblings and friends to gun violence and drugs, or had said goodbye to loved ones in prison, gangs or both. We'd also seen people give up on getting an education or a job that could turn into a career. Still, by luck, circumstance, determination or some combination of the three, we wound up on a positive path.

Sloly inspired a lot of us because he came from a place of optimism and trust—and we needed optimism and trust to have faith that our own lives would work out for the better. His message helped affirm that we weren't kidding ourselves by believing the world had some good things we could build on, not just bad things we had to break apart.

Darren, a young man from Toronto's black community, heard Sloly speak a few times, including once at a university event I helped organize. Darren grew up seeing cops mistreat youth in his neighborhood. Unlike me and others from similar backgrounds, Darren reacted to the distrust between youth and cops by deciding to become a police officer and fix these problems himself. He went to university with the intention of joining one of the police forces in the Toronto area. While working as a security guard and going through the police recruitment process, he stayed involved in community service activities in the neighborhoods he grew up in.

I met Darren through the community organizing work I was doing, and I could tell that the tough road he'd chosen was weighing on him. The police recruiting process was taking far longer than he'd hoped. Each passing month made him wonder if he really wanted to be the odd man out in a community where people fear and resent cops. I saw Darren sit silently in community meetings while other activists spoke about police officers as if they were foreign invaders. At times, I was concerned that the strength he needed to maintain his optimism in those rooms would fade before he got the chance to join the force and make a difference from the inside.

Meeting Sloly provided Darren with some of the inspiration he needed to keep going. His eyes lit up whenever Sloly was in the same room. He spoke more and projected greater confidence. Darren seemed less alone with his vision for a better world when he could draw on the strength of Sloly's message. Darren's own optimism was affirmed by this real-life example that you could be both a police officer and an activist at once.

Two years after he and Sloly first met, Darren was finally in the last stage of the recruitment process with a police department in a city neighboring Toronto. I was one of his references. A senior officer overseeing the hiring that year called me. I told him that from his interactions with Sloly, I thought Darren had learned how to encourage trust in communities with every reason to disengage, and how to manage people's expectations of his ability to make things better. I hoped that would mean something. I think it did. Darren was hired soon after. He now works as a police officer in one of the areas where I grew up.

Sloly's efforts to change law enforcement in Toronto left the door open for people who were different from him because he was committed to bringing together voices from inside and outside of policing, including those who criticized him and the police department he worked for. In spring 2015, however, Sloly was passed over for the post of chief of police, and under the new chief of police, Sloly no longer appeared in local media, did less public speaking and rarely participated in community events. Less than a year later, he resigned as deputy chief and took a job in the private sector. His departure was not without controversy, though: in a speech he made in January 2016, before he resigned, Sloly made headlines when he said, "I've never seen policing at this low a point in terms of public trust and legitimacy. I feel there's a crisis in the offing, not just here but right across North America. . . . We run around all over the city in the most unfocused way, reacting to what you call us for, as opposed to trying to understand what's going on and . . . putting our most important resources in the best place."[3]

Commenting on Sloly's resignation, *Toronto Star* columnist Royson James concluded, "He was too smart, too progressive for his own good. He dared to tell his colleagues he wanted them to reform policing, and he paid the price."[4]

Though he never held the top job in the Toronto Police Service, Sloly did leave a legacy as deputy chief. In addition to the reforms he led, such as the Police and Community Engagement Review, which issued thirty-one recommendations aimed at improving police–community interactions, Sloly proved that activists can come from unconventional places, including police departments. He also showed that a diversity of activism is helpful to engage people intent on pursuing change from all possible directions.

10

Diversity: Part II

■ ■ ■ ■

In the years after I graduated from law school, civil rights activism in North American cities quickly changed. At PLI, we started by having measured, thoughtful conversations about policing with cops, journalists, politicians and fellow activists. We made a documentary about the issues we wanted to change in Toronto. I even did a TEDx Talk to encourage people to file citizen complaints against officers when they experience police misconduct. We seemed to be getting somewhere—until it became too hard to hear each other over the literal and figurative shouting matches. Police departments became even more defensive, journalists chased conflict, politicians just wanted to avoid rocking the boat before rushing to make bad decisions and activism became synonymous with anger, cynicism and dramatic flair.

Black Lives Matter (BLM) was a primary influencer in these changes. BLM grew exponentially from a trending hashtag after the killing of Trayvon Martin in February 2012 to a large international network of activists. The group describes itself as working toward the goals of "broadening the conversation around state violence to include all of the ways in which Black people are intentionally left powerless at the hands of the state," and "talking about the ways in which Black lives are deprived of our basic human rights and dignity."[1] Inspired by the headline-grabbing protests and marches after police killings in Ferguson, Missouri, and New York City in 2014 and Baltimore in 2015, BLM quickly evolved into a powerful organization with chapters and solidarity efforts across the United States, Canada, Germany, the United Kingdom, Ireland, the Netherlands and South Africa.

A 2016 study of social media activity between June 1, 2014, and May 31, 2015, found that BLM was dominant in all Twitter conversations discussing police killings. Of the more than 40 million relevant tweets sent in that period, pro-BLM activity outnumbered politically conservative and mainstream news media tweets by nearly two to one.[2] Moreover, on Twitter's ten-year anniversary in 2016, the company published a list of the most-used hashtags in its history.[3] The hashtags #Ferguson and #BlackLivesMatter were first and third on the list, respectively. Additionally, #BlackLivesMatter was used eight times more often than #AllLivesMatter, a hashtag created to counter BLM's social media activity.

I was unprepared for how important Twitter would become to activism. I balked at the idea that social media was more influential than building relationships in person, on the ground. In 2010, the *New Yorker*'s Malcolm Gladwell articulated a similar skepticism, confidently declaring, "The revolution will not be tweeted." Comparing modern social media activism to the American civil rights movement of the 1960s, Gladwell argued that social media platforms are unable to create meaningful political or social change because social media "shifts our energies from organizations that promote strategic and disciplined activity and toward those which promote resilience and adaptability." Behind Gladwell's essay is a generational question about how modern activism compares to activism of the past. According to Gladwell, some activism (such as the American civil rights movement) is better suited for bigger changes because it can better include strategy and discipline. Other activism (such as online activism), which might be more resilient and adaptable, is helpful "if you are of the opinion that all the world needs is a little buffing around the edges."[4]

Gladwell's comments provoked passionate responses. Defenders of modern activism published reactions in *Wired*, the *Guardian*, the *Atlantic*, the *Huffington Post* and *techPresident*. Biz Stone, co-founder of Twitter, argued that Gladwell was "dismiss[ing] leaderless, self-organizing systems as viable agents of change" and that he didn't understand where political and social change can come from. Stone also pointed to the benefits of using social media, stating that it "allows many to move together as one—suddenly uniting everyone in a common goal."[5]

BLM's success is a testament to both Gladwell's and Stone's views. The group's popularity on Twitter has proven, as Stone argued, that the decentralized nature of social media can be harnessed to rally people around a common goal. But BLM's growth also required action on the ground, which Gladwell championed.

DeRay Mckesson, a leading voice in the BLM network, said the group grew quickly after the killing of Michael Brown because of conditions on the ground. "There was no one, two, or three people that founded the movement," he noted. "In the unrest in St. Louis on August 9 [2014], people came out of their homes because Mike's body was lying in the street for 4½ hours. And they refused to be silenced, and that was the beginning of what spread across the country."[6] Researchers from the Georgia Institute of Technology and the Qatar Computing Research Institute found that BLM is most successful at transitioning its online activism to on-the-ground protests when there's "a spike in the intensity of social media conversations, as well as an increase in negative affect and sadness."[7]

BLM grew so quickly that it became the dominant effort to change policing in North America. In *Wired* magazine, writer Bijan Stephen even credited BLM with changing the experiences of black people in America. "I see this in the way it has become a community reflex to record interactions with police—a habit that is empowering, even as it highlights black vulnerability," he wrote. "I see it in the rise of a new group of black public intellectuals and in the beginnings of a new political language."[8]

BLM's dominance is partly a result of the authority the group asserts in its activism. BLM implicitly claims to speak on behalf of those who believe black lives matter, which in turn creates a moral pressure for many people to support the group. This moral pressure is especially powerful for black communities, as was illustrated by the reaction to comments made about the group by New Orleans rapper Lil Wayne in 2016.

Asked for his thoughts on BLM during an interview on ABC's *Nightline*, Wayne responded with defiance. "I don't feel connected to a damn thing that ain't got nothin' to do with me," he said, before pointing to his own success as a sign that America understands black lives do matter "these days." Shortly after, Wayne pulled out the red bandanna associated with the Bloods street gang and told the interviewer, "I'm a gangbanger now."[9]

The outrage following Wayne's interview was directed not at his glorification of gangs and criminal subculture but at him personally for not supporting or identifying with BLM. Prominent Twitter personalities attacked him using words like "disgusted" and "ridiculous."[10] Fellow rapper and frequent collaborator T.I. criticized Wayne on Instagram, saying, "[You] MUST STOP this buffoonery & coonin' you out here doin."[11] *New York Magazine*'s Craig Jenkins accused Wayne of betraying his fans and of "poor role-modeling."[12]

Yes, Wayne's comments about being part of a street gang were *less controversial* than his refusal to be part of BLM. He was labeled a poor role model because of his rejection of Black Lives Matter, not because he self-identified as a gangbanger. He succumbed to the pressure he faced and issued an apology for what he'd said about BLM—but not for glorifying gangs.[13] Even if you agree with BLM's outrage in response to police killings of black citizens, the group has provided plenty of reasons for a fair-minded person to oppose it. BLM has broadened its scope well beyond challenging law enforcement—and taken several controversial and divisive positions in doing so.

As part of the coalition called the Movement for Black Lives, BLM articulated a broader vision for the world in a policy platform released in fall 2016. The platform argued for providing black communities with reparations for colonialism and slavery, adopting socialist economic reforms, divesting from fossil fuels, ending support for Israel, abolishing private education, funding "black" institutions and reforming campaign finance laws.[14] These policy ideas were developed in consultation with sixty progressive or radical activist groups, but not through any kind of broad and inclusive democratic process.

My former law school classmate Amanda Alexander, who is an assistant professor at the University of Michigan, has argued that groups like this Movement for Black Lives are an appropriately bold alternative to reformers who look to solutions like body cameras to achieve change. In her words, "Reformers are asking the wrong questions. They have turned to increased police training and altered use-of-force protocols to end this nightmare. Fortunately, some among us demand another way. Young black activists are not just asking, 'How do we make cops stop shooting us?' but instead, 'What do our communities need to thrive? How do we get free?'"[15]

Whether or not you agree with Alexander about the radical ideas BLM advocates, it's clear that these are ideas that would inspire a diversity of opinions among any segment of our society. Yet, as Lil Wayne's experience highlights, BLM's influence meant that black people and others were expected to fall in line behind the group. Individuals who exhibit a different way of thinking are shamed as if they have betrayed their race, creating a repressive environment for people who want to express different ideas.

The news media has played a significant role in forcing people to fall in line with BLM, despite its radical views. BLM was a preeminent voice in both traditional news media and social media, perhaps because of the significant overlap between the two types of platforms. Journalists, who determine traditional news media content, were the largest and most active verified group on Twitter as of 2015.[16] Such overlap can easily create an echo chamber, with dominant issues on one platform carrying over to the other.

Toronto-based writer Septembre Anderson has expressed dissatisfaction with the way news outlets pick and choose unelected voices, like members of BLM, to speak on behalf of black communities. "Black leaders are crowned not by the communities they are members of, but by media picking their most accessible faves," she wrote. "And for this reason the revolution will not be televised (or covered by the media). Instead of Black communities getting to elect their own leaders, we are presented ones that fill slow news cycles and token black pundit positions."[17]

Some activists or chapters in the BLM network may not intend to essentialize or undemocratically represent a community or cause in this way. But essentialism is an inherent risk in activism organizing around identity groups today. The American civil rights movement of the 1960s focused on changing laws and policies that imposed singular experiences on people based on race, such as the inability to vote or the segregation of public school students. Singular experiences don't exist in the same way anymore because of the success of leaders like Martin Luther King Jr. And that's a good thing. Trying to force a shared political agenda onto an entire identity group will inevitably lead to dismissing the genuine diversity of experiences, beliefs and political opinions that exists among people from the same identity group.

BLM's growing influence changed the environment all civil rights activists worked in. Everything became more conflict-oriented. People wanted to fight, not listen to each other. That was partially because of the nature of BLM's activism, but also because of how opponents of the group treated activists.

BLM's approach to activism focuses on having an enemy that must be defeated and forced to capitulate to the group's demands.

BLM is accusatory at its core. Even the name assumes that people who don't agree with its demands believe black lives *don't* matter. Most people who are targeted by BLM's activism, like police officers and government officials, are made defensive by the accusation that they don't care about black people.

Saul Alinsky wrote extensively about this kind of activism in the 1970s, following the success of the American civil rights movement. Alinsky, one of the leading thinkers in shaping modern community organizing, suggested that activism should have an "enemy." He distilled his experience into a famous list of ten "rules for radicals," the last of which is "Pick the target, freeze it, personalize it, and polarize it."[18] He elaborates on this by saying, "[As] it becomes increasingly difficult to single out who is to blame for any particular evil . . . the problem that threatens to loom more and more is that of identifying the enemy. Obviously, there is no point to [activist] tactics unless one has a target upon which to center the attacks."[19] BLM's enemies are usually individual police officers, entire police departments and politicians (who are treated as symbols of broader racism and inequality). Identifying an enemy is a very effective way of grabbing the world's attention and engaging lots of people. Pursuing change becomes a duel between good guys and bad guys, like a Hollywood movie.

Vocal opponents of BLM have tried to turn the tables and make an enemy out of the group itself. When protesters at an August 2015 BLM demonstration in St. Paul, Minnesota, were recorded chanting, "Pigs in a blanket, fry 'em like bacon," Fox News presented this as an example of BLM's mission. One Fox anchor went so far as to say, "[BLM's] agenda is it's okay to go ahead and kill cops."[20] This video has reappeared in news media many times since, to cast aspersions on BLM whenever a police officer is killed in the line of duty.

In such a confrontational environment, the loudest, most divisive voices take over the public conversation. Voices that aren't filled with anger become dull and boring to many. Those of us who choose not to participate in shouting matches are often accused by those doing the shouting of being watered-down centrists. Many existing activists were displaced or silenced by BLM's dominance, leaving only the most extreme critics to oppose the group.

In December 2014, I helped organize a meeting at Toronto city hall to talk about how local activists could support efforts to improve policing in Ferguson and New York City after the killings of Michael Brown and Eric Garner, while also pushing for changes at home in Toronto. The meeting was scheduled to start after a rally organized by BLM so that people who wanted to attend both events could do so. About forty people showed up to city hall that day, including many who were familiar to me.

As I outlined different policy ideas we could consider researching and presenting to government offices and law enforcement agencies, I detected tension in the room. Those who had just come from the BLM rally were more interested in being angry than talking about policy. Some of them looked at me like I was out of touch because I didn't speak as though the police were my enemy and I thought we should be engaging with them to change. After everyone in the room had a chance to share their ideas on how we all might move forward, I asked attendees to write down their email addresses if they wanted to help me put together a report about policies we could get behind. Of the forty people present, seven signed up.

The group of us who worked on the policy report finished it a couple of months later, in February 2015. We'd put a lot of effort into it, and we genuinely believed the ideas we explored could help prevent the problems highlighted by the Ferguson and New York City tragedies. These ideas included appointing special prosecutors for police killings, improving independent citizen complaint processes and citizen oversight boards, establishing more coroners' inquests and creating mobile crisis intervention teams with mental health expertise.

For months, we tried to get people to listen to our ideas. We couldn't get any traction. Politicians smiled but refused to start a dialogue. Journalists seemed bored when they realized we weren't fighting with the police. Cops reacted defensively, as if anyone who wanted them to change believed they were racists. Activists who might have been allies moved aside for BLM and weren't part of the conversations taking place.

As if in a supposed clash of civilizations, I felt like we were caught in the middle of the conflict, between those who sided with the police and those who sided with BLM. The space in between, where I had previously seen valuable activism take root, such as Peter Sloly's efforts, had shrunk significantly. Our policy report then met the same fate as many others: collecting dust on a shelf.

11

To Brussels

■ ■ ■ ■ ▬▬▬▬▬▬▬▬▬▬▬▬▬▬▬▬▬▬▬▬

For two years after law school, I tried to be an activist in local Toronto communities and work in the corporate world at the same time. I was a corporate lawyer or management consultant by day, and trying to change policing in my city at night and on weekends. I couldn't figure out how to earn a living as an activist and my heart wasn't in the corporate world, so I was stuck doing both. When reflecting on what I wanted to do with my career, I thought back to my time as a student in New Haven and Newark, where I learned ways that I could be helpful using my education to create opportunities for others. So I returned to universities, this time as a law professor. I was less interested in the academic life of law schools, and more interested in developing projects that would allow students to do what I did at Yale: find ways to share the resources, networks and skills at universities with disadvantaged communities outside of the university.

I started teaching at Toronto's Osgoode Hall Law School in fall 2015. The great students in my first seminar made the transition into teaching a lot easier than it could have been. Students in the class partnered up with nearby community organizations to create projects that would aim to increase voter turnout, lower the number of incarcerated youth and educate community groups about Ontario's new racial profiling legislation. We exceeded all expectations of what student activists could accomplish in one semester. I thought I'd be teaching again in the winter and spring, until the Paris attacks occurred in November 2015, and I was driven to start a research project in Brussels the following semester. With Osgoode Hall's support, I left for Brussels in February 2016 to learn how the ISIS terror cell there had become so influential and dangerous, and to see if I could find similarities between young men in Europe and the young men I'd been working to help and empower in Toronto.

In the years leading up to the Paris attacks, under the leadership of Abu Bakr al-Baghdadi, the Islamic State of Iraq and Syria gained international notoriety by capturing and governing territory in Syria and Iraq and orchestrating terrorist attacks in the Middle East, North Africa and Europe. Estimates of the number of ISIS members in these years vary widely, from tens of thousands to hundreds of thousands of people. Senator Ron Johnson, chair of the US Senate Committee on Homeland Security and Governmental Affairs, reported weeks before the Paris attacks that 28,000 foreign fighters—including at least 5,000 Westerners—had traveled to Syria and Iraq to join ISIS.[1]

ISIS's origins can be traced back to 1999. The group has a lengthy history in Iraq, including affiliations with Osama bin Laden and al-Qaeda. Despite the group's claim to be an Islamic state, it is not in line with mainstream Islam in most parts of the world. ISIS is a small minority within a minority of Muslims. It's part of the violent wing of the Salafist subgroup of Sunni Muslims. Guilain P. Denoeux, professor of government at Maine's Colby College, has authored a widely cited explanation of what distinguishes Salafism from other types of Islam: "Salafism urged believers to return to the pristine, pure, unadulterated form of Islam practiced by Muhammad and his companions. It rejected any practice (such as Sufi rituals), belief (such as the belief in saints) or behavior (for example, those anchored in customary law) not directly supported by the Quran or for which there was no precedent in Muhammad's acts and sayings."[2]

Notably, most Salafis are not jihadists. Jihadists are distinguished by their commitment to violence against those who don't agree with them, including most Muslims. The *Atlantic's* Graeme Wood, in an insightful piece titled "What ISIS Really Wants," explains that part of what makes ISIS unique is a "carefully considered commitment to returning civilization to a seventh-century legal environment, and ultimately to bringing about the apocalypse."[3]

ISIS's terror cell in Brussels executed the Paris attacks and, in doing so, captured the world's attention. I arrived in Brussels with a group of Canadian journalists also hoping to identify the roots of youth radicalization and what was being done to save young men from the extremists seeking them out. The Brussels-South train station was beautiful, as train stations tend to be in Europe's big cities. As we exited, I looked around and saw the city I'd expected: a diverse population, nice architecture, clean streets and tourists taking pictures. What stood out immediately, though, were the soldiers patrolling the station in uniform. They were in the main hall, at the exits, outside the exits—pretty much everywhere. I would later find out that the Belgian government had positioned these soldiers in public places partly in response to the Paris attacks.

We hailed a taxi to get to the Molenbeek district, which had become internationally known as the home of the Paris attackers. A meeting at the headquarters of the JES youth organization awaited us. JES (pronounced "yes") is a self-described urban laboratory that provides a range of education programs and social services to youth in Brussels, Antwerp and Ghent. The address we had for the JES office was in Flemish, and the taxi driver didn't know where it was. I thought we were just pronouncing it wrong, but when we showed him the name on a sheet of paper, he still wasn't sure where we were going. What we didn't know is that many streets in Brussels have both Flemish and French names, reflecting the city's place in the middle of a linguistically divided country. Our driver, who was of Moroccan background, didn't speak Flemish, but he did speak perfect French. This was an early sign of how difficult it can be for a newcomer in a city with two prevalent languages. We finally figured out the French name of the street by looking at the driver's old map book (the kind you haven't seen since the internet came along), and we were on our way.

We arrived at the JES office fifteen minutes later. Some of the reporting about Molenbeek had erroneously suggested that it was a suburb quite far from the city center, similar to the *banlieues* of Paris, but it wasn't very far at all. Along the way we saw, to our right, more of the old buildings that make up the city center and, to our left, a canal. We then turned onto a bridge to cross the canal into Molenbeek.

Once we'd crossed it, that canal seemed more like a border than a natural part of the landscape. Everything just felt different. The concentrated North African and Muslim population in that part of Molenbeek stood out immediately. Young men were hanging out with seemingly nothing to do, which is a common sign of people out of work and out of school. There were few businesses or employers, aside from small retail stores and modestly priced restaurants, and barely any tourists. There also looked to be far too little housing for the 100,000 or so people living in the district.

If you traveled to New York City, you might feel a similar difference where Manhattan turns into Harlem. In Chicago, you'd feel it when going from Hyde Park to Englewood or Fuller Park. In Toronto, you'd notice it traveling along parts of Finch Avenue West. In Brussels, it was crossing the canal into Molenbeek's historical center, which is also home to the district's municipal government offices. But what separated Brussels from the North American cities I've visited is how old everything looked. Roads and houses were made of stone. Public buildings looked like they were from another time period altogether. The age of the infrastructure made the visible markers of inequality seem more ingrained, even harder to change.

The entrance to the JES headquarters was behind a gate. I rang the bell and we were greeted warmly by some of the staff. The Canadian journalists and I were given a tour of the facilities and met some youth in passing, which made for a nice introduction to the community. But I detected a defensiveness or skepticism from some of the young Muslims participating in JES programs. After I asked a senior manager about the vibe I was getting, he told me to try speaking to them again without the journalists around. According to him, "The only thing people trust less than cameras here is police."

Two of the JES participants who didn't seem to want to talk to me on my first day in Molenbeek were Youness and Soufian, both young men around my age. On the second day, after the journalists had returned to London, Youness and Soufian were much friendlier.

Youness was born and raised in Molenbeek to parents who'd emigrated from Morocco. He did some time in prison but came to JES for its educational opportunities; he hoped he could own his own restaurant one day and work for himself. Youness said people from outside of Molenbeek think of him as a terrorist. He cited examples of border agents denying him entry into other European countries and police officers making comments after seeing "Molenbeek" on his national ID card. Youness's wife is a white Belgian woman who he said was fired from her job when her boss saw him pick her up from work one day. The appeal of owning his own business was that he wouldn't need to tolerate anyone else's prejudices— nor would his wife. Youness's eyes and body language reflected his exasperation. He looked tired.

Soufian had immigrated to Belgium from Morocco about five years earlier. He lived in Brussels, in a district other than Molenbeek. He didn't look nearly as exasperated as Youness did, but he also appeared very frustrated. For Soufian, Belgium offered the promise of better economic opportunities than he'd had in Morocco. And yet, he said, he felt less free there than he had in Morocco. Living in Brussels came with negative attention from the news media and the police that he hadn't had to contend with before. As we came to know each other, he passionately shared his frustrations about journalists and their portrayal of Molenbeek as a terrorist hotbed.

Youness and Soufian felt rejected by the world around them and had rejected parts of that world in turn. But not all of it. Their participation in the JES program signaled that they believed something good might be awaiting them—some opportunity they could seize despite the stigma they'd encountered. At JES they participated in the vocational cooking program, which is designed to give unemployed youth who are also out of school the opportunity to enter the food services industry. After completing the program, most participants are placed in an internship or job with a restaurant.

Youness and Soufian had interests similar to mine, in that they also wanted to talk about the rejection experienced by young men in Belgium's Muslim communities. For them, talking to people like me about the challenges in their community was a way to fight back against the news media's stereotyping. They wanted to take attention away from terrorists such as the Paris attackers and turn it toward what they saw as the bigger issues. One of the issues they were most concerned about was Molenbeek's 40 percent youth unemployment rate.[4] To them, this issue and others like it had made young men vulnerable to the influence of jihadists by contributing to a feeling of hopelessness. This hopelessness has been called a "no future" youth subculture by Rik Coolsaet, chair of the Ghent Institute for International Studies at Ghent University. Coolsaet has observed that for foreign fighters who leave Belgium to join ISIS, "going to Syria is an escape from an everyday life seemingly without prospects."[5]

Another issue mentioned by Youness and Soufian was Belgium's ban on hijabs (headscarves) in public schools, which I would later learn more about from women in the Baas over Eigen Hoofd (Boss over My Own Head) movement.[6] The ban on hijabs was a barrier for some Muslim schoolchildren and also prevented qualified Muslim women from working as teachers. It became a symbol for men and women alike of Belgian intolerance.

Religious freedom arguments aside, banning hijabs is a type of forced assimilation policy that has a track record of failing to promote the integration of minority groups. During and after the First World War, the United States barred people from speaking foreign languages in schools to force the assimilation of certain minority communities. Stanford University political science professor Vicky Fouka studied German families who were in the United States from 1917 to 1923 and found that these foreign-language prohibitions didn't have their intended effect. Germans affected by language prohibitions actually assimilated less than Germans elsewhere in the country. Her findings were based on observations that those affected by the prohibitions were less likely than other Germans to volunteer for the US military in the Second World War and more likely to marry within the German community and give their children German names. Fouka concluded her study by warning that "negative consequences of assimilation policies may be even more likely amongst poor marginalized groups—such as the Muslim population in Europe."[7]

I spent a couple of hours with Youness and Soufian at an event catered by their cooking class. The two of them had offered to help me meet more people in their community by inviting me to chat with their fellow students. The invitation meant a lot to me because it was a sign that they trusted me, even if only a little bit. The conversation I had with the cooking class went well, so JES invited me to sit in on other classes they offered: housekeeping, construction and part-time high school studies. I met sixty to eighty students from all over Brussels and from all different ethnic, religious and linguistic backgrounds. Most of them were between the ages of sixteen and thirty.

The people I met at JES shared a common dislike of news media. These students were frustrated by the lack of control they had over how people perceived their communities. They felt voiceless. The students also shared a common concern about the way immigrants and racial minorities are treated in Belgium, and they described the country as particularly hostile toward diversity. "You're not Belgian if you look like this," one student said, pointing at his brown skin. Youth of all races and backgrounds used the term "Belgian" to describe their white peers, rather than anyone who was Belgian by birth or citizenship. It was a telling comment about their sense of belonging in the country.

I also heard big differences of opinion on why young men are drawn to groups like ISIS. Many of the students I met agreed with Youness and Soufian that the main problem facing youth in areas like Molenbeek is rejection from mainstream society through unemployment and discrimination. Others, particularly those of sub-Saharan African background, pointed out that black communities in Belgium have similar struggles but don't have people joining ISIS. "It's not Christians, it's not black people, it's Muslims," one student of Congolese background said passionately. The debate between students about how much Islam is to blame for the Paris attacks became very combative.

Some students of Moroccan background suggested that more Islamic education would help ensure Muslim youth were less vulnerable to distorted interpretations of Islam, such as the preachings of jihadists. French philosopher Pierre Manent, who teaches at the School for Advanced Studies in the Social Sciences in Paris, has advocated for investing in local Islamic education as part of his vision for French nationalism. Manent views the growth of jihadist groups in France as a result of young Muslims being French on paper but not in their political attachment to the country. A central part of his plan to create this political attachment "involve[s] the government's insisting that mosques and cultural associations cut their ties with Algeria, Tunisia and other foreign countries and instead actively promote an indigenous French Islam."[8]

The conversations I had during my first few days in Molenbeek foreshadowed what most of my time in Belgium would be like. Muslims were defensive, as if the rest of Belgium had pointed its finger at them to say, "There is something wrong with you." And the news media had amplified that message.

Belgian politicians appeared to exacerbate this defensiveness. Bart De Wever, the mayor of Antwerp, the largest city in Belgium's Flanders region, had controversially singled out the Berbers, a mostly Muslim ethnic group, as a source of problems in the country. "They form an extremely closed society, with a distrust of government," he said.[9] The country's interior minister, Jan Jambon, put the blame for the Paris attacks on an entire district of 100,000 people when he vowed to "clean up Molenbeek."[10]

Of all the people I met at JES, the person who stood out the most was Sara, a sixteen-year-old student of Moroccan background in one of the part-time high school classes. Sara was petite with dark hair, and she wore a leather jacket. When I met her, other students in her class were outside, scaling a large metal structure used for physical exercise. But Sara wasn't feeling well, so she stayed inside, watching her classmates have fun through the window. I kept her company. Sara told me about her dreams of living in California someday, and about how much she loves American fashion. She also mentioned being a huge Marilyn Manson fan and wanting to go to one of his concerts. She even convinced me to download some of his songs. I did listen to them, as promised. They weren't on my phone for very long.

One of Sara's cousins, just a couple of years older than her, went to Syria to join ISIS. This bothered Sara, but she was confident in speaking about it. She explained how much of a surprise his departure was to her and her other family members. They knew he wasn't happy, she said, but had never expected him to make such a drastic decision.

I asked, "Why did your cousin want to join the Islamic State, but you didn't, even though you grew up in the same family and neighborhood?"

"I don't know," she said. "We think about it a lot, but we still don't know."

As we went back to talking about how weird Marilyn Manson is, I was struck by a certain insightful humility in Sara's comments about her cousin. People all over Belgium and across the world have tried to understand why people are influenced by jihadists. Sara was comfortable accepting the complexity of the problem. She wasn't self-conscious about saying she didn't know. Nor did she have some neat and tidy explanation that she wanted to argue about.

Sara's humility was a helpful way of thinking about the diverse reasons for the destruction young men cause. The "no future" youth subculture described by Youness and Soufian is commonly offered as an explanation for why young men are drawn to groups preaching conflict between Islam and the West. Other explanations focus less on what *pushes* youth toward these organizations and more on what *pulls* youth in their direction. Researchers have found that jihadist groups "may provide an outlet for basic existential desires that cannot find expression through legitimate channels."[11] Those who join jihadist groups are also motivated by the search for "greater purpose, meaning, identity, and belonging."[12]

Mohammed Hafez, chair of the Department of National Security Affairs at the Naval Postgraduate School in California, has compared the diverse explanations for jihadi radicalization to a jigsaw puzzle. The pieces of this puzzle, according to Hafez, are grievances, networks, ideologies and support structures. "Just as similarly structured jigsaw puzzles can reveal different images once their pieces are interconnected," he argues, "cases of radicalization can exhibit tremendous diversity even when the variables of radicalization are reoccurring. The puzzle metaphor is also useful to highlight the interdependent nature of radicalization variables, where one piece of the puzzle contains elements of the adjacent pieces."[13]

I needed several more years than Sara to learn to humbly acknowledge the complexity in the choices people make, but it's a lesson I learned from seeing people I care about make bad choices repeatedly. What was clear from speaking with people at JES was that whether we were talking about young men who have pledged allegiance to jihadists, have spent time in prison or need a job or an education, there was a gap between Molenbeek's youth and the country they call home. JES was trying to narrow that gap by serving as a mainstream institution for these youth to connect to.

I was still in Molenbeek when Youness and Soufian graduated from the JES cooking program some months later. I saw them the day they were awarded their certificates, signaling the next chapter of their lives. They had big smiles on their faces—Youness in particular. I greeted them with *félicitations* and wished them well. Young men like these are incredibly important to any efforts to make life better for communities where people grow up feeling hopeless. Their peers, and the generations behind them, will look to people like Youness and Soufian as the positive counterpart to the negative examples receiving the world's attention.

12

Faithless Radicals

■ ■ ■ ■ ▬▬▬▬▬▬▬▬▬▬▬▬▬▬▬▬▬▬▬

While I was in Europe, Muslims of all ages, in different cities and of different ethnic backgrounds, wanted to let me know that the two young men who made Molenbeek infamous by organizing the Paris attacks, Abaaoud and Abdeslam, were not practicing Muslims. I was told, many times, that these young men and their actions should not be associated with Islam—not only because their crimes were inconsistent with its teachings, but also because they were not devout in how they lived their lives. According to many of those I spoke with in Molenbeek, neither Abaaoud nor Abdeslam was considered to be part of a faith community.

This distinction—between people who are actively part of a faith community and the supposedly faithless radicals misusing religion—isn't always clear, but it does apply in many cases of ISIS-inspired activity in the West. Among the young men recruited by ISIS to execute terror plots, there are different levels of religious observance. Mohamed Lahouaiej-Bouhlel, who killed 86 people and injured more than 400 in Nice, France, on July 14, 2016, reportedly started attending his local mosque only months before he launched his attack. Omar Mateen, who one month earlier had killed 49 people and injured 53 in Orlando, Florida, appears to have been far more observant, attending his local mosque several times a week for years. The Manchester Arena bomber, Salman Ramadan Abedi, who killed 23 people and injured more than 100 in May 2017, reportedly attended a mosque in Manchester with his elder brother and father.

Self-identified Muslims with very little, if any, religious observance in their background seem to be a common type of jihadist in the West. In 2016, the Associated Press analyzed thousands of leaked ISIS documents summarizing 3,000 recruits' knowledge of Islam. Of these recruits, 70 percent were noted to have only a basic understanding of key elements of Islam, such as Sharia.[1] Also in 2016, French authorities monitored an estimated 10,000 young men and women suspected to be in the process of becoming radicalized. Four thousand of those were converts to Islam, meaning they did not grow up with the religion or come from a Muslim household.[2] In the United States, 2015 saw the largest number of arrests for terrorism-related offenses since the immediate aftermath of September 11, 2001. Of the fifty-six people arrested, 40 percent were converts to Islam.[3] This 40 percent figure appears to be consistent in Europe and North America. A study by the Henry Jackson Society in Britain looked at thirty-two ISIS terrorist plots in the West between July 2014 and August 2015 and also found that 40 percent of the people involved (mostly young men) were converts to Islam.[4]

ISIS's recruiting efforts have been described by the *New York Times* as appealing to "in-betweeners"—defined as "young adults whose identities have not yet solidified" and whose "uncertainty makes them vulnerable."[5] This uncertainty often comes from immigration and racial or religious identity, but it also comes from dissatisfaction with life. In promoting conflict between the West and Islam, ISIS is able to appeal to people who want to fight *against* the West as much as those who want to fight *for* Islam.

For example, a social worker I met in Europe told me about a young man in his late teens who was recruited by ISIS to fight in Syria. His family had fallen apart because of issues between his parents and one of his siblings. ISIS recruiters attributed these painful experiences to the ways of the West and claimed that the West undermines the traditional family because it's against Muslims and Islam. The message resonated, and the young man was close to giving up on the West as a place he could make a home when police and social workers intervened to keep him in the country.

Another example is Aaron Driver, a twenty-three-year-old white Canadian from a Christian family who pledged allegiance to ISIS and plotted a terrorist act in Ontario that was interrupted by law enforcement officials. Driver's father has noted that his son's radicalization followed his mother's death when he was sixteen—a period when he became "withdrawn" and "unwilling to talk about his grief."[6] He was unhappy with the world around him and wanted to attack it as a member of ISIS.

The supposedly faithless ISIS recruits in countries like Belgium have had more of a background in criminal activity than religious observance. Belgium's prison system has been labeled a breeding ground for jihadists because so many ISIS recruits have spent time behind bars there.[7] Prisons all over the world, but especially in Europe, are struggling with the growth of jihadi radicalization.[8] In Belgium, an estimated 20 to 30 percent of the prison population identifies as Muslim, compared to just 6 percent of the overall population.[9] In France, the disproportionality is even higher.[10]

Hind Fraihi, a journalist who documented the early signs of jihadi radicalization in Molenbeek some ten years prior to the Paris attacks, has observed that ISIS purposely recruits among criminals "because it needs them for their knowledge of guns, safe houses and the underground scene."[11] Criminal activity also helped fund ISIS activity. Khalid Zerkani, the now-imprisoned jihadist credited with building the ISIS terror cell in Brussels, is said to have "doled out cash and presents to the wayward youths he recruited as thieves and prospective fighters. They would target train stations and tourists, stealing luggage, even shoplifting for their cause. The profits, officials say, went to help cover the costs of sending recruits from Europe to the battlefields of the Middle East."[12]

As I spent more time in Belgium, community leaders explained the overlap between the worlds of petty criminals and jihadists. I stayed in and often walked through the historical center of Molenbeek when I was in Brussels. In my first few walks through this area, referred to by some locals as the Étangs Noirs–Ribaucourt–Bonnevie triangle for the three landmarks that delineate its informal border, I noticed the familiar signs of a high-crime neighborhood: young men hanging out with nothing to do, drug dealers and a couple of restaurants that appeared to serve as fronts for criminal activity.

I then walked through this same area with one of Molenbeek's local community leaders, and he pointed out that those I saw as drug dealers were alongside the guys who spread jihadist propaganda. I was shocked to learn that jihadist recruiters could operate so openly—and in a public park, no less. But it shouldn't have been surprising that areas where drug dealers operate in the open would also be areas where other criminals feel emboldened to act.

Another community leader—this time in a city north of Brussels—also gave me some insights into this overlap between petty criminals and jihadist radicals. He told me about some kids who were unhappy with their local youth center because one of them had been punished for stealing there. Local rumors said that these kids had set the youth center on fire late one night in retaliation, forcing it to close for months. Even with these rumors swirling, police couldn't get any witnesses to talk, and community members were reluctant to give any helpful information. Residents in this mostly Muslim and North African area were not willing to communicate with law enforcement, according to locals, because of a distrust of the police. Not coincidentally, this is also one of the neighborhoods where I heard concerns about the growth of jihadi radicalization. In areas where police and residents don't communicate, law enforcement agencies will likely not have the intelligence needed to combat the influence of jihadists.

In some social circles in Belgium, jihadist groups were viewed as trendy and Hollywood-esque (not unlike the gangster subcultures I'd embraced growing up). In an article given to me by a youth worker in Brussels, journalist Kurt Eichenwald labeled what he saw in Belgium as "pop-jihad" for "jihadi hipsters" who "know more about Tupac Shakur than they do about Osama bin Laden."[13] According to Eichenwald, the young men recruited by ISIS in Belgium love rap music, wear clothing made by popular companies like Urban Ummah, use Islamic-themed hashtags on social media and take selfies while wearing Middle Eastern fashion. A similar observation has been made by Mohamed Azaitraoui, a Muslim counselor who works with jihadists at a Brussels correctional home for minors. Azaitraoui believes many of the teens he works with "think they are Rambos" when they choose to leave for Syria.[14]

Other parts of Europe are home to pop-jihad, too. Raffaello Pantucci, director of international security studies at the Royal United Services Institute in London, has described jihadists in the United Kingdom as being drawn in by "the notion of becoming an international terrorist, a figure imbued with a sense of cool—an alternative James Bond—with concomitant visions of global travel, secret encounters overseas, participation in training camps with guns, all in aid of a world-changing ideology."[15]

These connections between crime and religion aren't unique to Belgium. When trying to change their lives, young men who participate in criminal subcultures often seek redemption from a life of immorality and look for help in building moral discipline where little to no such discipline exists. Iconic figures like Malcolm X and Stanley "Tookie" Williams, the leader of the West Side Crips street gang, stand out as examples of people who turned to religion to find redemption after a life of crime. The Pew Research Center's 2012 survey of prison chaplains in the United States found that Malcolm and Williams weren't alone in relying on religion to compensate for a life of crime. The survey reveals that religious conversion and religious extremism are common among inmates, and that three-quarters of chaplains consider religious programming critical to rehabilitation.[16]

Jihadist groups exploit these connections, and market their cause as a way of finding redemption for a life of sin. One Belgian investigator has noted the relationship between moral bankruptcy and jihadi radicalization. "We have one guy who comes home from Syria to visit people on breaks," he explained. "We know he's in Syria and he'll sneak back into the town, see his friends, and go clubbing. We have CCTV of him sniffing lines of coke and drinking in a club on one break before he goes back to Syria."[17] ISIS convinced this young man that he could indulge himself all he wanted on his breaks because his inevitable death in the name of their jihadist cause would erase all his sins.

This possibility for redemption is similar to what's offered to the petty criminals who are drawn to jihadist groups in prison or on the street. It's a way out—and it's a way out that makes you feel you're becoming a good person. The idea that a person can be a sinner and seek forgiveness through certain actions is offered in many religions.

During my visit with JES in Molenbeek, I met Hamza, a young man who was working through his own experiences with crime and religion. Hamza identified himself as a Muslim of Moroccan background. He had recently left jail after doing a few months inside. He'd had a child just before he was arrested, so his time in jail was especially hard on him. He was around my age but had no employable skills or education, so the prospect of taking care of a family was weighing heavily on his mind.

Young men like Hamza usually participated in cooking, construction or security classes at JES. He wasn't in any of those programs. Instead, I found him in a room I didn't expect: the housekeeping class. Hamza was the only man in the program, so he stood out. I tried to imagine what had drawn him to housekeeping. I know a lot of men who would be uncomfortable with the idea of becoming a housekeeper, and equally uncomfortable being the only man in a group of twenty getting trained for housekeeping jobs.

"Is it hard for you to be here as the only man?" I asked him.

"I'm here to change my life," he said with great maturity, like a man with purpose. "I need a job for my family. This is the job I can get. I was away from my daughter. Now I am here. I need to work." Hamza then shared some details about the circumstances of his arrest. He was part of a crew of guys who got into trouble together, he said, but he was the only one who went to prison.

"Are your friends trying to work like you?" I asked. "Are they changing their lives?"

"No. They are the same. I am different. I went to jail. I was away from my daughter. I change because I need to change."

Hamza said he was religious, and I saw some evidence of that. When one of his classmates criticized Islam in our discussion about Molenbeek, Hamza was infuriated. He argued passionately with her, but he was respectful and restrained. I could see the anger in his eyes when she made inflammatory comments about Muslims. He told me later that he didn't like people who said criminals such as the Paris attackers were Muslims. To Hamza, they were not. Now, as a man doing better things in the world, he believed he could say with confidence that he was a Muslim. He tried to explain the difference to his classmate, but she wouldn't listen. He probably felt some degree of guilt when he heard her words. After all, young men like him and his friends who were involved in crime gave people reasons to unfairly judge Islam as a violent religion.

Even though Hamza considers himself a Muslim now, he didn't

talk about religion or religious ideas when describing his way forward after jail, his redemption. He was focused on his family. "It is good I have a daughter," he declared. Behind those words was more than just idle talk about being a better person—there was also the knowledge that if he didn't have a family to give him focus, he might continue to make destructive choices and become vulnerable to the promise of redemption offered by dangerous criminals determined to radicalize as many young men as they can.

13

Fake News

■ ■ ■ ■ ▬▬▬▬▬▬▬▬▬▬▬▬▬▬▬▬▬▬

The arrest of Salah Abdeslam, the last alleged Paris attacker on the run, happened about a month into my stay in Belgium. He had been in hiding for more than four months, but he was like a mythical creature in the stories I heard in Brussels. Most people spoke with disdain of the crimes he had committed. Others said he was a diversion from the real issues that plague the country. To them, he was a distraction propped up by nefarious forces in the news media.

Abdeslam was arrested on a Friday night, March 18, 2016. I was in Antwerp that night, an hour north of Brussels, presenting some of my research to a Belgian youth organization. After the presentation, the organization's staff congregated outside the youth center, casually chatting, drinking and eating. Their good times were interrupted when they began to receive calls and texts from their colleagues in Brussels informing them that Abdeslam had been arrested. Police officers and soldiers had swarmed Molenbeek to make the arrest, and people were concerned about what that meant for all the innocent residents who had nothing to do with Abdeslam or ISIS. One staff member who lived in Molenbeek left immediately for home because she was concerned about what might happen next and wanted to be there for her family. "I need to go," she announced abruptly while gathering her things.

I arrived back in Molenbeek the next morning and walked around the neighborhood, chatting with people to get a sense of what had happened the night before. It sounded intense. I was told there was video of the arrest on YouTube, but I hadn't seen it yet. In the afternoon, I headed for one of the Molenbeek community centers, the Association des Jeunes Marocains. AJM was my favorite place in Brussels: a warm and inviting community center that provides meeting spaces and activities for youth and adults, in addition to a variety of education services. The heart of this center is a tight-knit group of youth and staff who welcomed me warmly. They made me feel like I had a home away from home.

Older members of Molenbeek's Moroccan community had founded AJM more than thirty-five years ago with the goal of creating a center for Moroccan young people who didn't have a place they could call their own. AJM is located near Bonnevie Park in the most stigmatized part of Molenbeek. It's in an old building with an aged sign bearing its name in French and Arabic. Below the sign are two blue metal doors that open up to a staircase connecting three floors: the first floor is a lounge area including couches, a television, a kitchen and a ping-pong table; the second floor has a gymnasium suitable for a variety of activities; the third floor has office space for employees and workspace for students and adult learners.

Most of the people who frequent the first-floor lounge area are young men, from teenagers to those in their midthirties. On a typical evening, ten to fifty men are there. They are the nucleus of a network of young men who use the lounge area as a default meeting place after school or work—somewhere to spend time with each other playing games, watching television, eating Moroccan-style sandwiches from nearby restaurants or talking about the latest news, sports and music.

On the day after Abdeslam's arrest, I walked into the AJM building and saw some familiar faces in the lounge, but I didn't see any staff members around. I was told they were upstairs, so I went up to find them. I was hoping to get their thoughts on what had happened the night before. In the third-floor offices I saw a group of people huddled around a laptop watching the YouTube video of Abdeslam's arrest. The group welcomed me to join them at the screen.

The short video shows dozens of police officers and soldiers approaching what looks like a townhouse or apartment in Molenbeek. They surround the door of this residence in a semicircle, blocking off any potential escape route. Abdeslam opens the door to a sea of uniformed men and women pointing guns in his direction. In what can only be described as a cartoonishly foolish act, he tries to make a run for it. Predictably, his strategy doesn't work. It looks as if he is shot in the leg before being easily apprehended.

After watching the video, the staff and youth continued to talk about it, describing the video as almost comical. One staff member sarcastically remarked, "They say this is some criminal genius international terrorist?" A youth in the huddle laughed, calling Abdeslam "stupid" for attempting to run through a crowd of police officers and soldiers.

To them, the video was evidence that Abdeslam wasn't the person the news media said he was. It was proof that he was a foolish scapegoat. A patsy, even. They replayed the video for another good laugh at how ridiculous Abdeslam looked when trying to get away. The huddle around the laptop then disbanded and just a few of us were left.

I asked one of the remaining staff members, "Why do you think people are making the Paris attacks about Abdeslam if he's not the real leader?"

"They want to say it's Molenbeek and Muslims," he explained.

"Who is 'they'?"

"The world has to fight something," he said. "After Communism they need something. To be the USA, you have to fight something, and they choose Islam. The West's view is against Islam. As Muslims, we don't have a goal to invade. We only want to live in Europe as Muslims."

Abdeslam's arrest fueled a number of alternative explanations for what exactly was happening in Belgium at that time. For example, in the video of his arrest, it appears that he has a note in his hand while he attempts to run away. That note is a blank canvas for anyone looking to add new dimensions to the story. The discovery of Abdeslam's hiding spot in Molenbeek also seemed dubious to some people I spoke with. Brussels police said they became suspicious when an "unusually large" pizza order was made for the apartment where Abdeslam turned out to be hiding. By their account, officers monitoring the area knew three people lived there, so when six large pizzas were ordered, they suspected more people were in the residence. This explanation was unconvincing to the skeptics I met in Molenbeek.

The most compelling evidence of a conspiracy was a news report that revealed a local law enforcement agency in the Belgian city of Mechelen had received but failed to act on a tip that might have led more quickly to Abdeslam's arrest after the Paris attacks.[1] A former employee who specialized in radicalization alerted the officers to the suspected radicalization of Abid Aberkan, who was a cousin of Abdeslam's. Mechelen police deemed this information "unreliable" and failed to share it with national law enforcement or Brussels police. Aberkan was later found to be the person hiding Abdeslam. The manhunt for Abdeslam might have been a lot briefer if Aberkan's suspected radicalization was more widely known. For people looking for conspiracy theories, this was evidence that law enforcement agencies weren't as committed to finding Abdeslam as they made it seem—perhaps because he wasn't as central to the terrorist threat as the official story made him out to be.

The skepticism I found in Belgium regarding Abdeslam and the Paris attacks reflected a much deeper and more widespread problem: distrust of news outlets as authorities on truth. Many people saw journalists as agents of misinformation and stigma, rather than gatekeepers of facts. News media losing credibility in this way creates a slippery slope. The official explanation becomes easy to dismiss, and in the absence of an official explanation, all sorts of ideas can take root, including conspiracy theories and propaganda.

I saw firsthand the distrust of the media in Molenbeek when the Canadian journalists who'd originally accompanied me to Belgium made a return visit to meet with several community leaders. Three of us walked from AJM to Bonnevie Park, which had become a special place to me because I saw a lot of the same problems there that I encountered in North America. Apart from the drug dealers and jihadists known to hang out there, the park was frequented by young guys just trying to be cool. Local tough guys occupied the park as if it were their own. Normally I didn't attract much attention from them because I was often accompanied by someone from AJM or could blend in with the crowd when by myself. My experience was very different when I went into the park with the journalists.

The cameraman with us set up his equipment next to the park's soccer pitch, hoping he could include some shots in a news story about Molenbeek. One of the local tough guys saw us and decided he would make himself known. I recognized him from an earlier visit to the park because he was wearing the same dark purple hoodie and black fitted baseball cap. He walked over and started cussing at us, demanding we leave. He spoke as if he had the authority of the entire park behind him.

Not wanting to be filmed is totally reasonable, but he delivered his objections in an almost cinematic manner. He treated the journalists as if they were paparazzi there to see him. The spectacle reminded me of the time when Tupac Shakur aggressively confronted the media on his way out of a police station. Wearing a Detroit Red Wings jersey, the rapper got in the face of the journalists, spitting at them numerous times. This guy in the purple hoodie didn't spit, but he was equally dramatic, flailing his arms and looking around to make sure people got the message he was trying to deliver. Needless to say, we were not in the park for very long.

At another community center, I met a young man who didn't have the kind of role models and mentors available at AJM. Mohammed, a young Muslim man of Italian background, had a long beard and wore traditional Arab clothing underneath his hoodie. We initially talked about what life is like for Muslims in Brussels, and he was very concerned about Islamophobia and discrimination. He was from a different district, a wealthier one where there are fewer Muslim residents. He said his neighbors often looked at him with suspicion and he didn't feel like a free person.

Mohammed focused a lot on the perceived inaccuracies of the news media when we talked. "They are telling lies about Muslims," he repeated many times when defending his faith and his community.

"Where do you get the real news?" I asked.

He pulled out his phone and showed me some of the articles he had been reading. Many were in French, which I could follow for the most part, and others were in Arabic, which I couldn't understand at all. He pointed to one in particular, as if he had the evidence to prove the Western news media is corrupt. "They don't show you this," Mohammed said, explaining that the article was about the Saudi Arabian government executing suspected terrorists and denouncing jihadist groups such as al-Qaeda and ISIS. He looked me in the eyes and said with strong conviction: "They don't show you what Saudi Arabia does so you will think all Muslims are terrorists."

Mohammed continued to go through news stories while I

talked to one of his friends. In a few moments, he interjected to show me another piece of "real news." This time it was an article claiming that Jewish businesses, synagogues and community centers received extra security from the Belgian military. Mohammed took that as proof of a conspiracy to associate Muslims with terrorism by denying them equal security, as if they were not also in danger. "Where is our security?" he asked with indignation.

Mohammed was so frustrated with the news media that it seemed like *anything* offering an alternative take was appealing. I asked him whom he talks to about the things he reads online and he dismissively replied, "People don't know the truth."

ISIS distinguished itself from other criminal organizations by expertly exploiting the media's eroding credibility and using social media platforms to spread conspiracy theories and propaganda. Thus, it's not surprising that ISIS would find success recruiting young men in communities where distrust of traditional news outlets is particularly high. ISIS social media channels are filled with text and videos promoting the group's successes in gaining control over physical territories in Syria and Iraq, calling to Muslims around the world to join the efforts to build a caliphate and disputing the claims of news outlets and governments.

Researchers from the University of Miami's Complexity Initiative examined ISIS's method for spreading conspiracy theories and propaganda through a series of "ad hoc virtual communit[ies] that anyone can create on social media sites." From January 1 to August 31, 2015, these researchers found 196 of these communities involving 108,086 individuals. These communities tended to be short-lived because they were quickly shut down by counterterrorism efforts, but they were prevalent enough that "any online 'lone wolf' actor will truly be alone only for short periods of time. . . . Any such lone wolf was likely either recently in [a virtual community] or will soon be in one."[2] The appeal of these virtual communities to young men unsure of what to believe isn't hard to understand. They offer some certainty when traditional authorities on truth, like the media, are torn down.

Young men who walk the halls of AJM or similar community institutions have role models and mentors in their lives who can help them navigate the conspiracy theories and propaganda to which they're exposed. The conversation I observed after watching the video of Abdeslam's arrest is an example of that. The young people at AJM can discuss what they see online with adults who are capable of debating with them and challenging their assumptions. Young men who lack these community supports are less likely to openly discuss the information they access, and thus are more likely to be influenced by conspiracy theories and propaganda.

My friend J. D. Vance, author of *Hillbilly Elegy*, has observed the erosion of the media's credibility in white working-class communities in the United States as well. According to Vance, the information gaps created by distrust of these authorities are quickly filled by conspiracy theories, such as the one suggesting that Barack Obama was born in Kenya. Vance explains that his community in southwestern Ohio "had lost any trust in the media as guardians of truth and consequently many were willing to believe all manner of conspiracies about our allegedly foreign-born president and his supposed grabs for power." Vance believes white working-class Americans and the challenges they face, such as opioid addiction and the decline of manufacturing jobs, have been underrepresented in news stories, largely because the people who write those stories don't live in or associate with working-class communities. That underrepresentation, in his view, is a primary contributor to the erosion of credibility of these "guardians of the truth."[3]

That eroding credibility is also intertwined with the rise of social media platforms as significant sources of information. Social media has made it easy for alternative news sources to reach the public—including those that may not meet journalistic standards. Anyone with a Facebook, Twitter or Instagram account knows how easy it is for misinformation to travel with the right image or video. But traditional media outlets have also emboldened these sources of alternative news, both accurate and inaccurate, because of their own credibility problems. People who don't trust the media will look elsewhere, and sometimes alternatives gain credibility just by being different.

After the 2016 US presidential election, concerns over the media's eroding credibility went mainstream. When Donald Trump won the presidency—blindsiding journalists who thought he had no chance of victory—people finally began to pay attention to the frustrations that had been articulated in places like Molenbeek and Vance's community for years. The term "fake news" emerged, initially, as a way of describing the inaccurate or illegitimate alternative news sources blamed for turning the election in Trump's favor; later Trump also used the term to attack news stories from credible outlets that he deemed unfair or biased.

BuzzFeed conducted a study of the popularity of "fake news" during Trump's campaign. The study found that "the 20 top-performing false election stories from hoax sites and hyperpartisan blogs generated 8,711,000 shares, reactions, and comments on Facebook," while "the 20 best-performing election stories from 19 major news websites generated a total of 7,367,000 shares, reactions, and comments on Facebook."[4] In other words, the top fake news stories got significantly more attention on Facebook than the top real news stories. One of the most popular of these false stories suggested that Hillary Clinton had connections to ISIS. In the wake of Trump's election, tech companies vowed to fight back against fake news. Google announced it would withhold its lucrative ads from news sites deemed fake.[5] Facebook introduced a sophisticated policy to monitor material posted by users with the help of third-party fact-checkers. Disputed stories would get tagged with disclaimers.[6] But while these efforts address fake news, they do nothing to tackle the credibility problem facing real news outlets, which helps create a demand for fake news in the first place. Nathan J. Robinson of *Current Affairs* magazine has argued that the problem facing the media can't be fixed by a Google or Facebook policy alone. "The only way to counter fake news is with real news," he asserts. "Not fake real news, or news that merely looks like news but is actually opinion or allegation. Actual real news. Substantive and serious reporting. A commitment to avoiding innuendo and anonymous sources. Transparency and a willingness to atone for mistakes."[7]

Weeks after Abdeslam's arrest, I attended a workshop in Belgium organized by the US State Department. The goal of the workshop was to help European Muslim community leaders learn some skills and strategies for strengthening civil society organizations. But the workshop quickly became a spirited discussion about the biases of media outlets and journalists.

The dozen or so people running the workshop were all Americans working for either the US government or organizations such as the Ford Foundation and Media Matters for America. The two dozen Muslim community leaders attending the workshop were Europeans from a diverse range of civil society organizations, including Scouts and Guides, local art theaters, youth groups and organizations promoting religious freedom.

Throughout the workshop, I detected a gap between the American organizers and the European attendees. Some of the issues discussed weren't connecting on both sides. For example, when the organizers brought up the idea of raising funds from private foundations, the community leaders seemed to think that was impossible in Europe. Corporations don't want to give money to Muslims, they said. Or when we talked about lobbying different levels of government, the attendees expressed a deep cynicism about whether European governments would care at all.

We had a breakthrough, though, when we talked about the media and negative stereotypes. One of the workshop presenters, Ali Noorani, the director of the Washington-based National Immigration Forum (NIF), discussed his organization's campaigns to help people understand the implications of the political debates Americans have about illegal immigration and Hispanic communities. One such campaign features a video titled "Jose's Story," about a young illegal immigrant's academic accomplishments and the positive influence he has on his peers at Queens University of Charlotte in North Carolina. Another NIF video, "Maria's Story," describes the perseverance of a young illegal immigrant and the adults who helped her realize her potential.

Hearing about the NIF campaign inspired some of the Muslim leaders in attendance to talk about their own struggles with the media. One of these leaders was a representative of the Boss over My Own Head movement. She had been quiet up to that point, but she began to speak passionately about how easy it is to find Muslims on European television when the topic is terrorism, but not when it's other political issues. She said, "They're on TV talking about headscarves and they don't have any Muslim women there. We don't see anything good about us [on television]— nothing about the good things in our community." Another community leader echoed these complaints by pointing to specific examples of newspapers ignoring positive stories about the academic accomplishments of Muslim students.

A workshop facilitator from the American Civil Liberties Union (ACLU) connected what he was hearing from the Boss over My Own Head representative with what he'd observed in Ferguson, Missouri, after the killing of Michael Brown. The ACLU's Missouri office had become involved in conversations about the importance of representative and authentic media reporting when the Ferguson police department banned journalists from recording officers on public streets and sidewalks.[8] This ban made it harder for people to tell their own stories and challenge the narratives put forward by media outlets and government agencies.

Frustrations with the media got these Europeans and Americans on the same page, but it wasn't because they were particularly passionate about journalism. Their passion came from seeing what's at stake on the ground when the news lacks the credibility that it should have.

14

Youth Workers Fight Back

■ ■ ■ ■

On March 22, 2016, just days after Abdeslam's arrest, I woke up to learn that three suicide bombers had attacked the Brussels airport and a subway station. I left the attic apartment I was renting in Molenbeek to walk the streets for hours, aimlessly. I wanted to get out there and see what was happening. I also didn't want to be alone. The streets were mostly empty, however. The downtown core, normally a bustling area full of tourists and locals, was a ghost town. Police, fire and ambulance sirens filled the air. Soldiers and police officers were patrolling every street corner. Onlookers seemed scared or, even more concerning, numbed by what had happened.

Brussels felt like a city in mourning. We were all part of one big funeral procession, but there was a diversity of reactions at this funeral. Among the people I spoke to, there was a lot of concern that another terrorist attack was imminent. I also heard fears about the political ramifications of these incidents for Muslims and immigrants, such as increased profiling and police raids.

The bombings had been orchestrated by members of the ISIS terror cell in Molenbeek, which was the same cell responsible for the Paris attacks. These young men had turned on their own hometown this time, killing 32 people and injuring 300 more. The three suicide bombers were all in their middle to late twenties. Less than three weeks later, five additional suspects were arrested for their alleged involvement in the bombings.

I didn't travel to Belgium expecting to find myself caught up in a terrorist attack. I'd expected to see a country trying to recover from the damage done by the Paris attacks. People far more knowledgeable about Brussels than I am weren't as caught off guard, though. They plainly told me that they had feared the worst because they hadn't seen enough changes made in their community after the Paris attacks. Evidently, they were correct.

Unsure of what to do with myself in the days after the attacks, I turned to the place I felt most at home in Molenbeek—AJM, where the staff and youth welcomed me with open arms. I wasn't the only young man in need of the community during those days. The first-floor lounge area was packed with dozens of people who probably felt like I did: scared, but unsure of what to do with that feeling. It was weird that we were all thinking about the attacks and the world's reaction to them, but none of us said anything about them to each other. We just watched television, played ping-pong and joked around like normal.

Some of the older men at AJM could tell there was a tension that needed to be broken. Or maybe a masculine wall of silence that needed to be overcome. They decided that on the Thursday after the Brussels attacks, we would have a group conversation about what was going on in Belgium and how we all felt about it.

The facilitator of the conversation, Bilal, was in his midthirties and grew up in Molenbeek. After completing a university degree in engineering, Bilal worked for one of the biggest corporations in the world. He left that company after several years and several promotions. He said that he saw too many barriers for Muslims in his time at university and in the corporate world. There was, as he put it, too much racism. He was constantly asked why he had a beard, or he was expected to explain news stories about Muslims to his colleagues.

Bilal left his cushy corporate job to return to his roots at AJM, where he had spent a lot of time growing up. He wanted to help other young people get the support he didn't have. He hoped he could help them find success in school and work, like he did, but also make them better prepared for the challenges they'd be likely to face as Muslims. Bilal once told me he saw his job at AJM as working with children to discover what they like to do, then supporting them to do those things. His passion for his community is obvious to anyone who meets him.

On the Thursday evening after the attacks, Bilal gathered everyone in the first-floor lounge. There were probably fifty of us in total, ranging from teenagers to people well into their thirties. It was an open group conversation aimed at giving all of us a chance to talk about our thoughts and feelings. The conversation lasted about an hour. I couldn't participate fully because it was hard for me to speak in a sophisticated way in French, but I could understand almost all of what was said. My language limitation was a blessing in disguise, because it meant I had to stay quiet and listen.

The first part of the conversation was focused on the question of who is a true Muslim, and many people in the circle condemned terrorists for promoting a distorted view of Islam. A few acknowledged that these tragedies happen in many other countries, and that each tragedy should be seen as equally horrible. "We [Westerners] don't care when it happens in other countries," one of the older men in the group asserted, while trying to explain that such tragedies happen elsewhere more frequently. A teenager raised his hand and said he expected more Islamophobia, racism and discrimination against his community as a result of the Brussels attacks. He was the first teenager to speak, and his comments emboldened others to speak up, too. A few more teenagers chimed in to lament the increased police presence in Molenbeek and the resulting tensions between police and youth.

A young man in his early twenties, wearing a gray hoodie and a blue puffer vest, signaled for Bilal's attention. I later learned his name was Nabil. He was one of the more popular guys at AJM. Nabil checked with Bilal to see if he could ask me a question. Bilal nodded. With Bilal's help translating, Nabil asked me what life is like for Muslims in Canada. I explained as best I could from the perspective of a non-Muslim. I said the politics around Islam aren't as extreme where I live. We don't have the same influence of jihadists, nor do we have the same anti-Muslim rhetoric from politicians. I also explained that Toronto is a very multicultural city with lots of minority groups that receive different kinds of media attention; Brussels, by contrast, has diversity but a uniquely intense media focus on Muslims. I did acknowledge that Canada is not immune to anti-Muslim politics. I pointed to the 2015 federal election as a time when many of my Muslim friends felt like they were being attacked by political rhetoric that focused on banning headscarves with face veils (known as niqabs) or encouraging Canadians to report the so-called barbaric cultural practices of their neighbors. Bilal then decided to make the conversation more personal. He asked each person in the group to talk about how he *felt* when thinking about what the attacks would mean for him personally as a young Muslim man in Molenbeek. Everyone's body language and tone changed. Instead of the spirited discussion we'd had about religion and politics, the conversation slowed down and took on a markedly somber vibe. Bilal made it easier for us by suggesting we should all take turns giving one-word answers.

Starting from one end of the room and moving to the other, each man said how he felt in a single word. The most common answers were *foncé* (dark), *morne* (bleak) and *noir* (black). Bilal took me aside afterward to make sure I'd understood what was said. He wanted me to see the personal side of how those men felt. I did. I understood not just the French words they used, but also the feelings they were struggling to express. They were worried that the Brussels attacks would make it even harder for them to feel that they belong in their country.

I left that evening's gathering feeling optimistic because I saw a group of young men dealing with the trauma of the Brussels attacks in a way that was far healthier than anything I knew how to do. I had never before seen young men be so open about their feelings in moments of fear and sadness. I also couldn't help but reflect on the many young men in Belgium and elsewhere who don't have community institutions like AJM to rely on in moments of vulnerability. Those men, I knew, were left to find a way to move forward on their own.

Despite the important role AJM was playing in the lives of young men, I observed how few people appreciated what the organization was contributing to its country. AJM hoped to expand its outreach efforts and education programs, but it lacked the financial resources to hire new employees. Following the Brussels attacks, I was hopeful that people would see the urgency of supporting groups that connected youth to positive community institutions. AJM's employees were very busy organizing programs, so I volunteered to explore funding opportunities, to see if it would be possible to expand into Bonnevie Park. They warned me it would be a dead end, but I optimistically tried anyway.

For weeks, I met with various organizations to see what funding AJM could apply for. I thought I would learn about all sorts of different programs and then come back to AJM with options to consider. I was wrong. People in the municipal and federal governments told me there was nothing available. All the money allocated in response to the Brussels attacks was going to the police and the military. European Union funding wasn't helpful, either, because these funds didn't target local initiatives and were instead focused on national and international projects. Private foundations, which should have had the most flexibility in their funding, considered AJM's expansion "too small" a project to get excited about.

Even after a terrorist attack that had captured the attention of the entire world, the people who control the resources were taking local community services for granted. The challenges in getting this funding signaled a communication gap between community leaders working with young men on the ground and people who sit in offices writing checks.

I saw this communication gap more clearly during a meeting

with the mayor of Molenbeek a few weeks after the Brussels attacks. A group of about ten people, including government officials, community leaders and Bilal, gathered at city hall for a reception for representatives from the Centre for the Prevention of Radicalization Leading to Violence. The CPRLV delegates were in the middle of a tour across Europe to meet people combating jihadi radicalization and exchange best practices.

The mayor of Molenbeek introduced the CPRLV representatives to the director of the district's de-radicalization office, a white Belgian man in his late thirties or early forties who was tasked with using government resources to stop jihadist groups from recruiting youth in Molenbeek. When this man spoke glowingly about his work, there was a palpable tension in the room. Those who didn't work for the government did not agree with the rosy picture being painted by officials. It was awkward. I tried to make eye contact with Bilal in hopes he might feel the urge to speak up and share his views, but he remained quiet. I even texted him, "dude u should speak," but he didn't respond.

The conversation ended as we approached the hour mark. I made my way to Bilal to express my disappointment. "Why didn't you say anything?" I asked.

"If I talk, we [he and the Molenbeek city officials] will just argue," Bilal replied. "They don't want to listen."

"But if you don't say anything, then what will happen? Nothing."

"I know them. I know these people. Trust me."

We were interrupted by a city employee ushering us out to an elaborate staircase for a group photo. Bilal said he had a phone call to make and walked down the stairs, out of the camera's sight.

Posing together felt dishonest. The picture might tell a story of a meeting that was diverse and inclusive. The truth is that the people who are closest to the problem of jihadi radicalization—those who work directly with vulnerable youth every day—were silent the entire time. That picture was a lie, and I knew that's why Bilal didn't want to be part of it.

This communication gap both is caused by and further reinforces a lack of awareness of the role of youth workers as local community leaders. The aspect of youth work that makes it successful in reaching vulnerable young men—its informal nature and flexibility—also makes it difficult to standardize and professionalize. Some youth workers are formally educated, while others are qualified based on lived experience and on-the-job training. Additionally, many of the organizations that employ (or should employ) youth workers don't always see how young people best fit. These organizations struggle to accept the limits of what they can do, and they often fail to recognize that they must rely on informal and flexible strategies to fill in the gaps. Governments and other funders also don't adequately support sustainable youth work because they don't properly value what young people can bring to the table.

The European Commission states, "Youth work seeks to create a safe, supportive and flexible environment for personal development and offers non-formal and informal learning opportunities, personal advice, guidance and support."[1] Bernard Davies, co-editor of the book *What Is Youth Work?*, says youth workers are distinct from teachers or social workers because they have a presence in many different environments, engage friendship groups (not just individuals) and encourage youth to pursue new experiences.[2]

Youth workers can be valuable guides for all young people, but they have a unique role to play in reaching those who are not attached to mainstream institutions. The parks, basketball courts, soccer pitches, street corners and alleyways—in other words, the places where you find some of the most disconnected young people—are where youth workers are supposed to be. Teachers aren't there. Parents aren't there. And if the cops are there, everyone else has left. Youth workers actively seek out young men who may not be engaged in school or work, may have negative relationships with police and may not have support at home. For young men trying to escape a negative lifestyle, youth workers can bring new opportunities to change their ways.

Howard Sercombe, former professor of community education at the University of Strathclyde in Glasgow, has observed the unique value of youth workers in fighting off destructive influences. "Youth workers do work with a problem, but the problem is not, in the first instance, the young people. The problem is the systems of exclusion that make it difficult for them to participate in the common wealth. . . . Youth workers also work with the consequences of exclusion for young people, including the violence, problematic drug use, poverty, isolation and alienation and ill health that predictably follows social disengagement."[3]

Almost everything I learned while in Belgium was made possible by youth workers at JES and AJM who connected me with young men in their communities and shared tremendous insights with me about the lives of young people who feel as though they're without a country. I observed a particularly impressive tradition of youth work in the city of Antwerp.

In April 2016, I joined thousands of others at the eleventh annual SHOOT! street soccer tournament, which is organized by JES and Kras Jeugdwerk, two of the largest youth-serving organizations in Belgium. Teams of five teenagers and young adults competed to call themselves champions, exhibiting incredible speed and skill. Players came from across Antwerp, and some even took the train in from Brussels.

Borgerhout, the Antwerp neighborhood where the tournament took place, has some important similarities to Molenbeek. It is locally referred to as "Borgerokko"—a combination of Borgerhout and Morokko, the Dutch name for Morocco—because it is home to a large population of Moroccan and Muslim families. Borgerhout is a growing, densely populated area of Antwerp with significant school dropout and unemployment rates. Jihadist groups like ISIS and Sharia4Belgium (which sought to bring the country under the rule of Sharia) have targeted Borgerhout, recruiting local young people and spreading propaganda.

The crowd for the street soccer tournament was lively, but the atmosphere skyrocketed to a new level of intensity for the semifinal game between the local Borgerhout team and the team from Kiel-Hoboken, a neighborhood on the other side of Antwerp. Almost everyone in the crowd was from one neighborhood or the other, and all screamed in support of their team as if their pride was on the line. As the clock ran out and it looked like the game would end in a draw, I could feel the intensity about to boil over. The referee blew the whistle and the crowd, made up almost entirely of young men, swarmed the pitch, one side for Borgerhout and the other for Kiel-Hoboken. In two distinct factions, the men started chanting for their respective neighborhoods in anticipation of what was next: penalty kicks.

There was a slight problem, however—the referees couldn't

start the penalty kicks because the crowd was covering the entire pitch. Testosterone was in the air and people were going crazy. I'd heard stories about a fight that broke out at a similar soccer game between the same two neighborhoods a couple of years earlier, and I was concerned that the same might happen here. There was cursing, even from small children, and yelling of all sorts of obscenities in the name of neighborhood pride.

To an outsider like me, it looked like chaos was unfolding, but I was lucky enough to have friends there who could show me the brilliance of youth workers in action. A handful of them— themselves young men from the two competing neighborhoods— were there as tournament organizers, coaches and referees. They made eye contact to remind the young men on the pitch of who they were, spoke with authority, called out the rowdiest by name and established themselves as leaders. Slowly but surely, the crowd calmed down and refocused on the game. The youth workers created enough space on the pitch for a player to get into position and take the first penalty kick. As soon as the ball went into the net, the crowd went crazy again, and men started running back onto the pitch and screaming. But the youth workers again restored order. After the second penalty kick, the same thing happened. And the cycle repeated itself until the winner was declared. What could have been chaos was remarkably well organized. In the end, everyone went their separate ways in peace.

Aziz was one of the youth workers who brought order to the tournament. He's a young man from Borgerhout and also a star indoor soccer player whose reputation as an athlete helps him build trusting relationships with youth. When he walked around between games, Aziz was swarmed by young people who wanted to play soccer with him. They told me he's like an older brother who looks out for them.

Karim, a young father who grew up in Borgerhout but had moved to a nearby town to start his family, was attending SHOOT! as a spectator. We observed the drama on the soccer pitch together. Karim credited youth workers like Aziz with bringing positive change to the neighborhood. He said he once viewed Borgerhout as full of destructive influences, but he now felt comfortable bringing his kids back to the neighborhood he grew up in. Events like the soccer tournament are part of that transformation, in Karim's eyes, because they give young people positive things to do and help them feel good about their community.

I had been invited to SHOOT! by Filip Balthau, a veteran youth worker in Antwerp. Filip, who's in his fifties and lives in Borgerhout with his wife and son, is at the heart of the strong tradition of youth work in the neighborhood. Filip grew up in a small town in the Flanders region, and his desire for adventure took him to Antwerp, where he launched a career as a social worker supporting people fighting addictions before entering the field of youth work in Borgerhout, which he enjoyed so much that he moved into the neighborhood.

On Filip's walk to and from work, young people and parents alike often greet him and talk about upcoming community events. For him, being a youth worker is more of an identity than a job. He has progressed to the level of a manager, and in that role, he oversees other youth workers and is able to bring them along in the tradition he practices, creating institutional knowledge and a legacy.

Filip's expertise also means he has the confidence and skills needed to innovate. For example, some of the youth workers he supervises are developing online outreach strategies to build relationships with people who may not come out to community events but spend a lot of time on social media. This strategy means youth workers are consistently interacting with young people online and keeping an eye out for destructive influences, like jihadist recruiters pushing propaganda.

Filip's success is largely a result of the effort he puts into ensuring that the value of youth work is recognized and understood by everyone willing to learn. He must fight for this understanding; it doesn't come easily. He regularly travels around Belgium to speak to local community groups, government offices and international organizations about the valuable contributions made by youth workers.

In his presentations, Filip introduces audiences to what he has called a "competence-based" approach to youth work. This approach is designed to emphasize young people's strengths, not their weaknesses. Filip and his colleagues describe the goals of this approach as (1) to help youth become "better aware of their own competences, [so] they can better navigate the labor market [and] choose their educational paths and leisure time activities," and (2) to translate the "experiences of young people into competences and [make] them measurable, so these competences can be validated in education and the labor market." To accomplish these goals, Filip seeks to establish a shared vision with youth (e.g., "What do I want and why do I want it?") and then create a plan to achieve that vision (e.g., "What steps do I have to take to reach my goal?").

The strength of Filip's message is that it helps everyone understand what young people are capable of. The better we understand that, the more we will appreciate and value those who work with youth to bring out their potential.

Ibrahim, one of the success stories of Antwerp's youth worker tradition, is an especially powerful voice in helping people understand how youth workers compete with negative influences in the struggle for a young man's future. We met when Ibrahim was a high school senior with a passion for activism. Community organizations looked to him as a local leader and a positive role model. He had become a local celebrity after he was stopped by police and arrested at gunpoint following the Paris attacks. Why? Apparently, he fit the description of somebody connected to ISIS.

Because of Ibrahim's eloquence as a public speaker, his story about being profiled, unfairly arrested and harshly treated went viral online and generated significant media attention. Ibrahim's ability to turn his traumatic experience into an opportunity to educate others about police profiling of Muslims earned him immense respect in his community, where he's now viewed as an authority on the experiences of Muslim youth. In his interviews and speeches, he often asserts that police profiling is partly why young Muslims feel like outsiders in Belgium and thus are vulnerable to the influence of jihadists.

I was honored to meet Ibrahim and very grateful that he made time for me, since he was a person in high demand. We attended several community events together and shared a number of meals. As we got to know each other, our conversations grew beyond talking about police profiling and I got to learn about his own personal journey. Ibrahim explained to me that when he was fourteen years old, he felt like he didn't belong in Belgium and was disheartened about his prospects in the country because of the racism and Islamophobia he'd experienced. He believes that if the option of going to Syria to join ISIS had been available to him at that age, he probably would have taken it. He was already open to the idea of a future in a faraway place he had never been—a place where he thought there wouldn't be any racism or Islamophobia.

While in high school, Ibrahim was approached by jihadists seeking to welcome him into their networks. He said that these recruiters would talk "10 percent about religion" and "90 percent about Belgium." They spent most of their time talking about the problems that afflict minority communities in the West and reinforcing the thoughts Ibrahim already had about his bleak future in Belgium. High unemployment rates, the banning of religious symbols in schools, special taxes imposed on immigrant entrepreneurs and police profiling—all were part of the outsider experience of young men like Ibrahim. These recruiters encouraged Ibrahim to give up on the West, then offered him membership in their groups as a way out.

ISIS recruiters in Europe rely on many of the same talking points that I saw Louis Farrakhan use to communicate with NOI members. British jihadist Anjem Choudary, who was sentenced to five and a half years in prison for actively supporting ISIS and is alleged to have helped at least a hundred people engage in terrorism in Europe, has employed some of the same themes as Farrakhan in his public comments.[4] In an interview with CNN, Choudary presented ISIS's territory as a misunderstood place, much as Farrakhan had claimed Saddam Hussein's Iraq was misunderstood. "There's peace, there's no corruption, there's no bribery, there is [no] usury, there is no alcohol and gambling. . . . By the way, we have videos of all Christians, coming back to Mosul, you can see this, embracing Islam. You don't show those because it doesn't fit your agenda."[5]

Choudary also mirrored Farrakhan in his attempts to identify

US foreign policy, not terrorists, as the real enemy of Muslims. "Where was freedom of religion and expression for people in Guantanamo Bay? What about the people being tortured in Abu Ghraib, Baghdad—was that freedom in practice? . . . Did you hold that up as [an] example of liberty and democracy, the American way, the American life? You know, George Bush flushed those down the toilet. He said, you know, we can flush them away because we're talking about terrorism."[6]

Ibrahim reminded me a lot of myself, but he was ahead of me in how young he was when he understood the importance of education. He had read Malcolm X's autobiography shortly before we met, so personal transformation was at the top of his mind. Malcolm was one of his heroes, and Ibrahim hoped to become as powerful a voice for his community as Malcolm X was for black Americans. His plan was to become a civil rights lawyer, and he expected to start law school after graduating from high school.

I asked Ibrahim about his transformation from someone who felt hopeless enough at fourteen to contemplate going to Syria into an all-star student aspiring to go to law school. He credited the youth workers in his neighborhood, saying they had found ways to give him the leadership opportunities he needed to grow and mature. For example, he was empowered to organize athletic activities for kids and to help build a playground near the housing complex he grew up in. Youth workers had encouraged him to be more involved in his student community at school, where he found additional role models and saw examples of Belgians embracing diversity. Once his mind had opened up to the possibilities youth workers showed him, he couldn't go back to thinking he didn't belong in his own country.

15

Jobs

■ ■ ■ ■ ▬▬▬▬▬▬▬▬▬▬▬▬▬▬▬▬▬▬▬

The conventional wisdom in most North American communities is that jobs are important to helping young men lead positive, healthy lives. I've attended plenty of community meetings and heard youth and parents ask for job opportunities as an answer to crime, addiction, broken families and a variety of other social ills. With decent jobs, these community voices say, young men will abandon negative behaviors and become positive contributors to society.

In the face of crisis, North American governments make these same assumptions about jobs. For instance, 2016 saw increases in gun violence across North America. Gang violence contributed to a 14 percent spike in the number of murders in the thirty largest American cities (as compared to 2015).[1] Chicago led the way with a 17.7 percent increase, accounting for almost half of the overall national increase. Gun homicides in Canada's largest city, Toronto, were up 54 percent in 2016 over the previous year.[2] Political leaders in both Chicago and Toronto had identical responses: we need more jobs.

Toronto mayor John Tory announced more funding for job programs, claiming, "This is going to engage [young people] in positive activity and keep them away from those who would have them engage in negative activity. A lot of the time it is idle hands that get in trouble, kids and adults."[3] This new funding was a response to calls from community leaders to do more.[4] In Chicago, Arne Duncan, the former head of Chicago Public Schools and a former US secretary of education, identified a lack of jobs as being at the root of the problem of gun violence in the city. "If we can work in communities and provide real training that leads to real skills that can lead to real jobs, I have confidence that these men and women will make different choices," he said.[5]

I encountered similar sentiments in Belgium after the Paris and Brussels attacks. During a kabob dinner with Muslim youth leaders in Antwerp in March 2016, I pressed people on what exactly should be done by the Belgian government to address the concerns of Europe's Muslim and Moroccan communities. The youth leaders represented different ends of the political spectrum, from those with harshly anti-American and anti-Western views to a moderate incremental reformist who firmly believed in Western democracies. To my surprise, despite their very different political leanings, people from both ends of the spectrum had the same answer: stop labor market discrimination against Muslims in Europe. Research published by the National Bank of Belgium suggests the country may have some unique problems in this area. The research showed that second-generation Belgians have the same challenges integrating into the labor market as first-generation newcomers to the country.[6]

In Belgium I nodded in agreement when people talked about jobs as the answer to keeping young men off paths of destruction, just as I've done in Chicago, Toronto and other North American cities I've visited or worked in. I'd never really questioned this way of thinking until I traveled to Egypt to learn about an organization called Education for Employment (EFE). While there, I saw people react to these ideas about jobs in a completely different way. Some were even offended by the suggestion that a person without a job is more vulnerable to destructive influences than those with jobs.

I landed in Egypt just days before EgyptAir Flight 804 crashed into the Mediterranean on May 19, 2016, in what was initially suspected to be an act of terrorism orchestrated by ISIS (and still is in some circles). It gave me another opportunity to see the deep sadness and fear that terrorism inflicts on a country. At that time, the Egyptian military was at war with a group called the Sinai Province, which had pledged allegiance to ISIS and was fighting for control of the Sinai Peninsula. Because of Egypt's domestic concerns, combined with events happening elsewhere in the world, terrorism and jihadi radicalization were common topics of conversation while I was in Cairo.

The organization that had inspired my trip to Egypt, EFE, is a network of nonprofits that offer job training to youth in the Middle East and North Africa. EFE sponsors programs in Egypt, Jordan, Palestine, Morocco, Tunisia, Yemen and Saudi Arabia. It was launched as a response to the 9/11 attacks: its founder, New York entrepreneur Ron Bruder, turned his attention to the lack of jobs for young Arabs in the Middle East and North Africa.[7] Bruder concluded that "existing institutions weren't giving young people the skills and training they needed to secure jobs and succeed in the workplace."[8] So he put up $10 million of his own money to start EFE. Bruder has compared the group's approach to the Marshall Plan. "After World War II, we [the United States] had reached out to the countries that we had been fighting with months earlier, rebuilt their economies, and made long-term allies out of them," he noted. "I felt we should be doing that in this region."[9]

The US government under George W. Bush and Barack Obama has supported Bruder's vision with financial contributions to EFE, and EFE was even listed as a counterterrorism organization on US State Department reports in 2008 and 2009.[10] The organization's Marshall Plan–inspired approach was very much in line with the Obama administration's view on jobs as a counterterrorism effort. In 2015, Marie Harf, then spokesperson for the US State Department, identified job creation as a key part of the Obama administration's counterterrorism strategy. The government's expressed goal was to answer the question "What makes these 17-year-old kids pick up an AK-47 instead of trying to start a business?"[11] Harf explained, "We can work with countries around the world to help improve their governance. We can help them build their economies so they can have job opportunities for these people."[12]

I wanted to learn about EFE because its approach to fighting terrorism seemed in line with crime-fighting strategies I'd learned about in North America. The World Economic Forum describes EFE as an organization that responds to two problems at the same time: "the skill gap resulting from educational systems that fail to prepare graduates for private-sector needs" and "the opportunity divide facing low-income, talented youth who do not have the contacts or the soft skills to enter the job market."[13] I thought there might be something to learn from EFE's work that could be applied in places like Antwerp, Chicago and Toronto, where people have high hopes for what jobs can do for the vulnerable young men in their communities.

When I contacted a member of EFE's communications team and said I wanted to learn more about the organization, they suggested I visit their Egypt office, which opened in 2008. It was described to me as one of their fastest-growing, which was unsurprising considering the far-reaching issues with youth unemployment there. Egypt is far younger than any country in the West, with 60 percent of its population under the age of thirty.[14] Of the Egyptians who are under thirty but of working age, one-third are unemployed.[15]

Almost every day for about two months I made my way from my apartment in the Abdeen district of Cairo through Tahrir Square (famous as the home of the 2011 Egyptian revolution), across the Nile and over to the Dokki district of Giza, where EFE's office is located. It was a beautiful half-hour walk when the heat wasn't too bad and traffic wasn't too overwhelming. During the month of Ramadan, it was also fascinating to walk back to my apartment. Cairo, a normally hectic and chaotic city, would be totally quiet for the hour when families were at home or in restaurants breaking their fast. Then people would slowly return to the city, spending time together until well after midnight.

EFE's Egypt office works with unemployed youth from humble economic backgrounds in different cities, including Cairo, Giza, Al Qalyubiyah, Alexandria, Al Minufiyah, Al Sharqiyah, Qina, Port Said and Al Minya. Most of the thousands of young people who've come through EFE's doors are graduates of public universities who require additional support or training to enter Egypt's labor market. EFE's programming is developed in partnership with employers, who look to the organization as a way to ensure that prospective hires are trained and supported as needed. These employers come from a variety of industries, such as retail, hospitality, manufacturing, information and communications technology, and business process outsourcing.

As I learned about EFE's programs, I also got an opportunity to see the people behind this work. The staff are well-educated, well-traveled and passionate people who are genuinely motivated by a certain kind of patriotic desire to see their country improve. Of the few dozen youth participants and alumni I spoke with, almost all were university graduates who learned about EFE from friends or the group's Facebook page. Most of them were drawn to EFE's programs because of the skills they hoped to gain and the possibility of getting a first job in a large company.

After attending an EFE class focused on English-language skills, I decided to ask people what they thought of job programs as a counterterrorism strategy in Egypt. I sat down with one of the participants, Tarek, to chat about his experience at EFE. He was a few years younger than me and had recently graduated from a public university. When I asked about jobs and terrorism, he looked at me with incredulity. Half jokingly and half seriously, he responded with a question of his own: "Do you think I would be a terrorist if I'm not here?"

Tarek explained that he didn't agree with the idea that unemployed youth are somehow more vulnerable to the influence of jihadists. He actually seemed offended by the idea, so I backed off for the moment. That evening, however, we continued our conversation as we both walked back to downtown Cairo from the EFE office in Giza. Before crossing the Nile, we sat down to chat at a pizzeria on the island of Zamalek. We overcame the awkwardness of our first conversation by chatting about our mutual love of hip-hop. Tarek had watched many of the same rap battles on YouTube that I had, from the Ultimate Rap League and King of the Dot, my hometown battle rap league in Toronto. We even had some favorite rappers in common.

Tarek told me he was a rapper himself and had recorded music in the past. I asked him where I could find some of his songs, but he had taken them all offline. He was afraid the Egyptian government would find them and consider him a threat because he rapped about political issues, such as economic inequality and democracy. It all seemed rather innocuous to me, but I knew the Egyptian government was openly harsh toward public figures who were critical of the military dictatorship, and the government's anti-free-speech agenda made a lot of people paranoid. Tarek confessed that he'd been hesitant to speak to me at first because he feared that I was a government agent.

We finished our pizza and I tried a second time to ask him about jobs and terrorism. He advised me to focus on religious extremism. "It's about how these boys grow up, what their parents tell them about religion," he asserted. From his perspective, being employed or unemployed doesn't change a person's religious views. He was offended by the suggestion that people are simply material beings whose economic circumstances can change their morals. He told me he believes a person's religious views are far more relevant to his susceptibility to terrorism than how much money he makes.

Tarek's comments were markedly different from what I've heard in Western cities, where most people I've met are more comfortable attributing violent crime to economics. My conversation with Tarek made me wonder if our insistence that jobs can save young men from paths of destruction is reducing them to material beings in exactly the way he feared. Are we saying that what's in their pockets is more likely to determine what they do with their lives than what's in their minds or hearts? What do we really mean when we tell a government that our kids will be more vulnerable to destructive influences if they don't have jobs? What does it mean when we allow a government to say that to us?

I asked more people in Cairo if job creation would help fight against terrorism in Egypt, and I learned that Tarek's views weren't unique. A friend of a friend, Mariam, smirked at me like I was an idiot when I told her about the US State Department's plan to fight terrorism with jobs. Mariam told her husband about it and he shared in her amusement. At a local coffee shop, a barista I'd befriended called it propaganda. A couple of guys my age who kindly showed me around town took my questions about jobs as a chance to share their views on the evils of American foreign policy. They completely dismissed the idea that more jobs would stop people from hating the West and its influence in the Middle East.

Even some of the youth and staff at EFE's office seemed to agree with Tarek to varying degrees. I didn't see the counterterrorism narrative from EFE's origin story present in how the organization operated, or even viewed itself. Terrorism never came up in conversations I was exposed to, nor was it part of how the organization presented itself to donors or employers. The focus was more on the untapped potential of educated Egyptian youth in need of opportunities, and on the positive effect these young people can have on the Egyptian economy. There was no sense that EFE's participants were at risk of being drawn into destruction. These were simply smart kids in need of a job.

Nevertheless, my questions about jobs and terrorism helped me learn that the problem of jihadi radicalization looks different depending on where you are and who you're talking to. Like other complex problems, radicalization isn't one-dimensional. In Egypt, for example, many jihadists are motivated to fight against secular governments with the goal of establishing Sharia as the law of the land. This clash between secular and religious governance was an important issue in the 2011 Egyptian election (won by the Muslim Brotherhood), and it has been an unresolved issue since a military coup took place in 2013.

Egypt's president since the 2013 coup, General Abdel Fattah al-Sisi, has tackled jihadi radicalization as a religious problem in his efforts to rid the country of the Muslim Brotherhood, which is now considered a terrorist organization in Egypt, Russia and a handful of countries in the Middle East.

In a 2015 interview with the *Wall Street Journal*, in which he was labeled "Islam's improbable reformer," General Sisi explained that his strategy to counter jihadists is to emphasize the failures of the Muslim Brotherhood when they had a chance to govern. "What brought the Muslim Brotherhood to power was Egyptian sympathy with the concept of religion," he said. "Egyptians believed that the Muslim Brothers were advocates of the real Islam. The past three years have been a critical test to those people who were promoting religious ideas. Egyptians experienced it totally and said these people do not deserve sympathy and we will not allow it."[16]

I also learned that jihadi radicalization in Egypt occurs as part of a broader landscape of religious intolerance and sectarian violence. During my stay in Egypt, there were a number of incidents in which Christian minority communities were attacked by Muslim groups. The incident that received the most public attention while I was there was an attack on a village in Minya Province. A seventy-year-old Christian woman was stripped naked and paraded through the streets in an act of humiliation. What provoked the attack was a rumor that the woman's son was in a romantic relationship with a girl from a Muslim family.[17] This was part of a larger pattern of attacks on Christians in Egypt.

A staff member at EFE told me about Catholic Relief Services (CRS), a group she used to work for that's trying to stop such conflicts. According to her, groups like CRS are directly addressing terrorism concerns, while groups like EFE are focused on a different set of problems. In 2013, CRS launched a program in Egypt called Tolerant Attitudes and Leadership for Action, which provides training in conflict resolution and mediation to clan and religious leaders in areas beset by sectarian violence. Roger Fahmy, who oversees this initiative, explained the theory behind such peace-building initiatives as follows: "If influential Muslims and Christians actively collaborate to resolve conflict and promote tolerance, and if communities take action across religious lines, then there will be less conflict because the moderate majority will have relationships, skills and the leadership to respond to situations in a nonviolent way."[18]

The questions Tarek raised with me, and the support his views seemed to have among many other Egyptians, pushed me to reevaluate some of my longest-held assumptions. I wasn't quite sure what to say when people pushed back, and that was probably a good thing. I needed to listen and reflect.

When I left Egypt, my conclusion wasn't that community

groups advocating for jobs in the West were wrong. Nor was it that the folks I'd met in Egypt were wrong about what jobs can and can't do for young men in their country. Rather, my conclusion was that we need to better understand what jobs mean to young men in different places and not assume a universal response.

In Western cities where I've heard community groups ask for jobs to keep people safer, it's not just because of the material benefits that work brings. Jobs are also a way of keeping young men connected to mainstream society by giving them a place in the economy. With that connection in place, young men can be guided away from destructive influences, or at a minimum, they can be given a chance of finding a positive path in life. A job is a life raft of normalcy to kids who may have nothing normal in any other part of their lives. This is how jobs impact the minds and hearts of young men, not just their pockets.

These views from the ground are supported by academic research. In 2014, Sara Heller of the University of Chicago's Crime Lab published an article showing that a part-time, minimum-wage summer jobs program for 1,634 Chicago youth reduced violent crime by 43 percent over a sixteen-month period. The reasons for this decrease are uncertain, but Heller points out that the summer jobs program reduced violent crime but not always other types of crime—suggesting that the strength of the program is in its social and cultural impact, not necessarily its economic one. "The fact that [the summer jobs program] only reduces violent crime is perhaps most consistent with a role for improvements in self-control, social information processing, and decision-making, which . . . are more central to violent behavior than to other types of crime. Other interventions that target these skills through either explicit curricula or mentorship have also reduced youth delinquency with very few contact hours."[19]

Jobs can also have a significant impact on the well-being and family life of men, in a way that extends beyond just having money in their pockets. David G. Blanchflower of Dartmouth College and Andrew J. Oswald of the University of Warwick conducted a study of happiness in the United States and the United Kingdom and found that unemployment "hits a male harder than it does a female." Additionally, their study revealed that "the costs of unemployment are large relative to the costs from taking a cut in income."[20] In other words, men's happiness is more strongly associated with working than with earning a higher salary.

Harvard University sociologist Alexandra Killewald found, in a study of more than 6,000 heterosexual American couples, that male unemployment significantly threatens marriages, while female unemployment does not. Killewald's study revealed that unemployed or underemployed men were 33 percent more likely to be divorced than men working full-time. Killewald concluded, "Contemporary husbands face higher risk of divorce when they do not fulfill the stereotypical breadwinner role, by being employed full-time."[21] The likelihood of divorce is constant across all income levels, not just among wealthier or poorer families, suggesting that the harm posed by male unemployment is less about the money earned and more about what the dignity of working means to men and their families.

When communities ask for jobs as a way to bring their young men to positivity, they're asking politicians and business leaders to understand these realities. It's about more than money—it's also about finding a place to belong.

16

Isolating Extremists

■ ■ ■ ■ ▬▬▬▬▬▬▬▬▬▬▬▬▬▬▬▬▬▬

While visiting Belgium and Egypt, I encountered many young men who felt misunderstood as Muslims. They believed the Western world had drawn negative conclusions about them on the basis of their religious identity, and they asserted that their individuality had been partly denied to them by those in the West who wished to link them to extremists for no reason other than the God they prayed to.

I returned to North America in time to see Donald Trump win the 2016 US presidential election. Trump won with a campaign that involved stereotyping Muslims in many of the ways that frustrated the young men I had met in Belgium and Egypt. Yet, ironically, I found some Trump supporters and white Americans expressing similar frustrations. They too wanted to show that they shouldn't be linked to violence and hate because they shared an identity (in their case, a white racial identity) with extremists.

Trump was one of several politicians around the world dubbed the "new nationalists" by the *Economist*.[1] In Europe, many of these nationalists emerged as voices of dissent aiming to break up the European Union. The United Kingdom's June 2016 Brexit referendum, when a majority of voters chose to leave the European Union, was an inspiration for many other nationalists in Europe, and it set the tone for Trump's election later that year.

These new nationalists reflected populism's growth in the West over the preceding decades. In August 2016, the Harvard Kennedy School published a paper by Ronald F. Inglehart and Pippa Norris that tracked the growth of populism in the West since the 1960s. According to the paper's findings, the average share of votes for populist parties increased from 5.1 percent to 13.2 percent, and the number of seats held by these parties more than tripled, from 3.8 percent to 12.8 percent.[2] Inglehart and Norris attribute the growing influence of populist politicians in part to changes in who feels like an outsider in their own country. They identify a number of factors that may explain changes in the outsider experience, including the labeling of traditional values as politically incorrect, growing economic inequalities, the successes of progressive politics, increased immigration and shifts in demographics.[3]

In his analysis of 2016's new nationalists, St. John's University law professor Mark L. Movsesian points out that nationalism can be positive or negative. "Especially when tied to ethnic claims, [nationalism] has led to great horrors," he asserts. "On the other hand, it had a major role in resisting, and ultimately defeating, fascism and communism in the 20th century. And a cultural nationalism such as the United States has had for much of its history, which welcomes immigrants from across the globe provided they assimilate to local traditions, can do much to promote social peace and tolerance."[4]

Taken at face value, Trump's three campaign pillars—"sovereignty, immigration ruled by law, and economic policies meant to promote social stability"—could be compatible with the positive nationalism that Movsesian describes.[5] However, Trump toxically mixed these ideas with divisive identity politics. He denigrated Mexicans, vowed to ban Muslims from entering the country and made inflammatory comments about women and black Americans. Consequently, to many observers, Trump's discussion of national sovereignty and immigration ruled by law became synonymous with anti-immigrant sentiment and yearning for a more homogenous past. Many people also perceived Trump's nationalist economic policies as linked to a sort of zero-sum game in which ethnic and religious groups must compete for a share of the economic pie.

The night of the US presidential election, I watched the returns at an Irish pub in Toronto where at least a hundred people had gathered for a party hosted by a young professionals network. The party was initially upbeat and positive because most people there expected Hillary Clinton to win. It felt as though the home team was playing in the championship game and everybody was absolutely certain they would win.

We were celebrating prematurely. As the election results poured in, the vibe in the room changed. A Trump presidency suddenly became likely with the Republicans ahead in such key states as Ohio, Florida, Pennsylvania, Michigan and Wisconsin. People left the party early, like football fans leaving in the fourth quarter to beat the traffic once it's clear their team is going to lose.

The pub was down to fewer than fifteen people when Trump was officially declared the victor. Several people across the room made comments about how the election was rigged and ordered shots, hoping to drink away their frustrations. A young couple visiting Toronto from the United States were in tears and screaming at the television. Others were denouncing America and pointing to Trump's victory as a sign of something wrong with the country.

Eight years and two Barack Obama victories had made my friends feel as if the world was trending in the right direction after the George W. Bush years. President Obama had been the leader of the free world for most of our adult lives. Our reality—in which ethnic and religious diversity is a priority and a virtue—was affirmed when he was elected for the first time, marking a new day in American politics. His reelection told us that the first one wasn't a fluke.

Trump's victory, like the Brexit referendum, indicated that we weren't as in touch with where the world was going as we thought we were. Most of those who were in the pub on election night saw the results as a victory for various isms and phobias, such as racism, sexism, xenophobia and Islamophobia. CNN's Van Jones captured this sentiment when he described the results as a "whitelash against a changing country"—meaning white voters showed up to the polls for Trump because he'd promised to resist changes to American society.[6]

The election occurred at a time when demographic changes in the West were especially intense, lending some degree of credence to Jones's "whitelash" comment. More than 1 million people applied for asylum in Europe in 2015–16, contributing to a 1 percent increase in immigrant share of the population in several European countries.[7] From 2010 to 2014, immigrant share of the US population grew to 13.3 percent. In 2014, that increase was driven by the arrival of more than 1 million immigrants, 11 percent more than the year before.[8] Canada welcomed 320,000 newcomers between July 2015 and July 2016, which was the largest annual number of immigrants to settle in the country since at least 1971.[9] The United Kingdom took in 330,000 newcomers in 2015, the second-highest number in the country's history.[10]

Not coincidentally, Trump's campaign targeted the two fastest-growing immigrant communities in the West: Hispanics and Muslims. In 2014, Hispanics made up the largest portion of American immigrants, at 46 percent.[11] Europe's Muslim populations have grown steadily for decades. Muslims were expected to be 8 percent of the entire continent by 2030, and they claim much higher population shares in certain countries, such as Germany and France.[12]

Ryan Enos, of the Institute for Quantitative Social Science at Harvard University, has documented how intergroup hostilities can grow alongside these kinds of demographic changes. In 2014, Enos conducted an experiment involving train commuters in Boston. The experiment placed Spanish-speaking commuters at train stations to interact with Anglophone white commuters. Survey results from before and after the experiment indicated white commuters experienced an increase in exclusionary attitudes after the experiment, as demonstrated by them being "far more likely to advocate a reduction in immigration from Mexico" and "far less likely to indicate that illegal immigrants should be allowed to remain in this country" than they were before the experiment. Enos also observes that "the casual presence of outsiders causes an exclusionary reaction, perhaps because of the activation of negative stereotypes." He concluded, "The findings here indicate that continued demographic change in Western nations will be accompanied by impulses for intergroup exclusion and that regions predicted to become more diverse should expect initial conflict."[13]

How many of Trump's 63 million voters were motivated by such exclusionary reactions? To what extent was Trump's victory a "whitelash"? How many Trump supporters were motivated by his three campaign pillars rather than his identity politics?

For some of my Muslim friends and relatives, who were unsure if they or their families would be able to travel to and from the United States because of Trump's proposed travel ban, it was certainly hard to resist blaming his supporters. At best, Trump supporters were accepting enough of his identity politics that they would vote for him despite his campaign promise to make life harder for Muslims. At worst, Trump supporters were motivated by a shared desire to make life harder for Muslims.

Still, among some of my white friends and relatives, I noticed a displeasure with the "whitelash" narrative explaining Trump's election win, because it put them in the company of racists. To them, there were many reasons to vote for Trump, not just his identity politics, and, even if some Trump voters were racists, that didn't mean all of them were. They also pointed to the fact that most white Americans didn't vote for Trump because many didn't vote at all. Their displeasure with news coverage mirrored the ways I've seen Muslim communities react to being vilified following incidents of jihadist terrorism.

One example of the "whitelash" narrative in action was a piece written by Canadian journalist Doug Saunders two days after the election. Saunders was one of the journalists whose insightful writing about Molenbeek had motivated me to visit Belgium after the Paris attacks. In his article about Trump supporters, titled "The Real Reason Donald Trump Got Elected? We Have a White Extremism Problem," Saunders labeled Trump's platform a type of ethnic nationalism. Implicitly drawing parallels to jihadists, Saunders addressed white communities, writing, "It was our turn to experience the cold shock of discovering that a significant part of our community has been radicalized, sometimes over the Internet, into a form of intolerant extremism that rejects conventional Western values and threatens the integrity of entire countries."[14]

I shared Saunders's article with some of my white relatives and friends because I wanted to see how they felt about this kind of news coverage. I expected them to react much as my Muslim relatives and friends do to news coverage broadly linking them to extremism. I was correct. Even those who didn't vote for Trump felt implicated in the "whitelash" narrative in some way and rejected it in turn.

My younger cousin, who's in her midtwenties, wasn't happy. "My thing is this: correlation does not imply causation," she explained. "Trump had a majority of white voters, but I don't think it's fair to suggest guilt by association . . . like associating all Muslims as terrorists. I personally know three Trump supporters, and they're not racist."

Another member of my mom's family thought Saunders had missed the mark. "I read the article at least three times," he said, "and it bothered me when Saunders describes white people and Trump voters as extremists, radicalized and pessimistic. I don't think these words are a fair description of this group."

A lawyer who grew up in the South and voted for Trump replied with sarcasm: "I assume there will be a comprehensive discussion of the importance of positions on trade, traditional energy production, and other critical blue-collar co-variants, right? Hmmm. Strange. I'm not seeing one. Just that all uneducated whites are inherently extremist."

Another friend who voted for Trump, an academic researcher from the Midwest, felt the nationalism he was inspired by was being misrepresented. "I am really bothered by the term 'ethnic nationalism' to describe what I would regard simply as nationalism," he said, "because it evokes racial underpinnings."

Trump supporters and white Americans are large enough groups that they can decide the fate of the American presidency. On the surface, it might be hard to believe they have the ability to share in the frustrations of minority groups in the West. But as the comments from my friends and relatives indicate, nobody reacts well to feeling stereotyped. Regardless of whether you're part of a majority or minority group, being denigrated and denied your individuality feels the same. If my white friends and relatives used this as an opportunity to better understand how my Muslim friends and relatives feel when somebody like Trump targets them, I think they'd have a hard time voting for Trump again or defending anyone who did.

Whether we're discussing nearly 2 billion Muslims, more than 200 million white Americans or 63 million Trump voters, associating large groups of people with extremists overstates the influence of actual extremists and makes it difficult to isolate them and their ideas. Overstating the influence of extremists also makes it harder to distinguish those who might be persuaded by better political ideas from those who are primarily moved by extreme views. A sizable number of extremists supported Trump and celebrated his victory. Chief among the extremist groups that identified with Trump is the alt-right. The alt-right garnered significant attention during the 2016 presidential campaign for its online activity, which often took the form of social media harassment. The group is made up mostly of young white men. The Anti-Defamation League offers a helpful definition: "Though not every person who identifies with the Alt Right is a white supremacist, most are and 'white identity' is central to people in this milieu. In fact, Alt Righters reject modern conservatism explicitly because they believe that mainstream conservatives are not advocating for the interests of white people as a group."[15] Richard Spencer, a leading figure of the alt-right, has promoted "peaceful ethnic cleansing" and a "new society, an ethno-state that would be a gathering point for all Europeans."[16] Shortly after Trump's election, Spencer shouted, "Hail Trump, hail our people, hail victory!" as members of the audience responded with Nazi-like salutes at a conference in Washington, D.C.[17]

Like some of his detractors, Trump has failed to isolate the alt-right members among his supporters. During the first year of his presidency, for example, the alt-right organized a white supremacist rally in Charlottesville, Virginia. The rally turned violent when a car was driven through a group of counterprotesters opposing the white supremacists. Twenty-year-old James Alex Fields Jr. was charged, and later sentenced to life in prison. Following the attack, Trump refused to use his bully pulpit to condemn the alt-right. He tried to spread the blame for what happened in Charlottesville equally between white nationalists and those protesting against them, effectively granting shelter to extremists looking for somewhere to hide from public scrutiny. *National Review*'s David French described the need for moral clarity that Trump failed to provide perfectly. "There is a bloodlust at the political extremes," French warned. "Now is the time for moral clarity, specific condemnations of vile American movements—no matter how many MAGA hats its members wear—and for actions that back up those appropriately strong words."[18]

Joshua M. Roose, of the Institute for Religion, Politics and Society at Australian Catholic University, offers insights that can help achieve the moral clarity that moments like the Charlottesville terrorist attack require. In his study of Islam and masculinity in Australia, Roose notes, "For some young Muslim men in the West [seizing state power] is undoubtedly an ideal and one they may seek to contribute to." By contrast, he adds, "for many others, Islam guides their daily lives and actions as they seek to shape the world around them in accordance with their guiding principles. Yet this stands well removed from seizing state power and, in fact, may result in substantive contributions to society."[19] Roose believes the distinction between these two groups—extremists who seek to radically transform our societies by forcing their ideology onto others and non-extremists who don't—is important to successfully politically engaging young Muslim men in the West. I'd argue this distinction is equally important to politically engaging any other segment of our societies. By making such a distinction, we are better positioned to morally condemn extremists with precision rather than condemning or implicating broader groups. Such clarity is especially important to understanding the white supremacist networks that can inspire and organize violent attacks, and why these groups gain influence over young men. If we can't isolate the extremists among large groups of people, we will fail to ask the right questions and fail to develop the right solutions.

White supremacist networks have a lengthy history of using the internet to organize, long before the term "alt-right" was coined or Trump was president. Dating back to the early 1990s, the white nationalist and Holocaust denial online message board Stormfront, which was founded by a former member of the Ku Klux Klan terrorist group, has served as a way for white supremacists around the world to connect. Stormfront describes itself as "the first White Nationalist website on the Web" and has maintained a base of users for decades, as demonstrated by the fact that the website featured 70,000 new discussion forum threads per year from 2012 to 2015.[20] Stormfront provides a window into how online white supremacist networks serve to spin current affairs to advance racial conflict. The "Politics & Continuing Crisis" section of the website, for instance, is filled with posts titled "Jews are dangerous," "the Islamic disease," "STOP WHITE GENOCIDE" and "Anti-racist is a codeword for anti-White!" A news story about jihadist terrorism or a crime committed against a white person by a black person is shared in these categories as evidence.

Members of these white supremacist networks feel like they're part of a fight for the future of their race, religion and country. Their worldview assumes a clash of civilizations between the West and Islam, whites and non-whites, race nationalists and race traitors. And they must turn to the internet to communicate what they think is *really* happening in the world, because mainstream news outlets aren't on their side. News from Stormfront or other white supremacist outlets reinforces this worldview and undermines any competing ways of understanding the world.

The alt-right has been particularly effective at reaching young men by posing as authorities on masculinity. Members of the alt-right make use of the term "cuck" (short for "cuckold," which traditionally refers to the husband of an unfaithful woman) to describe men who don't share in their white nationalist solidarity against other races and cultures. The alt-right attempts to emasculate young white men who don't identify with white supremacists and refers to them as weak beta males. The young men who gravitate to the alt-right feel disconnected from their country much as ISIS recruits do, but what's distinct is a feeling of decline. In their worldview, the West used to be theirs but is no longer because "cucks" have allowed Europe and North America to be overtaken by various minority groups.

Counterintuitively, white nationalist ideologies cultivate a minority identity among white men. Yes, white supremacists identify with the West, claiming Europe and North America to be testaments to the supremacy of white communities. But, to build a following, white supremacists spread a message of "us against the world," offering victim status to disaffected white men unhappy with their lives. The world must be rigged against them, too, in order for their violent messages to be justifiable.

Online white supremacist networks have been linked to a series of murders since the alt-right became well known during the 2016 US presidential campaign. For example, on May 26, 2017, thirty-five-year-old Jeremy Joseph Christian allegedly (as of this writing, these charges haven't been proven in court) entered a train in Portland, Oregon, made anti-Muslim remarks to two young female passengers and then killed two other passengers who came to their aid. The Quebec City mosque shooting on January 29, 2017, is another example. A lone gunman entered a mosque and opened fire after evening prayers, killing a total of six people and injuring others. Twenty-seven-year-old university student Alexandre Bissonnette pleaded guilty to the killings. Other attacks linked to online white supremacist networks since the alt-right achieved infamy include the killings of black men in New York City and Maryland, and the Kansas murder of an engineer who'd emigrated from India. FBI agent Loren Cannon attributed the Portland train attack and similar incidents to networks of white nationalists: "These are political acts of violence that are the responsibility of white nationalists. . . . We're talking about an unstable person that was led into a mindset of violent revolution and egged on until he kind of burst."[21]

These murders are examples of white supremacist networks creating a bridge between their online activities and offline violence. The creation of such a bridge can sometimes be purely ideological: an isolated, mentally unhealthy young man consumes enough conflict-oriented propaganda that his mind and heart fill with hate, fear and rage. Other times, creating a bridge is a more deliberate, organized process of recruiting a young man to join a violent group that could be far away or nearby.

Maxime Fiset, now a project associate at the Centre for the Prevention of Radicalization Leading to Violence in Montreal, has seen the bridges between online activity and offline action firsthand. He was once considered a prospect for joining the Canadian neo-Nazi skinhead group Sainte-Foy Krew, going so far as to shave his head and to write propaganda for and help distribute the group's magazine. He founded his own white nationalist group, the Federation of Old Stock Quebecers, in 2007. In 2008, he was arrested for inciting hatred. He was also an active member of Stormfront, even being promoted to moderator of the website's francophone section. All of this happened before his twenty-fifth birthday. Now in his thirties, Maxime has changed his ways, and he works to end youth radicalization. He credits becoming a father with partly inspiring his transformation.

I learned of Maxime's story after he appeared in news media articles about the 2017 Quebec City mosque shooting, trying to shed light on the causes of white supremacist terrorism. We had the chance to speak after appearing together on a Canadian radio show about struggling young men.

On Stormfront, Maxime explained to me, there are sections for white supremacists in the same city to connect with each other and potentially arrange meetings. "That's not what necessarily leads to violence," Maxime clarified. "This can be something that prevents violence. If you join a group that shares propaganda but is dead set against violence, you can be protected [from becoming violent]. But if the group is violent, or you're too mentally ill to fit into a group, you can become violent." Maxime also explained that even nonviolent white supremacist groups are trafficking in potentially violent ideas, so it's important to fight against both racist ideas and the personal alienation that makes such ideas appealing to young men. "Alienation has this way of making you feel bad about the rest of the world, [which] you cut yourself off from when it makes you feel bad and you turn to what makes you feel better.

These [online and offline groups] give you somewhere to be yourself, to feel good."

Maxime also shared a story with me about how he is helping other young men avoid the mistakes he made. He is active on Facebook, and a young man who was part of the alt-right reached out to him for advice after the Quebec City mosque shooting. Shaken by the tragedy, the young Facebook user asked Maxime, "Did our [the alt-right's] ideas fuel this massacre?" and, wanting to change, "How are you not Islamphobic anymore?" Maxime built a relationship with him, including taking the young man to meet a professor who could explain that Islam is not as simple as the alt-right believes it is. Maxime's protégé is now back at school and working; according to Maxime, his protégé finds life easier "now that he doesn't have to cope with this mental baggage you carry when you are radicalized."

Stories like Maxime's and the work he does get lost when we fail to isolate extremists. There are dangerous groups seeking influence over young men in the West, and these groups won't be defeated if we can't or don't tell them apart from the populations they claim to be fighting for.

17

Broken Democracy

■ ■ ■ ■ ▬▬▬▬▬▬▬▬▬▬▬▬▬▬▬▬▬▬▬▬▬▬▬▬

For nearly four years, I sat on the board of directors of the Children's Aid Society of Toronto. CAST is a nonprofit organization that is primarily funded by the Ontario government and provides child welfare services, including care for children who can't remain with their parents. CAST oversees foster care and adoptions, and responds to calls concerning child safety, which come mostly from teachers and police officers.

I joined the CAST board right after I graduated from law school because its employees work with the most vulnerable youth in my hometown. My life—and my father's—taught me about the importance of having strong social services for children and parents. And I was concerned about the large overrepresentation of black families in the child welfare system. Black youth make up a staggering 41 percent of those in CAST's care, which is five times the share of black residents in Toronto's overall population. That's not only a lot of kids, but also a lot of parents.

I was part of a group of CAST board members and managers working to understand why so many black families were in the system, and to try to change that overrepresentation where it made sense to do so. We took a number of steps designed to improve services and ensure that the organization was taking a close look at its own operations, including hiring a director of diversity and anti-oppression, commissioning research reports and creating a stakeholders' advisory group.

As we introduced these initiatives, I was hopeful that CAST could do its part to lead changes. In the back of my mind, though, I always felt as if our hands were tied. In many cases, we were reacting to conditions that were beyond our control.

It wasn't within our power to help families get out of poverty, for example, nor could we support families in the ways they needed before being at risk of breakdown. But we knew the racial disparities we were trying to change take root before the child welfare system is ever involved. For instance, one-third of black households in Toronto are considered food insecure.[1] Black youth are twice as likely as other young people to be unemployed.[2] Black families in the suburbs of Toronto are also 20 percent more likely to live in poverty.[3] Like others, we looked to our provincial government— the people paying CAST's bills—to solve many of these problems.

As I struggled to figure out what to do about the problems outside of CAST's control, we had a breakthrough in our efforts to understand why we had such a large overrepresentation of black families in the system. Our director of diversity and anti-oppression and her team conducted a robust data analysis of a year's worth of calls made to CAST. Their goal was to identify patterns in when and why black children were being referred to children's aid workers. At a public board meeting, we discussed the results of the data analysis. What we learned is that in trying to understand racial disparities, local neighborhoods matter. A large number of the referrals of black children to CAST came from three particular areas: Guildwood/Morningside/West Hill in Scarborough, Malvern/Rouge in Scarborough and Downsview/Jane and Finch in North York. These areas were identified from records of postal codes of the children being referred.

Unsurprisingly, these are parts of Toronto that are struggling with a host of complex challenges. People in these neighborhoods are more prone to poverty and more likely to be dependent on public housing. And then there are the public policy failings, including limited local economic development, insufficient newcomer services and inadequate transit access. When I looked at this problem from a local neighborhood perspective, it was clear to me that the overrepresentation of black families in the child welfare system needed to be viewed in tandem with other inequalities afflicting these particular neighborhoods.

After four years of volunteer service at CAST, I recognized that it was the right moment for me to leave. The team I was part of had made a strong case for significant transformation in Toronto's disadvantaged neighborhoods—but this needed transformation was far beyond the scope of what one individual child welfare organization could do. Staying with CAST would have meant feeling handcuffed, unable to say or do what I thought was best, because I would have been tied to the government—and thus to the status quo—in some way.

The government officials overseeing the issues affecting these neighborhoods had good intentions. But the reality is that the provincial government as a whole was a slow-moving giant that couldn't always act with the speed or precision needed to improve conditions on the ground. Having the same people put their hands on every issue facing disadvantaged neighborhoods made it difficult to have honest, open conversations about what needed to be changed and who needed to do the changing.

Instead of taking a government-centered look at my city, I wanted to focus on empowering people locally, sharing power with civil society and businesses, decentralizing decision-making to local organizations and supporting families to solve their own problems whenever possible. The Toronto-based Wellesley Institute has described this as a "shared responsibility" lens, which is based on the belief that "fostering a healthy society requires investment from individuals, communities, private institutions, and public services."[4] No one segment of society can solve these intractable problems, and allowing any group to monopolize influence does a disservice to disadvantaged neighborhoods.

Shortly after leaving the CAST board, I began conducting research on child welfare issues in Columbus, Ohio. Specifically, I helped lead a project looking at the role of kinship guardians in providing care to vulnerable Ohio youth. Kinship guardians are relatives who assume the responsibility of caring for children in their families. These arrangements are sometimes informal (that is, a child may be living with his or her relative without any legal change of custody), and other times formal (when child protective services places a child in the legal custody of a relative).

Because informal arrangements are usually undocumented, it's hard to know exactly how many children are in kinship care. Data from the US Census Bureau showed that 5 percent of children in Ohio were being raised by kinship guardians in 2015, compared to 3 percent across the country.[5] The number of children in kinship care has grown significantly in recent years, and experts on the ground expect that figure to move well beyond 5 percent because of Ohio's struggles with the opioid crisis. The Ohio health department reported in 2015 that since 2007, "unintentional drug overdose continued to be the leading cause of injury-related death in Ohio." Overdoses climbed to 3,050 deaths in 2015, the highest on record at the time.[6] The crisis put greater strain on children's services and contributed to an 11 percent increase in the number of children in state custody.[7] In response to the growing need for grandparents and other relatives to step up as guardians, the Ohio House of Representatives set aside $20 million for kinship caregivers as part of a $170.6 million plan to fight opioid abuse in 2017.[8]

The research project I was part of sought to identify ways to make life easier for families relying on kinship guardians, such as increasing funding for support services or modernizing consent laws so kinship guardians could access medical and education records. Meeting people affected by the crisis was a quick and emotional introduction to the intergenerational trauma caused by opioid addiction.

In Portsmouth, Ohio (a town described in the *Columbus Dispatch* as "the epicenter of the pill mills believed to have incubated the Ohio opioid epidemic"), a group of community leaders gathered to discuss the harm opioids have inflicted on their neighborhoods.[9] We heard from a twenty-five-year-old rehabilitation counselor, a recovering addict himself, who recalled what it was like losing his own father to prescription pills and alcohol years earlier. Another person told us about an addicted eight-year-old boy she is trying to help. This child started taking prescription pills when his parents gave them to him as a reward for transporting drugs from one house to another.

Community Action Agencies in Ross County, Ohio, also showed us the depth of the opioid crisis. Ross County, which is home to 77,000 people, lost forty-four citizens to drug overdoses in 2016.[10] We were told by many that the numbers were trending higher for 2017. Very quickly I learned that it's hard for people in a small community not to feel each one of those deaths personally. Dozens of relatives and friends are attached to each person struggling with addiction.

The transformative impact of the opioid crisis was a common theme in Ross County. A municipal court judge powerfully explained, "None of us are doing the job we trained for." He said judges, police and probation officers, teachers, coroners, social workers and others working on the ground have seen their jobs change significantly over the past decade. A police officer echoed this sentiment: "Groups that used to not work together are now forced to be partners. We need all the help we can get."

On a more positive note, in Lancaster, Ohio, I spoke with a social worker who shared stories about local churches that were tackling the opioid crisis head-on. These churches had organized a series of opioid forums that had a huge turnout. The social worker mentioned that grandparents at these forums would find her and ask for advice on raising their grandchildren.

Ohio's opioid crisis created significant suffering and increased hardship. The crisis also created a sense of urgency for communities, civil society organizations and families to step up and try to improve their situations, with kinship guardians leading the way. The situation was markedly similar to what I had observed in neighborhoods threatened by jihadists or gangs. People had to act at a faster pace than was possible for governments. And in this case, they needed to get officials to support those who had been responding to the opioid crisis long before it became a government priority.

Dissatisfaction with government is a common sentiment I've encountered in my life and work, so my desire to find opportunities for change independent of government bureaucracy isn't new. I've seen people express this dissatisfaction with various aspects of the democratic process, particularly voting and joining political parties.

For many, voting feels like a no-win situation, in which the choice is between candidates who equally fail to prioritize their needs. Controversial hip-hop artist Paris articulated this feeling when he talked about what it's like for his community during election campaigns. Paris described it as being "pressured to vote for the lesser of two evils," and thus "rarely" feeling satisfied with political choices. He believes this contributes to lower voter turnout. "For many, the desire to keep the 'greater evil' out of public office isn't a good enough reason to engage in a democratic process that seems rigged, [or is] designed to maintain the illusion of choice while protecting the status quo."[11]

Maria Sobolewska, a political analyst for the United Kingdom's British Election Survey, has argued that left-wing parties take some minority communities for granted and right-wing parties ignore them altogether—with the result that many voters don't consider their options when exercising their democratic rights.[12] Furthermore, political parties create self-fulfilling prophecies when they treat voters as static and predictable groups rather than individuals with a diverse range of opinions. Arturo Vargas, the executive director of the California-based National Association of Latino Elected and Appointed Officials (NALEO) Educational Fund, described how this self-fulfilling prophecy works in his community: "In addition to the injury of not being contacted, they [organizations and candidates] insult us by lamenting that Latinos underperform in elections even though they spent no time and no resources engaging us."[13]

Joining a political party is also dissatisfying for many. Consider, for example, that although there are a sizable number of social conservatives in British Muslim and black American communities, these people are rarely engaged by right-wing political parties because of identity politics. ICM Unlimited's 2016 survey of 100,000 Muslims in the United Kingdom found that 52 percent of respondents believed same-sex marriage should be illegal, compared to 22 percent of non-Muslims.[14] Pew's annual polling of Americans on same-sex marriage found that just 42 percent of black Americans expressed support for the idea in 2016, compared to 57 percent of white Americans.[15] Right-wing parties could be vehicles for Muslim and black social conservatives to participate in Western democracies, just as they are for Christian and white social conservatives. But these parties have not become those vehicles because of the influence of ethnic and religious identity politics, which alienate or neglect Muslim and black communities.

In left-wing parties that seek out electoral advantages by appealing to ethnic and religious minority voters, as well as to women, white men have often become targets of divisive political rhetoric. Following the 2016 US presidential election, the Democratic Party was beset by infighting between backers of presidential hopeful Bernie Sanders (whose supporters tend to be whiter and younger than the average party member) and backers of other potential leadership hopefuls. RoseAnn DeMoro, the executive director of National Nurses United, described the anti-Sanders wing of the party as wanting "to classify everyone as a 'Bernie Bro'—as a white guy, an angry white man."[16]

I've seen two friends I met in university struggle to find a political voice amid this dissatisfying environment. Marcus has long grappled with whether he should identify as a conservative. He has always been a big believer in free market economics as a way to create better opportunities for his neighborhood, which is made up of mostly black, immigrant and low-income families. Marcus's optimistic belief in the power of free markets comes from seeing firsthand how little social mobility is created by relying on government programs and government-funded nonprofit organizations. He half-jokingly describes the situation in his neighborhood as a "nonprofit industrial complex," because it strikes him that people in positions of political and economic influence are more interested in propping up charities that serve his neighborhood and others like it than in creating any kind of economic development for people in need of jobs.

Marcus's hopes for what free market economics can do for his community mirror what Malcolm X called "the economic philosophy of black nationalism" in his famous 1964 speech "The Ballot or the Bullet." "When you spend your dollar out of the community in which you live," Malcolm said, "the community in which you spend your money becomes richer and richer, the community out of which you take your money becomes poorer and poorer. . . . And then you have the audacity to complain about poor housing in a rundown community, while you're running down yourselves when you take your dollar out."[17]

Conservative politicians are typically the most vocal advocates for free market solutions to society's problems, so Marcus tends to gravitate toward right-wing political thinking. However, he has never felt welcome in conservative circles. Marcus is black and just a few years older than me, so he grew up with many of the same political assumptions I did, especially the belief that progressives care about black and poor people, while conservatives don't. Conservative politicians have never done much to change this widely held belief—and this is especially true of local politicians, who Marcus says never show their faces in his neighborhood.

Even if Marcus got to a point where he was comfortable in conservative circles, I think it would be very difficult for him to publicly identify as a conservative. He would still have to contend with the negative reactions of many in his community and risk being less politically relevant to the people he cares most about. He would inevitably be called a sellout by some for aligning with politics inconsistent with the expectations of him as a black person from a struggling neighborhood. He'd feel like he was choosing between his ideas for bettering his community and the community itself.

Another good friend of mine from university, Salim, has

expressed frustrations to me about the political status quo in North America. I met Salim through Marcus, and the two of them have a lot in common. But they also have some important differences. Like Marcus, Salim is the child of immigrants from Africa, and he is particularly concerned with the struggles experienced by black families in low-income neighborhoods. Unlike Marcus, he is very progressive on economic issues and favors more socialist economic reforms. Salim is also a devout Muslim, and he wishes progressive political parties had more space for people who openly practice their faith and have some socially conservative views.

If he felt Muslims were welcomed in all political parties, I could see Salim being an independent voter who supports whichever candidate he believes will be best in a given election cycle. He doesn't feel welcome in conservative circles, though, so he gravitates toward left-wing parties. Like Marcus, Salim has viewed the hostility to diversity from right-wing political parties as an attack on his citizenship in the West. As he told me once, "I'm not even at a point where I can talk about taxes. I just want to feel welcomed here. When I don't have to worry about people hating me, then I'll worry about taxes."

A consequence of putting people like Marcus and Salim in this position is that their voices are stifled and their contributions are undermined. They are not empowered to advocate for what they think is best for their families and neighbors. Their belief of what's politically possible in their communities is limited.

The three of us have always been excited by ideas that would improve disadvantaged neighborhoods independently from ineffective government agencies. Each of us has seen talented local leaders have their positive influence reduced because they're too far away from centers of power. We've also seen government bureaucracy, politics or incompetence slow down or kill innovation.

One idea that has given us optimism over the years is charter schools, which are semi-autonomous public schools that operate under a charter approved by a state government, regional school board or other charter-granting entity. We've often talked about charters as a helpful vehicle to empower local leaders and provide the education services their communities need. Just one Canadian province, Alberta, has legalized charters, however, so the idea has never been adequately explored in our hometown, Toronto.

Charter schools are more common in the United States. The American charter school movement began in Minnesota in 1991, with the passing of the first charter school laws by a group that included both Democrats and Republicans.[18] The bipartisan origins of the charter school movement reflect its broad appeal to people seeking innovative ways to address inequalities in educational attainment. Nearly 6,400 charters were used by 2.5 million public school students in 2015.[19]

Regulation of charters varies from state to state, but their independence from a school district gives them flexibility to create their own academic programs, establish unique school cultures, hire non-union staff and teachers and set alternative class schedules. Charters are often managed like private schools, but they use public funds redirected from traditional schools.

Much of the growth of the charter school movement stems from its popularity in inner-city communities, where large numbers of young people are disengaged from schools or receive inadequate education. Educators in these communities have turned to charters as a way to reach students the traditional district public schools cannot. Charters are also an opportunity for local grassroots groups to exercise control in areas where government policy has failed to transform the lives of struggling youth.

Geoffrey Canada, founder of the Harlem Children's Zone, turned to charter schools in 1990 as a way to improve a neighborhood similar to the one he grew up in. "I have been heartbroken as I have watched generations of black and Latino students failed by our public school system, then descend into unemployment, drugs, crime and, often, untimely deaths. This has been going on since I was a public-school child myself in the South Bronx in the 1960s."[20] Canada views charter schools as key to improving American education.

Derek W. Black, of the University of South Carolina School of Law, has explained the appeal of charters in black communities by pointing to two particular values: "the importance of individual choice" and "the power of markets to produce beneficial outcomes."[21] Black argues these values uniquely resonate with the experience of some inner-city residents. "Many inner-city communities have been disaffected from the educational system for some time, as meaningful and stable school desegregation never occurred and adequate resources, teachers, curriculum, and pedagogy have generally been in short supply. In addition, some inner-city communities see public schools as simply a small piece of a much larger system designed to move poor minority students seamlessly toward jail."[22]

Monica Almond, of Claremont Graduate University, conducted a 2013 study to learn why black students are disproportionately enrolled in charters. Her results indicated broad dissatisfaction with the traditional school system in American cities. She identified the following factors in the appeal of charters: a safer learning environment, higher expectations for students, individualized attention and an atmosphere that encourages attending college.[23]

There have undoubtedly been some strong opponents of charter schools in black communities. These opponents are important voices because people in the same ethnic or religious community should freely express as diverse a range of opinions as any other collection of people. In Mississippi, for example, community members have argued that charters are "being imposed by outsiders" onto local communities.[24] Moreover, in 2016, the NAACP approved a resolution calling for a ban on privately managed charters because of a concern that "charter schools with privately appointed boards do not represent the public but make decisions about how public funds are spent."[25]

Charter critics have also accurately pointed to the inconsistencies in the academic performance of these schools. Quality control is difficult to maintain from school to school because charters don't have a central organizing body resembling traditional school boards. Additionally, regulatory oversight of charters has been toothless in some states, allowing for schools to fail to meet even the average academic performance levels of traditional public schools. In Michigan, for example, during the 2012–13 school year, 38 percent of charters performed below the 25th percentile of public schools in the state. In 2013–14, Michigan charters had lower levels of reading proficiency than traditional public schools.[26]

These criticisms have not slowed the popularity of charters, however, in large part because they perform better than traditional public schools on average. A 2015 study conducted by the Center for Research on Education Outcomes (CREDO) at Stanford

University found that, on average, inner-city charters do indeed outperform traditional public schools.[27] CREDO also found that urban charter students received the equivalent of forty additional learning days per year in math and twenty-eight additional days in reading. Learning gains for black, Hispanic, low-income and special education students were larger, at least in part because the flexibility of charters allows them to meet the specific needs of student populations.

Charters also continue to grow because of the inspiring success stories they can tell. The network of all-boys charter schools called Urban Prep Academies, for example, has sent 100 percent of its graduates to college for the better part of a decade. Urban Prep operates three schools in Chicago, including the first charter high school for boys in the United States. Most of their students come from low-income communities in Chicago, where for decades young men have fallen victim to gun violence or been incarcerated at alarming rates. And many of these students arrive at Urban Prep having fallen behind in numerous subject areas. Part of getting all of Urban Prep's graduates ready for college is instilling in them a creed, which states in part, "We are the young men of Urban Prep. . . . We are exceptional—not because we say it but because we work hard at it. . . . We have a responsibility to our families, community and the world. We are our brothers' keepers. . . . We believe."[28]

Not all charters are as successful as Urban Prep, but empowering communities to act independently of government agencies certainly has the potential to give children a chance at a better life. That potential is why the responsibility of improving disadvantaged neighborhoods should be shared, and not centralized in the hands of a select few.

18

My Brother's Keeper

■ ■ ■ ■ ▬▬▬▬▬▬▬▬▬▬▬▬▬▬▬▬▬▬▬

Talking about the experiences of young men and the challenges they face isn't always easy. In my efforts to do so, I've encountered resistance from multiple sources.

From young men themselves, there's often an aversion to being expressive about their feelings and sharing their struggles. This has been a dominant theme in my life and my work. It's why my father broke down crying at the side of my bed when I was eight, why King Pikeezy from Fathers NOW described himself as wearing a mask, why I turned to the internet as a teenager to find role models and why Bilal and AJM created opportunities for dialogue in Molenbeek following the Brussels attacks.

A literature review published in the *Journal of Advanced Nursing* identified trends suggesting that how men think about their masculinity significantly influences their willingness to seek out help, even when they're sick. A sense of masculinity that denies weakness or vulnerability makes men less likely to ask for help. "Indeed, theories prevalent among international men's health discourse contend that men are not permitted to be expressive in their illness behavior, or are 'unable' because of the construction of traditional masculinity, or an effort to conform to a socially prescribed male role where weakness and need for help are not believed to be masculine."[1]

Another reason many young men have withdrawn from society is to have more leisure time, taking their own voices out of public conversations in the process. In neighborhoods where people are most in need of opportunities to improve their lives, I've seen hundreds of young men choose marijuana, opioids, alcohol or other substances instead of doing something constructive. Playing video games has also become a common way for young men to use their time. University of Chicago economist Erik Hurst has argued that the popularity of video games explains why many young men work less than those in previous generations.[2]

In their online surveys of 20,000 young men, psychologists Philip Zimbardo and Nikita Coulombe identified what they call an "entitlement" among respondents because of their willingness to "seek long-term shelter either with Mom and Dad or within their marriages or relationships with a live-in partner" and their unwillingness to "work at jobs that will bring in money or even help out with household chores that will keep their living space tidy."[3] This entitlement means fewer men are out in the world making their voices heard, and more are at home or looking for fun elsewhere.

Resistance to talking about young men also comes from people who react defensively to discussions of masculinity. Feminists have developed valuable tools to discuss gender, but those tools can't be applied if any mention of masculinity is treated as an attack on men. Certain men's rights activists and opponents of feminism have equated conversations about gender with silencing male voices and denying male experiences.

Salon's Amanda Marcotte has written about men who have made it difficult to talk openly about masculinity—especially toxic masculinity, which she defines as "a specific model of manhood, geared towards dominance and control." Marcotte says that whenever she starts talking about toxic masculinity, she encounters "a chorus of whiny dudes who will immediately assume—or pretend to assume—that feminists are condemning all masculinity, even though the modifier 'toxic' inherently suggests that there are forms of masculinity that are not toxic."[4]

Other resistance comes from people who treat any discussion of masculinity as an attack on women and feminism. In the West, the male identity has historically functioned to exclude women and assign privileges and benefits to men. As a result, men have benefited from a psychological wage. W. E. B. Du Bois coined the term "public and psychological wage" to describe the benefits white workers received over black workers in late-nineteenth-century America. Being white offered benefits beyond the material benefits of a job, like "public deference and title of courtesy," access to police and courts, voting rights, better education and news media that catered to their interests.[5] Many similar benefits based on gender have historically worked to empower men and disempower women. Those who perceive the mere act of talking about the needs of men as an attack on women and feminism assume these efforts are designed to protect the psychological wage men have received, to return society to a time when men had great advantages in school and work, or otherwise to resist progress made in creating equal opportunities for women.

Equating talking about men with attacking others means that it's safer to discuss negative aspects of masculinity than positive aspects, because that invites less confrontation. But there's a lack of affirmative discussion about what we want boys and young men to grow up to be, and how we can empower young men to lead positive lives.

A friend of mine is a lawyer who represents youth expelled from public schools, and she has gathered some valuable insights into how this particular resistance to masculinity works in practice. Most of the students she represents are male, and often these boys and young men get into trouble for fighting, inappropriate touching of girls, talking back to teachers and generally disobeying the instructions of authority figures. My friend has recommended that schools and other organizations that work with male students try to develop programs and initiatives focused on encouraging healthy forms of masculinity. She believes more dialogue with boys about masculinity could help them mature and be more thoughtful about how they treat each other and their female classmates. But in response, she has been told that such initiatives would "promote patriarchy" and not be inclusive enough.

Barack Obama introduced an innovative approach to tackling the challenges faced by young men with My Brother's Keeper (MBK). Launched in 2014, MBK began with the stated goals of "broadening the horizons for our young men and giving them the tools they need to succeed." The initiative is described as a "focused effort on boys and young men of color who are having a particularly tough time."[6] MBK's strategy is to provide stewardship to a coalition of foundations, businesses, state and local governments, faith leaders and nonprofit organizations committed to the same goals.

The White House task force report that led to the creation of MBK made the case for a national initiative focused on young men by emphasizing the unique inequalities and disproportionalities that affect them. Specifically, the report mentions rates of poverty, fatherlessness, high school incompletion, unemployment and incarceration in black, Hispanic, American Indian, Alaskan Native, Southeast Asian and Pacific Islander communities.[7] To steer more young men toward positivity, the task force recommended emphasizing six milestones in their lives:

1. Entering school ready to learn
2. Reading at grade level by third grade
3. Graduating from high school ready for college and career
4. Completing postsecondary education or training
5. Successfully entering the workforce
6. Reducing violence and providing a second chance[8]

These milestones were dubbed the "Cradle-to-College-and-Career Approach," because helping young men advance through each milestone would theoretically bring them all the way from infancy to life as a working adult.

MBK was inspired in part by the success of a schools-based program in President Obama's hometown, Chicago, called Becoming a Man (BAM). This initiative of the nonprofit organization Youth Guidance offers classes to nearly 2,000 young men in schools and community centers in thirty-week cycles.[9] The group promotes six core values through its classes: integrity, accountability, self-determination, positive anger expression, visionary goal setting and respect for women.

The BAM program features frequent and honest group conversations to pierce the veil of tough-guy bravado, as well as self-reflection about male–female relationships. Marlin, a nineteen-year-old BAM graduate, has high praise for these group conversations. "Some of the guys were disrespectful of women. . . . The guys were treating women as a conquest or object or just fun, instead of an individual with thoughts, feelings, plans. [After the group conversations in BAM,] they are owning up to more than they may have otherwise."[10]

What distinguishes BAM from similar programs is the academic evaluation performed to assess its effectiveness. A study published by the National Bureau of Economic Research found that in 2009–10 and 2013–15, participation in the program "reduced total arrests during the intervention period by 28–35%, reduced violent-crime arrests by 45–50%, improved school engagement, and in the first study where we have follow-up data, increased graduation rates by 12–19%."[11] The study's authors, including Sara Heller of the University of Chicago's Crime Lab, credit BAM's ability to "directly help youth recognize their automatic assumptions and responses and make better decisions in high-stakes situations."[12] The study concluded, "The rate of return to investing in helping youth make better judgments and decisions in high-stakes moments seems promising" compared to interventions focused on building academic or vocational skills and changing the benefits and costs of crime or schooling.[13]

In 2016, the White House's two-year progress report on MBK indicated that private-sector partners had committed more than $600 million and foundations $200 million to the group's priorities. MBK also helped create mentorship programs across the country, grants for job programs, a pilot project to fund education and training for incarcerated Americans, gang intervention programs, preschool initiatives and entrepreneurship and STEM programs. Additionally, a new nonprofit called the My Brother's Keeper Alliance was formed to formalize MBK and its mission.[14]

Like any organization tasked with solving complex problems, MBK has its limitations and areas for improvement. Critics say the initiative isn't doing enough. The Brookings Institution, for example, published an analysis of MBK that argued the initiative doesn't adequately address structural issues in American society most relevant to struggling young men because it pays too much attention to cultural issues, such as fatherlessness, and focuses on policies outside the purview of the federal government.[15]

In writing this book, I drew inspiration from MBK because it provides the big-picture thinking, cultural leadership and political voice needed to strengthen work being done to keep young men connected to their countries. Throughout my career, I've had the chance to learn from thousands of young men and people who work with them in Europe and North America. An initiative like MBK could make a positive difference for every single one of them if it lived up to its potential.

My friend Chris Blackwood is someone I think about often because he's on the front lines working with young men without the support MBK could offer. Chris is a few years older than me and is from northwest Toronto. He works as a youth worker in the same neighborhood he grew up in, Jane and Finch, which has a high percentage of young, black, immigrant and low-income families living in public housing. Chris's presence in Jane and Finch is much needed. In 2013, the neighborhood was named "the most dangerous place to be a kid" in Toronto because of the high number of young people lost to gun violence.[16] A year later, the city ranked the Jane and Finch area as the "least livable" of its 140 neighborhoods based on a number of quality-of-life metrics, including employment, education attainment and mortality.[17] After he completed his bachelor's degree, Chris returned there to set his sights on becoming a youth worker. As he puts it, "I had a one-year-old daughter waiting for me at home, so I knew I had to make a career out of becoming a community leader mentoring youth. Especially because I was a parent myself."

Chris is now a father of four young children. Most days you'll catch him dressing in a way that reflects where he comes from and the young people he works with: a fitted baseball cap and hoodie or crewneck made by his younger brother's Grandslammer$ clothing company. He isn't tall, but he made his name in the community as a talented basketball player. He even played ball at university. The reputation Chris built for himself as an athlete gives him instant credibility with youth in the neighborhood.

Chris uses his reputation and skills to help organize an annual basketball tournament in honor of two young men he went to school with who were lost to gun violence as teenagers. He registers teams for the tournament and ensures they have proper coaches and referees. He also organizes basketball programs throughout the year for high school and middle school students. A lot of the young men he engages with through basketball are considered "at-risk," and basketball is a way for him to hold on to them and help guide them toward positivity. Other young men he engages with are already on a positive path, and basketball helps bring them around positive influences who can keep them there.

Chris has also been an innovator in combining his basketball programs and mentorship with other opportunities for youth, and that's when we've been able to work together. For example, Chris worked with students in my seminar at Osgoode Hall Law School to design political organizing training modules, and he then integrated them into his basketball programs by giving players homework after practices and discussing government and policy during breaks from play.

Through his efforts to engage youth, Chris is able to build the kind of trusting relationships necessary to make a difference in the lives of young people. I attended a community event with him and saw the depth of his relationships on display. The event was a discussion about the future of transportation in Toronto, hosted at the Jamaican Canadian Association's offices near Jane and Finch. A group of sixty people had gathered on a cold November evening to hear from representatives of the biggest transportation organizations in the city, including the Toronto Transit Commission (TTC), which operates buses and subways, and Uber, the technology company operating ride-sharing and food-delivery mobile apps.

The chance to hear from transportation experts brought people in the door, but Chris made the biggest impression. He gave a presentation about the experiences of youth in Jane and Finch when using transportation services. His most compelling message, which captured the entire room's attention, was about safety. He explained that students riding buses after school often feel unsafe because of fighting and bullying. The schools are supervised, but the buses are not, and therefore some kids in the community feel vulnerable.

Chris said the lack of supervision on buses particularly affects male students because they aren't offered the same safety considerations that female students rightfully receive. The TTC has a helpful policy of dropping passengers off between stops after dark upon request. Chris said that he knows of young men who would like to make use of this program, but it's often made available only to women passengers. "They worry about bullying, about being robbed when they get off the bus. They don't feel safe," he said of the young men he works with. Chris recalled an instance when a male high school student asked a bus driver to let him off between stops after dark, and the bus driver laughed. "We only do that for girls," the driver replied.

Chris moved all of us with his stories that night. TTC representatives acknowledged his concerns and explained that while it's in the rules that all customers can request a stop, not all drivers apply the rules properly. They vowed to take Chris's message back to their colleagues. It was a powerful moment of grassroots experience informing decision-makers. The Jane and Finch residents in attendance were proud of Chris for speaking truth to power. You could tell it was meaningful to see a person who understood them share the spotlight with influential people from other parts of the city.

For the young men Chris works with, it's taboo to talk about feeling unsafe or insecure on their way home. There is an expectation that they're going to be hard, tough, fearless and, too often, emotionless. Many of them grow up like I did, looking to rappers and Hollywood gangsters as role models who project an aggressive bravado. Most people in the lives of those young men will never get that kind of honesty from them. Chris is a safe person for them to go to, and a person who has built credibility in the community by spending years in the schools, at the community centers, on the basketball courts, in the streets and at their homes.

Chris is an example of a young man stepping up to be a voice for his community. The impression he made in the room shows why more men should consider becoming youth workers. William Marsiglio, a professor of sociology at the University of Florida, has advocated for more men to choose careers like Chris's. In his study of male youth workers, Marsiglio shared his hopes for what more men could accomplish: "If more men were inspired to work and volunteer with youth, men's greater participation in youth work would foster positive cultural change, prompting men to be more vocal public advocates for kids. . . . With high rates of divorce, single parenting, and dual-earner families, the time is right to encourage more men to share with women the responsibility for mentoring, teaching, nurturing, monitoring, and supporting kids of all kinds, their own and other people's."[18]

Unfortunately, Chris's contributions to his neighborhood aren't adequately recognized or supported. He has spent most of his career in an unstable position, working several part-time jobs because he can't find one organization willing and able to pay him the kind of salary he needs to support his growing family. Every day he spends an hour or two driving to different jobs in different neighborhoods, which eats up many hours each month. The programs he leads in the community never scale up to the extent they could because he doesn't have the time or resources to push his ideas to the maximum. There is also no institutional sustainability to the work Chris does. If he ever moved out of the neighborhood or changed careers, no one would be ready to build on his legacy.

If an initiative like MBK was available to Chris, it could make a world of difference by giving him a supportive network. MBK might ensure that organizations in his neighborhood have the resources needed to employ him. The initiative could also help him institutionalize what he has learned and exchange best practices with youth workers in other parts of the city. Above all, it would help legitimize the work he does to people who don't understand why expertise in empowering young men is both valuable and needed.

Shortly before leaving the White House in January 2017, President Obama renamed MBK the Task Force on Improving the Lives of Boys and Young Men of Color and Underserved Youth. The expressed goal of this new name was to "help ensure that the federal work continues, and that it remains a priority at the White House."[19] As Obama handed President Trump the keys to the White House, it was unclear what this name change would mean, but the attention brought to the name underscored some of the decisions made in shaping MBK.

From the beginning, President Obama had focused MBK on young men *of color*. The new name expands that group, presumably to white men as well, but as part of no more than a miscellaneous add-on of "underserved youth." I can't speculate as to why the White House chose to leave white men out of its young men's initiative, but an examination of the issues MBK was founded to address would indicate that some white communities face these struggles as much as the minority groups included in MBK.

Poverty and unemployment in particular have contributed to growing despair among working-class white men. University of Akron psychology professor Ronald F. Levant has commented on this despair: "With globalization, automation, the evolution of manufacturing, the increase in disparity of both income and wealth, there are all kinds of things going on that have had a devastating impact on white working-class men." The generation that raised today's young white men has struggled significantly. Because of alcohol and substance abuse, as well as suicide, death rates for middle-aged white Americans with no college education have been going up, while death rates for racial minority groups have gone down.[20]

From my experience, it's easier to talk about young men to many audiences when also talking about racial or religious minority groups. Adding other identities into the conversation makes it easier for people to sympathize with a group that's otherwise easy to overlook, fear or associate with privilege because of historical or modern-day sexism.

Most of this book has been set in racial or religious minority communities because those are the communities I've lived and worked in. I hope I have told these stories in a way that helps people look beyond racial and religious differences, to see some of the common challenges and experiences of young men, and the ways they can be better included, supported, held accountable and empowered.

EPILOGUE

What Went Unsaid

■ ■ ■ ■ ▬▬▬▬▬▬▬▬▬▬▬▬▬▬▬▬

Shortly after I turned twenty-nine, I finally asked my mom about the Nation of Islam book that she took from our kitchen table eleven years earlier. We were at a nice restaurant with my two younger sisters, Jasmine and Janine, to celebrate Jasmine's birthday. Before I arrived, I'd been working on this book, so the day when I couldn't find my friend's copy of *Message to the Blackman in America* was fresh in my mind. As I'm occasionally known to do, I complicated a casual night out by raising some serious questions.

Mom admitted for the first time that she had thrown the book in the trash. I asked her why. "I don't remember why," she said, "but I did throw it out."

I then brought up how difficult it had been for the two of us to communicate when I was a teenager. We never talked about what was in that book, for example—nor did we talk about much else that was going on in my life.

Mom folded her arms. Her face turned slightly red. She looked away at other tables in the restaurant. I thought we were going to leave the conversation there, but she turned back to me and shared her own perspective on that time in our lives.

"When you were a teenager," she said, "I knew you were going through something and I was worried to death about where you were headed. I didn't know how to deal with the situation."

I looked in her eyes and saw how much she feared being judged. She then reminded me of some of the attempts she'd made to better understand me.

"I drove you to the bus station on some of the days you went off on your own so I could ask you questions about what you were doing." She was referring to days when I accompanied my friend Brandon to the Nation of Islam mosque or hung out with Lucas on the other side of the city.

Mom recalled asking if she, as a Christian and a white woman, could attend one of the Nation of Islam meetings with me. She also mentioned asking to meet some of my other friends, including those who were getting into trouble. I don't remember any of those questions—which is fitting, since she couldn't remember me paying attention or taking her questions seriously.

Driving me to the bus station is one of the things Mom did for me that regrettably slipped my mind when I looked back on my teenage years. But hearing her perspective on that period of my life helped me see that those short car rides were important to her. They were her way of staying connected to me at a time when she feared losing me to negative influences. She also often drove me to the bus station when she knew I was at risk of skipping school so I would at least show up in the morning. Those car rides put us in proximity to each other, and without them our relationship might have totally disintegrated. But they couldn't get us beyond proximity to successful communication.

The conversation we were having at my sister's birthday dinner was an example of successful communication, though. I was optimistic that we might have turned a corner after years of rebuilding our bond as mother and son. I felt that I understood my mom better than ever before. And for the first time, she confidently and comfortably asked me to share my thoughts on what was going on in my life back when I was a teenager. Little did she know how prepared I was to do so!

In the months following, as I finished writing this book, I periodically sent parts of the manuscript to my mom and called her up to talk about what I'd written. She found answers to her questions about who I'd been spending my time with and what I was doing back when I was a teenager. She read about the people and ideas competing with her to influence me as a young man. She also saw that the struggles she experienced as a parent are part of bigger, more complex challenges across the West, which meant she wasn't alone.

During one of our conversations about the book, my mom remarked on how much the two of us had changed. "I used to feel sad that you couldn't share some things with me so I could be there for you. Today was more open. We actually had a conversation that helped me understand that you were searching for something that was missing in your life back then."

ACKNOWLEDGMENTS

*God is our refuge and strength, an ever-present help in
trouble. Therefore we will not fear.*

PSALM 46:1–2

I didn't go from "illiterate" high school student at sixteen to published author by the age of thirty without help along the way. Many
people from different walks of life deserve credit for what I've
learned over the years, and for seemingly small things, like sharing
a kind word of encouragement when I needed to hear one, and big
things, such as hiring me for a job. I'd like first to thank anyone
who ever made an effort to teach me something about myself or
the world around me. I appreciate you.

Thank you to the doctors and nurses at Toronto's North York
General and Sunnybrook hospitals, Michael "Pinball" Clemons
and Kingdom House Christian Centre in Brampton, Ontario, for
saving my life. Without you, I might not have finished this book or
seen its release.

My mom, Pam, and my sisters, Jasmine and Janine, are a source
of optimism and confidence when I most need them.

Those acknowledged below taught, supported, challenged and inspired me during the specific period I wrote this book.

Thanks, Jim Gifford, for editing *Why Young Men*, and believing I would find my voice long before I did.

Thanks, Adam Bellow, for additional editing of *Why Young Men* and his vision for what this book could be on an international scale.

I'm also grateful to the many talented people at HarperCollins Canada and All Points Books/St. Martin's Press for sharing their expertise and publishing this book.

Bruce Westwood and Meg Wheeler's representation made this book possible.

Kailyn and Christie inspired me to practice what I preach. Keep being a good man, Kailyn.

Thanks to Harvey Lam, Gavin Dia, Amina Farah Dia, Patrick Byam and Dionne Woodward for looking out for me and my family while I'm away from home. I'm also thankful to the MacFarlanes, Spirlings and Jardenicos for the same.

The published authors I'm lucky to call friends made a world of difference throughout the writing process. J. D. Vance showed me what's possible when young men share their stories. Amy Chua helped build my confidence. Nahlah Ayed encouraged me to write. James Forman Jr. set an example for how to be an author and an activist at once.

At Torys LLP, Mitch Frazer, Frank Iacobucci, Les Viner, Konata Lake and Ebad Rahman have been excellent mentors. I'm grateful to the firm at large for being such a supportive and talented community of lawyers.

At Osgoode Hall Law School, Michael Thorburn's research assistance, creativity and dedication were invaluable. Lorne Sossin opened the law school's doors to me as a dean truly committed to innovation. Students in my Community Organizing and the Law seminar motivated me to be the best researcher and writer I can be.

For providing diverse feedback to my ideas, including agreements and disagreements, I'm grateful to Abdi Aidid, Sujoy Chatterjee, Esete Kabtamu, Sofia Nelson, Jamelia Morgan, Samson Mesele, Usha Chilukuri Vance, James Eimers, Kyle Walsh, Matthew Penny, Sam Kyung-Gun Lim, Renatta Austin, Corey Black and Sean Speer.

Wes Hall, Heather Gerken, Sharon Brooks, Mike Thompson and Jai Chabria have provided invaluable mentorship through various challenges and opportunities.

Colleagues at the Children's Aid Society of Toronto, especially David Rivard and Nicole Bonnie, helped me keep the most vulnerable youth in mind during the writing process.

Toronto's Jane and Finch community is where I learned how to listen to and be held accountable by youth. Thanks to Kwesi Opoku, Chris Blackwood, Harpreet Gill, the Goulbourne family, the congregation at Lisle Memorial Baptist Church, Andrew Newsome and Westview Centennial Secondary School staff and students.

In Belgium, I'm grateful to more people in Molenbeek and Borgerhout than I can name here. Staff and youth at the Association des Jeunes Marocains and JES went above and beyond in teaching me about young men in their communities and the importance of humility in trying to answer complex questions. Leaders of both organizations graciously opened their doors to me. At AJM, Ali

Moustatine, Hazedin Dellah and Yann Conrath treated me like a brother. At JES, Patrick Manghelinckx, Koen Hanssens, Liselotte Vanheukelom, Duchka Walraet and Bram De Ridder graciously connected me with the communities they serve. I received incredible support from Filip Balthau, Joke Cortens and Luis Leon, who gave me a home away from home.

In Egypt, the staff and youth at Education for Employment gave me an opportunity to learn, as they do for many young people in their country. Nouran Soliman welcomed me to Cairo.

My Kenyan friends and relatives offered insightful perspectives on the lives of young men and efforts to support them. They encouraged the honest self-reflection needed to write this book. Thanks to Rizz Jiwani, Glena Jiwani, Albanus Muindi, Peter Mulli Mweu, Joseph Kyalo and the Mully Children's Family charity.

Finally, I'm grateful to all the young men I have had the privilege to learn from and whose stories I've been fortunate to tell.

NOTES

1. ROLE MODELS

1. National Fatherhood Initiative, "The Proof Is In: Father Absence Harms Children," https://www.fatherhood.org/fatherhood-data-statistics.
2. Sara McLanahan, Laura Tach and Daniel Schneider, "The Causal Effects of Father Absence," *Annual Review of Sociology* 39 (July 2013): 422.
3. W. Bradford Wilcox, "The Distinct, Positive Impact of a Good Dad," *Atlantic*, June 14, 2013, https://www.theatlantic.com/sexes/archive/2013/06/the-distinct-positive-impact-of-a-good-dad/276874.
4. W. Bradford Wilcox, "Sons of Divorce, School Shooters," American Enterprise Institute, December 16, 2013, http://www.aei.org/publication/sons-of-divorce-school-shooters.
5. American Psychological Association, "Marriage and Divorce," http://www.apa.org/topics/divorce.
6. Centers for Disease Control and Prevention, "Unmarried Childbearing," http://www.cdc.gov/nchs/fastats/unmarried-childbearing.htm.
7. National Center for Fathering, "The Extent of Fatherlessness," http://www.fathers.com/statistics-and-research/the-extent-of-fatherlessness.
8. Statistics Canada, "Portrait of Families and Living Arrangements in Canada," December 22, 2015, http://www12.statcan.gc.ca/census-recensement/2011/as-sa/98-312-x/98-312-x2011001-eng.cfm.
9. Office for National Statistics, "Families and Households: 2015," November 5, 2015, https://www.ons.gov.uk/peoplepopulationandcommunity/birthsdeathsandmarriages/families/bulletins/familiesandhouseholds/2015-11-05.
10. Chloe E. Bird and Kai Ruggeri, "UK and Europe Are Behind the Times for Single Mothers and Their Children," RAND Corporation, March 11,

2015, http://www.rand.org/blog/2015/03/uk-and-europe-are-behind
-the-times-for-single-mothers.html.

11. Michiko Kakutani, "Jay-Z Deconstructs Himself," *New York Times*, November 22, 2010, http://www.nytimes.com/2010/11/23/books/23book
.html.

12. Ed Stourton, "The Decline of Religion in the West," BBC News, June 26,
2015, http://www.bbc.com/news/world-33256561.

13. Conrad Hackett and David McClendon, "Christians Remain World's
Largest Religious Group, but They Are Declining in Europe," Pew Research Center, April 5, 2017, http://www.pewresearch.org/fact-tank
/2017/04/05/christians-remain-worlds-largest-religious-group-but
-they-are-declining-in-europe.

14. Pew Research Center, "America's Changing Religious Landscape,"
May 12, 2015, http://www.pewforum.org/2015/05/12/americas-changing
-religious-landscape.

15. Sofie Vanlommel, "Jonge Vlaamse Moslims Schrijven Eigen Kinder-
boek," *De Morgen*, May 10, 2016, http://www.demorgen.be/boeken
/jonge-vlaamse-moslims-schrijven-eigen-kinderboek-bc789c2a.

16. Richard Alexander Nielsen, "The Lonely Jihadist: Weak Networks and
the Radicalization of Muslim Clerics," PhD diss., Harvard University,
2013.

17. Stourton, "Decline of Religion."

18. US Department of Education Office for Civil Rights, "Gender Equity in
Education," June 2012, https://www2.ed.gov/about/offices/list/ocr/docs
/gender-equity-in-education.pdf.

19. Lehigh University, College of Education, "The Reverse Gender Gap,"
https://coe.lehigh.edu/content/reverse-gender-gap.

20. Richard Adams, "Young Men Miss Out as University Gender Gap Remains at Record Levels," *Guardian*, February 4, 2016, http://www
.theguardian.com/education/2016/feb/04/young-men-miss-out-as
-university-gender-gap-remains-at-record-levels.

21. Organisation for Economic Co-operation and Development, "Gender
Gap in Education," March 2016, http://www.oecd.org/gender/data
/gender-gap-in-education.htm.

22. Anne McDaniel, Thomas A. DiPrete, Claudia Buchmann and Uri Shwed,
"The Black Gender Gap in Educational Attainment: Historical Trends
and Racial Comparisons," *Demography* 48, no. 3 (August 2011): 889–914.

23. Jamie Doward, "Young Muslim Women Take Lead over Men in Race
for Degrees," *Guardian*, April 2, 2016, http://www.theguardian.com
/education/2016/apr/02/muslim-women-men-degrees-jobs-market
-british-universities.

24. Raj Chetty, Nathaniel Hendren, Frina Lin, Jeremy Majerovitz and
Benjamin Scuderi, "Childhood Environment and Gender Gaps in

Adulthood," National Bureau of Economic Research, January 2016, http://www.nber.org/papers/w21936.

25. Anna Brown and Eileen Patten, "The Narrowing, but Persistent, Gender Gap in Pay," Pew Research Center, April 3, 2017, http://www.pewresearch.org/fact-tank/2017/04/03/gender-pay-gap-facts.

26. Eileen Pollack, "Why Are There Still So Few Women in Science?," *New York Times Magazine*, October 3, 2013, http://www.nytimes.com/2013/10/06/magazine/why-are-there-still-so-few-women-in-science.html.

2. NEW ARRIVALS

1. Statistics Canada, "Immigration and Ethnocultural Diversity in Canada," May 2013, http://www12.statcan.gc.ca/nhs-enm/2011/as-sa/99-010-x/99-010-x2011001-eng.cfm.

2. Orlando Patterson, "A Poverty of the Mind," *New York Times*, March 26, 2006, http://www.nytimes.com/2006/03/26/opinion/a-poverty-of-the-mind.html.

3. Akilah N. Folami, "From Habermas to 'Get Rich or Die Trying': Hip Hop, the Telecommunications Act of 1996, and the Black Public Sphere," *Michigan Journal of Race and Law* 12 (Spring 2007): 235.

4. Alex Ballingall, "Q and A with Toronto Raptors Superfan Nav Bhatia," *Toronto Star*, May 25, 2016, https://www.thestar.com/sports/raptors/2016/05/25/toronto-raptors-q-and-a-with-the-superfan.html.

5. Noreen Ahmed-Ullah, "Brampton, a.k.a. Browntown," in *Subdivided: City-Building in an Age of Hyper-Diversity*, ed. Jay Pitter and John Lorinc (Toronto: University of Toronto Press, 2016), 247.

6. Penguin Random House, "A Conversation with Thomas Chatterton Williams," http://www.penguinrandomhouse.com/authors/245784/thomas-chatterton-williams.

7. Canadian Press, "5 Things to Know About Surrey's Gang War," June 21, 2015, http://www.cbc.ca/news/canada/british-columbia/5-things-to-know-about-surrey-s-gang-war-1.3122074.

3. CRISIS OF DISTRUST

1. World Bank, Worldwide Governance Indicators 2016, http://info.worldbank.org/governance/wgi/index.aspx#home.

2. World Justice Project, "Rule of Law Index 2016," http://worldjusticeproject.org/rule-of-law-index; Transparency International, "Corruption Perceptions Index 2016," January 25, 2017, http://www.transparency.org/news/feature/corruption_perceptions_index_2016.

3. World Justice Project, "Rule of Law"; Transparency International, "Corruption Perceptions."

4. Al Jazeera, "Exclusive: Kenyan Counterterrorism Police Admit to Extrajudicial Killings," December 8, 2014, http://america.aljazeera.com/articles/2014/12/8/kenyan-counter-terrorismpoliceconfesstoextrajudicialkillings.html; Reuters, "Kenya: Halt Crackdown on Somalis," April 11, 2014, https://www.hrw.org/news/2014/04/11/kenya-halt-crackdown-somalis.

5. Anthony Langat and Jacob Kushner, "Kenya's Anti-Terror Police Are Inflicting Terror of Their Own," Public Radio International, July 29, 2015, http://www.pri.org/stories/2015-07-29/kenyas-anti-terror-police-are-inflicting-terror-their-own.

6. Barack Obama, "Remarks by President Obama and President Kenyatta of Kenya in a Press Conference," White House Office of the Press Secretary, July 25, 2015, https://www.whitehouse.gov/the-press-office/2015/07/25/remarks-president-obama-and-president-kenyatta-kenya-press-conference.

7. Ben Hayes, "A Failure to Regulate: Data Protection and Ethnic Profiling in the Police Sector in Europe," *Justice Initiatives* (June 2005): 37, https://www.opensocietyfoundations.org/publications/justice-initiatives-ethnic-profiling-police-europe.

8. Nima Elbagir, Bharati Naik and Laila Ben Allal, "Why Belgium Is Europe's Front Line in the War on Terror," CNN, March 24, 2016, http://www.cnn.com/2016/03/21/europe/belgium-terror-fight-molenbeek.

9. Hugh Muir, "Metropolitan Police Still Institutionally Racist, Say Black and Asian Officers," *Guardian*, April 21, 2013, https://www.theguardian.com/uk/2013/apr/21/metropolitan-police-institutionally-racist-black.

10. New York Civil Liberties Union, "Stop-and-Frisk Data," May 23, 2017, https://www.nyclu.org/en/stop-and-frisk-data.

11. Jim Rankin and Patty Winsa, "Carding Drops but Proportion of Blacks Stopped by Toronto Police Rises," *Toronto Star*, July 26, 2014, https://www.thestar.com/news/insight/2014/07/26/carding_drops_but_proportion_of_blacks_stopped_by_toronto_police_rises.html.

12. Jessica Glenza, "'I Felt Like a Five-Year-Old Holding On to Hulk Hogan': Darren Wilson in His Own Words," *Guardian*, November 25, 2014, https://www.theguardian.com/us-news/2014/nov/25/darren-wilson-testimony-ferguson-michael-brown.

13. "Immortal Technique: Rock the Boat (Part I)," *XXL Magazine*, April 4, 2006, http://www.xxlmag.com/news/2006/04/immortal-technique-rock-the-boat-part-i.

14. W. E. B. Du Bois, *The Souls of Black Folk* (1903; repr., New York: Penguin Classics, 2002), 215.

15. Du Bois, *Souls of Black Folk*, 11.

16. Tom R. Tyler, "Procedural Justice, Legitimacy, and the Effective Rule of Law," *Crime and Justice* 30 (2003): 345.

17. Quoctrung Bui and Amanda Cox, "Surprising New Evidence Shows Bias in Police Use of Force but Not in Shootings," *New York Times*, July 11, 2016, http://www.nytimes.com/2016/07/12/upshot/surprising-new-evidence-shows-bias-in-police-use-of-force-but-not-in-shootings.html.

4. CAPACITY TO ASPIRE

1. Arjun Appadurai, "The Capacity to Aspire," in *Culture and Public Action*, ed. Vijayendra Rao and Michael Walton (Stanford, CA: Stanford University Press, 2004), 59–84.
2. Barack Obama, preface to the 2004 edition of *Dreams from My Father: A Story of Race and Inheritance* (New York: Three Rivers Press, 2004), x–xi.
3. Ben Shapiro, "The 'Radical Islam' Shibboleth," *National Review*, June 15, 2016, http://www.nationalreview.com/article/436632/obama-trump-radical-islam-dispute-both-are-wrong.
4. Paul Sperry, "Obama Was as Clueless About 9/11 as He Is About ISIS," *New York Post*, February 28, 2015, http://nypost.com/2015/02/28/when-obama-refused-to-blame-islam-for-terrorism.
5. Clark McCauley and Sophia Moskalenko, *Friction: How Radicalization Happens to Them and Us* (Oxford: Oxford University Press, 2011), 68.

5. COMPETING FOR THE FUTURE: PART I

1. Samuel P. Huntington, "The Clash of Civilizations?," *Foreign Affairs* 72, no. 3 (Summer 1993): 24.
2. "Political Islam: The Power of Religion," *Economist*, July 13, 2013, http://www.economist.com/news/special-report/21580618-islamists-government-proving-harder-opposition-power-religion.
3. Amarnath Amarasingam and Jacob Davey, "What About the Terrorism of the Far Right?," *New York Times*, June 21, 2016, https://www.nytimes.com/2017/06/21/opinion/finsbury-park-terrorist-attack-far-right.html.
4. Neil MacFarquhar, "Nation of Islam at a Crossroad as Leader Exits," *New York Times*, February 26, 2007, http://www.nytimes.com/2007/02/26/us/26farrakhan.html.
5. Martha F. Lee, "The Nation of Islam and Violence," in *Violence and New Religious Movements*, ed. James R. Lewis (Oxford: Oxford University Press, 2011), 305.
6. "The Process of Radicalization Leading to Violence," Centre for the Prevention of Radicalization Leading to Violence, https://info-radical.org/en/prevention-en/tools.

7. Elijah Muhammad, preface to *Message to the Blackman in America* (Phoenix: Secretarius MEMPS Publications, 2007), v.

8. Michelle Shephard, "How Can We End Terrorism Without Feeding It?," *Toronto Star,* May 28, 2016, https://www.thestar.com/news/atkinsonseries/generation911/2016/05/28/how-can-we-end-terrorism-without-feeding-it.html.

6. COMPETING FOR THE FUTURE: PART II

1. Louis Farrakhan, "Saviours' Day Speech," C-SPAN, February 25, 2007, http://www.c-span.org/video/?196795-1/saviours-day-speech.

7. SOCIAL (IM)MOBILITY

1. Joshua Hart and Christopher F. Chabris, "Does a 'Triple Package' of Traits Predict Success?," *Personality and Individual Differences* 94 (2016): 221.

2. Heather Patrick, Clayton Neighbors and C. Raymond Knee, "Appearance-Related Social Comparisons: The Role of Contingent Self-Esteem and Self-Perceptions of Attractiveness," *Personality and Social Psychology Bulletin* 30 (April 1, 2004): 503.

3. Office of Public Affairs and Communications, Yale University, "Investment Return of 3.4% Brings Yale Endowment Value to $25.4 Billion," *Yale News,* September 23, 2016, http://news.yale.edu/2016/09/23/investment-return-34-brings-yale-endowment-value-254-billion.

4. Jed Finley and Finnegan Schick, "Faculty, Students Respond to High Admin Salaries," *Yale Daily News,* November 7, 2014, http://yaledailynews.com/blog/2014/11/07/faculty-students-respond-to-high-admin-salaries.

5. DataHaven, "New Haven County: Key Facts," 2015, http://www.ctdatahaven.org/profiles/new-haven.

6. City-Data.com, "Crime Rate in New Haven, Connecticut (CT)," http://www.city-data.com/crime/crime-New-Haven-Connecticut.html.

7. Macy Corica, "New Haven Crime Rate on Steady Decline," WTNH.com, May 11, 2016, http://wtnh.com/2016/05/11/new-haven-crime-rate-on-steady-decline.

8. Nicholas Keung, "Jobseekers Resort to 'Resumé Whitening' to Get a Foot in the Door, Study Shows," *Toronto Star,* March 17, 2016, https://www.thestar.com/news/immigration/2016/03/17/jobseekers-resort-to-resum-whitening-to-get-a-foot-in-the-door-study-shows.html.

9. Nicholas Eberstadt, *Men Without Work: America's Invisible Crisis* (West Conshohocken, PA: Templeton Press, 2016), 144.

10. James B. Jacobs, "European Employment Discrimination Based on Crim-

inal Record II—Discretionary Bars," Collateral Consequences Resource Center, January 13, 2013, http://ccresourcecenter.org/2015/01/13 /european-discretionary-employment-discrimination-based-criminal -record; Shannon Young and Julie Labrie, "I've Got a Criminal Record. How Can I Get a Job?," *Globe and Mail*, May 10, 2015, http://www .theglobeandmail.com/report-on-business/careers/career-advice/life-at -work/ive-got-a-criminal-record-how-can-i-get-a-job/article24331295.

11. Raj Chetty, David Grusky, Maximillian Hell, Nathaniel Hendren, Robert Manduca and Jimmy Narang, "The Fading American Dream: Trends in Absolute Income Mobility Since 1940," National Bureau of Economic Research, December 2016, http://www.nber.org/papers/w22910.

12. Brent Orrell, Harry J. Holzer and Robert Doar, "Getting Men Back to Work: Solutions from the Right and Left," American Enterprise Institute, April 20, 2017, 1, http://www.aei.org/publication/getting-men-back -to-work-solutions-from-the-right-and-left.

13. Orrell, Holzer and Doar, "Getting Men Back to Work," 3.

14. International Labour Organization, *World Employment Social Outlook: The Changing Nature of Jobs* (Geneva: ILO, 2015), http://www.ilo.org /wcmsp5/groups/public/- - - dgreports/- - - dcomm/- - - publ/documents/ publication/wcms_368626.pdf.

8. REENTRY

1. Joshua Wilwohl, "Report: Newarkers Among New Jersey's Poorest," *Patch Newark*, November 7, 2011, http://patch.com/new-jersey/newarknj /report-newarkers-among-new-jerseys-poorest.

2. Les Christie, "Most Dangerous U.S. Cities," CNN, January 23, 2013, http://money.cnn.com/gallery/real_estate/2013/01/23/dangerous -cities/6.html.

3. Meredith Kleykamp et al., "Wasting Money, Wasting Lives: Calculating the Hidden Costs of Incarceration in New Jersey," Drug Policy Alliance, 2012, http://www.drugpolicy.org/resource/wasting-money-wasting-lives -calculating-hidden-costs-incarceration-new-jersey.

4. Sharon Adarlo, "Newark Program Encourages Fathers to Get Involved in Children's Education," *Star Ledger*, September 21, 2009, http://www .nj.com/news/index.ssf/2009/09/newark_program_encourages_fath .html.

5. Richard S. Grayson, "Localism the American Way," *Public Policy Research* 17, no. 2 (June–August 2010): 78.

6. Grayson, "Localism," 78.

7. Chanta L. Jackson, "Fatherhood Program Helps Men Grow One Day at a Time," NJ.com, June 18, 2009, http://www.nj.com/newark/index.ssf /2009/06/fatherhood_program_helps_men_g.html.

8. Jackson, "Fatherhood Program."
9. Alisa Hauser, "Chicago Gang Members Explain Why They're 'In for Life,'" *DNAinfo*, September 1, 2016, https://www.dnainfo.com/chicago/20160901/west-town/what-convicted-felons-will-tell-us-about-todays-chicago-gangs/.
10. National Public Radio, "Barbershop: Former Members Talk About What Led Them to Join Gangs in Chicago," January 7, 2017, https://www.npr.org/2017/01/07/508722513/barbershop-former-members-talk-about-what-led-them-to-join-gangs-in-chicago.
11. Jean Marie McGloin, "The Organizational Structure of Street Gangs in Newark, New Jersey: A Network Analysis Methodology," *Journal of Gang Research* 15, no. 1 (Fall 2007).
12. Mollie Shauger, "Bloomfield Man Admits He Used Twitter for Gang Recruitment," *Northjersey.com*, July 28, 2017, https://www.northjersey.com/story/news/crime/2017/07/28/bloomfield-man-admits-he-used-twitter-gang-recruitment/519906001.
13. Andrew V. Papachristos, "Social Networks Can Help Predict Gun Violence," *Washington Post*, November 3, 2013, https://www.washingtonpost.com/opinions/social-networks-can-help-predict-gun-violence/2013/12/03/a15b8244-5c46-11e3-be07-006c776266ed_story.html.

9. DIVERSITY: PART I

1. Timothy Appleby, "His Rise up the Ranks Started with Policing at an All-Time Low," *Globe and Mail*, September 16, 2009, http://www.theglobeandmail.com/news/toronto/his-rise-up-the-ranks-started-with-policing-at-an-all-time-low/article4216054.
2. Malcolm Johnston, "Deputy Police Chief Peter Sloly on Running to Succeed Bill Blair, and the First Item on His Agenda If He Does: Race," *Toronto Life*, January 26, 2015, http://torontolife.com/city/deputy-police-chief-peter-sloly-qa.
3. Betsy Powell, "Deputy Chief Peter Sloly Slams Bloated Police Budget," *Toronto Star*, January 18, 2016, https://www.thestar.com/news/gta/2016/01/18/deputy-chief-peter-sloly-pushes-for-change-amid-low-point-and-looming-crisis.html.
4. Royson James, "Sloly Was Too Smart and Progressive for His Own Good," *Toronto Star*, February 11, 2016, https://www.thestar.com/news/gta/2016/02/11/sloly-was-too-smart-and-progressive-for-his-own-good-james.html.

10. DIVERSITY: PART II

1. "About," Black Lives Matter, http://blacklivesmatter.com/about.
2. Deen Freelon, "The Measure of a Movement: Quantifying Black Lives

Matter's Social Media Power," working paper, School of Arts and Sciences, University of Pennsylvania, 2016.

3. Monica Anderson and Paul Hitlin, "The Hashtag #BlackLivesMatter Emerges: Social Activism on Twitter," Pew Research Center, August 15, 2016, http://www.pewinternet.org/2016/08/15/the-hashtag-blacklives matter-emerges-social-activism-on-twitter.

4. Malcolm Gladwell, "Small Change: The Revolution Will Not Be Tweeted," *New Yorker*, October 4, 2010, http://www.newyorker.com/magazine /2010/10/04/small-change-malcolm-gladwell.

5. Biz Stone, "Exclusive: Biz Stone on Twitter and Activism," *Atlantic*, October 19, 2010, https://www.theatlantic.com/technology/archive /2010/10/exclusive-biz-stone-on-twitter-and-activism/64772.

6. Kimberly Ricci, "DeRay Mckesson on Black Lives Matter and Refusing to Be Silenced," *Uproxx*, August 24, 2016, http://uproxx.com/news/deray -mckesson-interview-black-lives-matter/2.

7. Munmun De Choudhury, Shagun Jhaver, Benjamin Sugar and Ingmar Weber, "Social Media Participation in an Activist Movement for Racial Equality," in *Proceedings of the Tenth International AAAI Conference on Web and Social Media, May 17–20, 2016* (Palo Alto, CA: AAAI Press, 2016), http://www.munmund.net/pubs/BLM_ICWSM16.pdf.

8. Bijan Stephen, "Get Up, Stand Up: Social Media Helps Black Lives Matter Fight the Power," *Wired*, November 2015, https://www.wired .com/2015/10/how-black-lives-matter-uses-social-media-to-fight-the -power.

9. Linsey Davis, Chris James and Alexa Valiente, "Rapper Lil Wayne Says He Doesn't Feel Connected to the Black Lives Matter Movement," ABC News, November 2, 2016, http://abcnews.go.com/Entertainment/rapper -lil-wayne-doesnt-feel-connected-black-lives/story?id=43247469.

10. "Lil Wayne Slammed on Twitter over Black Lives Matter Comments," CBS New York, November 2, 2016, http://newyork.cbslocal.com/2016 /11/02/lil-wayne-black-lives-matter.

11. Max Weinstein, "T.I. Calls Out Lil Wayne for 'Unacceptable' Black Lives Matter Comments," *XXL*, November 5, 2016, http://www.xxlmag.com /news/2016/11/ti-responds-lil-wayne-black-lives-matter.

12. Craig Jenkins, "Lil Wayne's Black Lives Matter Comments Were a Betrayal of His Fans," *Vulture*, November 2, 2016, http://www.vulture.com /2016/11/lil-waynes-blm-comments-were-a-betrayal.html.

13. "Lil Wayne Sorry for BLM Rant," TMZ, November 2, 2016, http://www .tmz.com/2016/11/02/lil-wayne-nightline-black-lives-matter-apology.

14. "Platform," Movement for Black Lives, https://policy.m4bl.org/platform.

15. Amanda Alexander, "Those Who Focus on Police Reform Are Asking the Wrong Questions," *Globe and Mail*, July 29, 2016, https://www .theglobeandmail.com/opinion/police-reform-isnt-enough-for-black -america/article31166356.

16. Benjamin Mullin, "Report: Journalists Are Largest, Most Active Verified Group on Twitter," Poynter Institute, May 26, 2015, https://www.poynter.org/2015/report-journalists-are-largest-most-active-group-on-twitter/346957.

17. Septembre Anderson, "Why Black Lives Matter Doesn't Speak for Me," *NOW Magazine*, July 13, 2016, https://nowtoronto.com/news/why-black-lives-matter-toronto-doesnt-speak-for-me.

18. Saul Alinsky, *Rules for Radicals: A Practical Primer for Realistic Radicals* (New York: Random House, 1971), 130.

19. Alinsky, *Rules for Radicals*, 131.

20. Jessica Lussenhop, "How Black Lives Matter Was Blamed for Killing of US Police Officers," BBC News, September 14, 2015, http://www.bbc.com/news/world-us-canada-34135267.

11. TO BRUSSELS

1. Ron Johnson, "Threats to the Homeland," opening statement to the US Senate Committee on Homeland Security and Governmental Affairs, Washington, DC, October 8, 2015, https://www.hsgac.senate.gov/media/majority-media/opening-statement-of-chairman-ron-johnson-threats-to-the-homeland.

2. Guilain P. Denoeux, "The Forgotten Swamp: Navigating Political Islam," *Middle East Policy* 9, no. 2 (June 2002), http://www.mepc.org/journal/forgotten-swamp-navigating-political-islam.

3. Graeme Wood, "What ISIS Really Wants," *Atlantic*, March 2015, https://www.theatlantic.com/magazine/archive/2015/03/what-isis-really-wants/384980.

4. Johan Leman, "Is Molenbeek Europe's Jihadi Central? It's Not That Simple," *Guardian*, November 17, 2015, https://www.theguardian.com/commentisfree/2015/nov/17/molenbeek-jihadi-isis-belgian-paris-attacks-belgium.

5. Rik Coolsaet, "Facing the Fourth Foreign Fighters Wave: What Drives Europeans to Syria, and to Islamic State? Insights from the Belgian Case," Royal Institute for International Relations, Egmont Paper 81, March 2016, http://www.egmontinstitute.be/facing-the-fourth-foreign-fighters-wave.

6. Open Society Foundations, "Restrictions on Muslim Women's Dress in the 28 EU Member States: Current Law, Recent Legal Developments, and the State of Play," April 1, 2018, https://www.opensocietyfoundations.org/sites/default/files/restrictions-on-women%27s-dress-in-the-28-eu-member-states-20180425.pdf.

7. Vicky Fouka, "Backlash: The Unintended Effects of Language Prohibition in US Schools After World War I," working paper, Center for International Development, Stanford University, Stanford, CA, December 2016, 26.

8. Sohrab Ahmari, "How Nationalism Can Solve the Crisis of Islam," *Wall Street Journal*, May 26, 2017, https://www.wsj.com/articles/how-nationalism-can-solve-the-crisis-of-islam-1495830440.
9. Derek Blyth, "Protest in Antwerp Against Mayor's Remarks About Berbers," *Flanders Today*, March 26, 2015, http://www.flanderstoday.eu/politics/protest-antwerp-against-mayors-remarks-about-berbers.
10. Laurens Cerelus, "How Jan Jambon Will 'Clean Up Molenbeek,'" *Politico*, December 28, 2015, http://www.politico.eu/article/jan-jambon-clean-up-molenbeek-plan-vtm-police.
11. Simon Cottee and Keith Hayward, "Terrorist (E)motives: The Existential Attractions of Terrorism," *Studies in Conflict and Terrorism* 34, no. 12 (November 2011): 963.
12. Lorne L. Dawson, Amarnath Amarasingam and Alexandra Bain, "Talking to Foreign Fighters: Socio-Economic Push versus Existential Pull Factors," working paper, Canadian Network for Research on Terrorism, Security and Society, July 2016, http://tsas.ca/wp-content/uploads/2016/07/TSASWP16-14_Dawson-Amarasingam-Bain.pdf.
13. Mohammed Hafez and Creighton Mullins, "The Radicalization Puzzle: A Theoretical Synthesis of Empirical Approaches to Homegrown Extremism," *Studies in Conflict and Terrorism* 38, no. 11 (September 2015): 970, http://hdl.handle.net/10945/47758.

12. FAITHLESS RADICALS

1. Aya Batrawy, Paisley Dodds and Lori Hinnant, "'Islam for Dummies': IS Recruits Have Poor Grasp of Faith," Associated Press, August 15, 2016, http://bigstory.ap.org/article/9f94ff7f1e294118956b049a51548b33/islamic-state-gets-know-nothing-recruits-and-rejoices.
2. Nathalie Goulet, "We in France Must Face Terrorism Without Losing Our Soul," *Guardian*, July 17, 2016, https://www.theguardian.com/commentisfree/2016/jul/17/france-terrorism-massacre-nice.
3. Lorenzo Vidino and Seamus Hughes, "ISIS in America: From Retweets to Raqqa," Program on Extremism, George Washington University, December 2015, https://extremism.gwu.edu/isis-america.
4. Robin Simcox, "'We Will Conquer Your Rome': A Study of Islamic Terror Plots in the West," Henry Jackson Society (London), September 29, 2015, http://henryjacksonsociety.org/2015/09/29/we-will-conquer-your-rome-a-study-of-islamic-state-terror-plots-in-the-west-2.
5. Scott Shane, Richard Pérez-Peña and Aurelien Breeden, "'In-Betweeners' Are Part of a Rich Recruiting Pool for Jihadists," *New York Times*, September 22, 2016, http://www.nytimes.com/2016/09/23/us/isis-al-qaeda-recruits-anwar-al-awlaki.html.
6. "Aaron Driver: Troubled Childhood, ISIS Supporter, Terror Threat Suspect," CBC News, August 11, 2016, http://www.cbc.ca/news/canada

/manitoba/aaron-driver-troubled-childhood-isis-supporter-1
.3716222.

7. Steven Mufson, "How Belgian Prisons Became a Breeding Ground for Islamic Extremism," *Washington Post*, March 27, 2016, https://www.washingtonpost.com/world/europe/how-belgian-prisons-became-a-breeding-ground-for-islamic-extremism/2016/03/27/ac437fd8-f39b-11e5-a2a3-d4e9697917d1_story.html.

8. "UNODC Tackles Radicalization to Violence in Prisons," United Nations Office on Drugs and Crime, January 7, 2016, https://www.unodc.org/unodc/en/frontpage/2016/January/unodc-tackles-radicalization-to-violence-in-prisons.html; Noemie Bisserbie, "European Prisons Fueling Spread of Islamic Radicalism," *Wall Street Journal*, July 31, 2016, http://www.wsj.com/articles/european-prisons-fueling-spread-of-islamic-radicalism-1470001491.

9. Mufson, "How Belgian Prisons Became a Breeding Ground."

10. Christopher de Bellaigue, "Are French Prisons Finishing Schools for Terrorism?," *Guardian*, March 17, 2016, https://www.theguardian.com/world/2016/mar/17/are-french-prisons-finishing-schools-for-terrorism.

11. Andrew Wiggins and Kimiko de Freytas-Tamura, "A Brussels Mentor Who Taught 'Gangster Islam' to the Young and Angry," *New York Times*, April 11, 2016, http://www.nytimes.com/2016/04/12/world/europe/a-brussels-mentor-who-taught-gangster-islam-to-the-young-and-angry.html.

12. Anthony Faiola and Souad Mekhennet, "The Islamic State Creates a New Type of Jihadist: Part Terrorist, Part Gangster," *Washington Post*, December 20, 2015, https://www.washingtonpost.com/world/europe/the-islamic-state-creates-a-new-type-of-jihadist-part-terrorist-part-gangster/2015/12/20/1a3d65da-9bae-11e5-aca6-1ae3be6f06d2_story.html.

13. Kurt Eichenwald, "Belgium: Pop Goes the Jihad," *Newsweek Middle East*, April 6, 2016, http://newsweekme.com/belgium-pop-goes-the-jihad.

14. Reuters, "'Rambo' Appeal, Not the Mosque, Lures Brussels Youths to Islamic State," November 24, 2015, http://blogs.reuters.com/faithworld/2015/11/24/rambo-appeal-not-the-mosque-lures-brussels-youths-to-islamic-state.

15. Raffaello Pantucci, *"We Love Death as You Love Life": Britain's Suburban Terrorists* (London: Hurst, 2015), 11.

16. "Religion in Prisons: A 50-State Survey of Prison Chaplains," Pew Forum on Religion and Public Life, Pew Research Center, March 22, 2012, http://www.pewforum.org/2012/03/22/prison-chaplains-exec.

17. Mitch Prothero, "Chasing ISIS: Inside the World of ISIS Investigations in Europe," *BuzzFeed*, August 21, 2016, https://www.buzzfeed.com/mitchprothero/why-europe-cant-find-the-jihadis-in-its-midst.

13. FAKE NEWS

1. "Korpschef Mechelen: 'Fouten Gemaakt Binnen het Korps,'" *Het Laatste Nieuws*, March 25, 2016, http://www.hln.be/hln/nl/36484/Aanslagen -Brussel/article/detail/2657653/2016/03/25/Korpschef-Mechelen -Fouten-gemaakt-binnen-het-korps.dhtml.

2. Neil Johnson, "The Secret Behind Online ISIS Recruitment," *New Republic*, June 17, 2016, https://newrepublic.com/article/134393/secret -behind-online-isis-recruitment.

3. J. D. Vance, "How Donald Trump Seduced America's White Working Class," *Guardian*, September 11, 2016, https://www.theguardian.com /commentisfree/2016/sep/10/jd-vance-hillbilly-elegy-donald-trump-us -white-poor-working-class.

4. Craig Silverman, "This Analysis Shows How Fake Election News Stories Outperformed Real News on Facebook," *BuzzFeed*, November 16, 2016, https://www.buzzfeed.com/craigsilverman/viral-fake-election -news-outperformed-real-news-on-facebook.

5. Shanika Gunaratna, "Facebook, Google Announce New Policies to Fight Fake News," CBS News, November 15, 2016, http://www.cbsnews.com /news/facebook-google-try-to-fight-fake-news.

6. Davey Alba, "Facebook Finally Gets Real About Fighting Fake News," *Wired*, December 15, 2016, https://www.wired.com/2016/12/facebook -gets-real-fighting-fake-news.

7. Nathan J. Robinson, "The Necessity of Credibility," *Current Affairs*, December 6, 2016, https://www.currentaffairs.org/2016/12/the-necessity -of-credibility.

8. "Michael Brown Shooting in Ferguson," American Civil Liberties Union of Missouri, last updated January 28, 2016, https://www.aclu-mo.org /legal-docket/michael-brown-shooting-in-ferguson.

14. YOUTH WORKERS FIGHT BACK

1. "The Contribution of Youth Work to Address the Challenges Young People Are Facing, in Particular the Transition from Education to Employment," European Union Work Plan for Youth for 2014–15, European Commission, http://ec.europa.eu/assets/eac/youth/library/reports /contribution-youth-work_en.pdf, 5.

2. Bernard Davies, "What Do We Mean by Youth Work?," in *What Is Youth Work?*, ed. Janet Batsleer and Bernard Davies (Exeter, UK: Learning Matters, 2010).

3. Howard Sercombe, *Youth Work Ethics* (London: Sage Publications, 2010), 23–24.

4. Vikram Dodd, "Anjem Choudary Jailed for Five and a Half Years for Urging Support of Isis," *Guardian*, September 6, 2016, https://www

.theguardian.com/uk-news/2016/sep/06/anjem-choudary-jailed-for
-five-years-and-six-months-for-urging-support-of-isis.

5. Fareed Zakaria, "Why They Hate Us," CNN Live Event/Special, aired
May 23, 2016, http://transcripts.cnn.com/TRANSCRIPTS/1605/23/se
.01.html.

6. Zakaria, "Why They Hate Us."

15. JOBS

1. Josh Sanburn, "Murders Up in U.S. Cities—But Crime Rate Still Near
Record Lows," *Time*, December 20, 2016, http://time.com/4607059
/murder-rate-increase-us-cities-2016.

2. Chris Doucette, "Sharp Rise in Murders in Toronto in 2016," *Toronto
Sun*, December 27, 2016, http://www.torontosun.com/2016/12/27
/sharp-rise-in-murders-in-toronto-in-2016.

3. Codi Wilson, "Additional $600K Invested in Youth Jobs to Help Curb
Gun Violence in Toronto," CP24, June 20, 2016, http://www.cp24.com
/news/additional-600k-invested-in-youth-jobs-to-help-curb-gun
-violence-in-toronto-1.2953214.

4. Shawn Jeffords, "Black Leaders Say Jobs, Not Coupons, Needed to Stem
Violence," *Toronto Sun*, June 8, 2016, http://www.torontosun.com/2016
/06/08/black-leaders-say-jobs-not-coupons-needed-to-stem-violence.

5. Alexia Elejalde-Ruiz, "Arne Duncan Takes Aim at Chicago's Violence
with Youth Jobs Initiative," *Chicago Tribune*, March 17, 2016, http://www
.chicagotribune.com/business/ct-arne-duncan-youth-jobs-initiative
-0318-biz-20160317-story.html.

6. Vincent Corluy, Joost Haemels, Ive Marx and Gerlinde Verbist, "The
Labour Market Position of Second-Generation Immigrants in Belgium,"
working paper, National Bank of Belgium, Brussels, September 2015,
https://www.nbb.be/doc/oc/repec/reswpp/wp285en.pdf.

7. Reed Karaim, "Helping Jobless Youth Develop 'Soft' Skills," in *Issues for
Debate in American Public Policy: Selections from CQ Researcher* (Los Angeles: CQ Press, 2014), http://library.cqpress.com/cqresearcher
/document.php?id=cqrglobal2012030600.

8. "Ron Bruder's Education for Employment Gets to Work on Middle East
Unemployment," Synergos, Spring 2012, http://www.synergos.org
/globalgivingmatters/features/1206bruder.htm.

9. "Enterprising Ideas: Jobs for Jordan," *NOW*, PBS, 2008, http://www.pbs
.org/now/enterprisingideas/efe.html.

10. "Basic Education in Muslim Countries," chapter 5.8 in *Country Reports
on Terrorism*, Office of the Coordinator for Counterterrorism, US Department of State, April 30, 2008, https://www.state.gov/j/ct/rls/crt
/2007/104117.htm.

11. Steve Benen, "We Cannot Kill Our Way out of This War," MSNBC, February 18, 2015, http://www.msnbc.com/rachel-maddow-show/we -cannot-kill-our-way-out-war.

12. Michael Tomasky, "Yes, I'll Say It: Marie Harf Had a Point," *Daily Beast*, February 18, 2015, http://www.thedailybeast.com/articles/2015/02/18 /yes-i-ll-say-it-marie-harf-had-a-point.html.

13. "Breaking the Binary: Policy Guide to Scaling Social Innovation," Schwab Foundation for Social Entrepreneurship, World Economic Forum, 2013, http://reports.weforum.org/social-innovation-2013.

14. Patrick Kingsley, "Egyptian Population Explosion Worsens Social Unrest," *Guardian*, February 16, 2014, https://www.theguardian.com /world/2014/feb/16/egypt-population-explosion-social-unrest.

15. Adel Abdel Ghafar, "Youth Unemployment in Egypt: A Ticking Time Bomb," Brookings Institution, July 28, 2016, https://www.brookings.edu /blog/markaz/2016/07/29/youth-unemployment-in-egypt-a-ticking -time-bomb.

16. Bret Stephens, "Islam's Improbable Reformer," *Wall Street Journal*, March 20, 2015, http://www.wsj.com/articles/the-weekend-interview -islams-improbable-reformer-1426889862.

17. Associated Press, "Muslim Mob in Egypt Strips 70-Year-Old Christian Woman," *Guardian*, May 26, 2016, https://www.theguardian.com/world /2016/may/26/muslim-mob-in-egypt-strips-elderly-christian-woman -in-violent-attack.

18. Nikki Gamer, "Muslim, Christian Peacebuilding in Egypt," Catholic Relief Services, April 30, 2015, http://www.crs.org/stories/muslim-christian -peacebuilding-egypt.

19. Sara B. Heller, "Summer Jobs Reduce Violence Among Disadvantaged Youth," *Science* 346, no. 6214 (December 5, 2014): 1222.

20. David G. Blanchflower and Andrew J. Oswald, "Well-Being over Time in Britain and the USA," *Journal of Public Economics* 88 (2004): 1374–75.

21. Belinda Luscombe, "Men Without Full-Time Jobs Are 33% More Likely to Divorce," *Time*, July 27, 2016, http://time.com/4425061/unemployment -divorce-men-women.

16. ISOLATING EXTREMISTS

1. "League of Nationalists," *Economist*, November 19, 2016, http://www .economist.com/news/international/21710276-all-around-world -nationalists-are-gaining-ground-why-league-nationalists.

2. Ronald F. Inglehart and Pippa Norris, "Trump, Brexit, and the Rise of Populism: Economic Have-Nots and Cultural Backlash," working paper, John F. Kennedy School of Government, Harvard University, Cambridge,

MA, August 2016, https://research.hks.harvard.edu/publications/getFile
.aspx?Id=1401, 2.

3. Inglehart and Norris, "Trump, Brexit and the Rise of Populism,"
   29–31.
4. Mark L. Movsesian, "The New Nationalism," Online Library of Law and
   Liberty, December 8, 2016, http://www.libertylawsite.org/2016/12/08
   /the-new-nationalism.
5. Michael Dougherty, "Trumpism Without Trump in the U.K.," *National
   Review*, May 22, 2017, http://www.nationalreview.com/article/447837
   /theresa-may-practices-trumpism-better-trump-does.
6. Josiah Ryan, "'This Was a Whitelash': Van Jones' Take on the Election
   Results," CNN, November 9, 2016, http://www.cnn.com/2016/11/09
   /politics/van-jones-results-disappointment-cnntv/index.html.
7. Phillip Connor and Jens Manuel Krogstad, "Immigrant Share of Population Jumps in Some European Countries," Pew Research Center, June 15,
   2016, http://www.pewresearch.org/fact-tank/2016/06/15/immigrant
   -share-of-population-jumps-in-some-european-countries.
8. Jie Zong and Jeanne Batalova, "Frequently Requested Statistics on Immigrants and Immigration in the United States," Migration Policy Institute, April 14, 2016, http://www.migrationpolicy.org/article/frequently
   -requested-statistics-immigrants-and-immigration-united-states.
9. Tavia Grant, "320,000 Newcomers Came to Canada in Past Year, Highest Number Since 1971," *Globe and Mail*, September 28, 2016, https://
   theglobeandmail.com/news/national/canada-welcomed-320000
   -immigrants-in-past-year-highest-number-since-1971/article32102991.
10. "Net Migration to UK Rises to 333,000—Second Highest on Record,"
    BBC News, May 26, 2016, http://www.bbc.com/news/uk-politics-eu
    -referendum-36382199.
11. Zong and Batalova, "Frequently Requested Statistics."
12. Conrad Hackett, "5 Facts About the Muslim Population in Europe," Pew
    Research Center, July 19, 2016, http://www.pewresearch.org/fact-tank
    /2016/07/19/5-facts-about-the-muslim-population-in-europe.
13. Ryan D. Enos, "The Causal Effect of Prolonged Intergroup Contact on
    Exclusionary Attitudes: A Test Using Public Transportation in Homog-
    enous Communities," *Proceedings of the National Academy of Sciences* 111,
    no. 10 (March 11, 2014): 3704, https://scholar.harvard.edu/files/renos/files
    /enostrains.pdf.
14. Doug Saunders, "The Real Reason Donald Trump Got Elected? We Have
    a White Extremism Problem," *Globe and Mail*, November 11, 2016,
    http://www.theglobeandmail.com/news/world/us-politics/the-real
    -reason-donald-trump-got-elected-we-have-a-white-extremism
    -problem/article32817625.
15. "Alt Right: A Primer About the New White Supremacy," Anti-Defamation

League, https://www.adl.org/education/resources/backgrounders/alt
-right-a-primer-about-the-new-white-supremacy.

16. Chris Graham, "Nazi Salutes and White Supremacism: Who Is Richard
Spencer, the 'Racist Academic' Behind the 'Alt Right' Movement?," *Telegraph*, November 22, 2016, http://www.telegraph.co.uk/news/0/richard
-spencer-white-nationalist-leading-alt-right-movement.

17. Robinson Meyer, "YouTube Removes the 'Hail, Trump' Video from
Search," *Atlantic*, March 20, 2019, https://www.theatlantic.com/technology
/archive/2018/03/youtube-removes-the-atlantics-hail-trump-video
-from-search/555941/.

18. Maura Conway, "Determining the Role of the Internet in Violent
Extremism and Terrorism: Six Suggestions for Progressing Research,"
Studies in Conflict & Terrorism 40, no. 1 (2017): 84, https://doi.org/10
.1080/1057610X.2016.1157408.

19. David French, "The Alt-Right's Chickens Come Home to Roost," *National Review*, August 12, 2017, http://www.nationalreview.com/corner
/450433/alt-rights-chickens-come-home-roost.

20. Joshua M. Roose, *Political Islam and Masculinity: Muslim Men in Australia* (London: Palgrave Macmillan, 2016), 15.

21. Lizzy Acker, "Who Is Jeremy Christian? Facebook Shows a Man with
Nebulous Political Affiliations Who Hated Circumcision and Hillary
Clinton," *Oregonian/Oregon Live*, June 2, 2017, http://www.oregonlive
.com/portland/index.ssf/2017/05/who_is_jeremy_christian_facebo
.html.

17. BROKEN DEMOCRACY

1. Toronto Foundation, "Gap Between Rich and Poor," in *Toronto's Vital Signs
2016 Report*, http://torontosvitalsigns.ca/main-sections/gap-between
-rich-and-poor.

2. Government of Ontario, "Ontario's Black Youth Action Plan," March 7,
2017, https://news.ontario.ca/mcys/en/2017/03/ontarios-black-youth
-action-plan.html.

3. Social Planning Council of Peel, "The Black Community in Peel: Research Summary from Four Reports," United Way Peel Region, 2015,
http://www.unitedwaypeel.org/faces/images/summary-sm.pdf, 6.

4. Nishi Kumar and Kwame McKenzie, "Thriving in the City: A Framework for Income and Health in the GTA," Wellesley Institute, September 13, 2017, http://www.wellesleyinstitute.com/publications/thriving
-in-the-city-a-framework-for-income-and-health.

5. Generations United et al., "GrandFacts: State Fact Sheets for Grandparents and Other Relatives Raising Children," Grandfamilies.org, http://
www.grandfamilies.org/State-Fact-Sheets.

6. Ohio Department of Health, "2015 Ohio Drug Overdose Data: General Findings," https://www.odh.ohio.gov/-/media/ODH/ASSETS/Files /health/injury-prevention/2015-Overdose-Data/2015-Ohio-Drug -Overdose-Data-Report-FINAL.pdf.

7. Public Children Services Association of Ohio, "Opiate Epidemic 2015," http://www.pcsao.org/programs/opiate-epidemic.

8. Jackie Borchardt, "House Republicans Propose $170.6 Million in Budget to Fight Ohio's Opioid Crisis," Cleveland.com, April 25, 2017, http:// www.cleveland.com/metro/index.ssf/2017/04/house_republicans _earmark_1706.html.

9. Marty Schladen, "Strapped for Funds, Ohio Coroners Likely Undercounting Opioid Epidemic," *Columbus Dispatch*, May 28, 2017, http:// www.dispatch.com/news/20170528/strapped-for-funds-ohio-coroners -likely-undercounting-opioid-epidemic.

10. Jona Ison, "44 Dead from Overdoses Breaks Record, Again," *Chillicothe (OH) Gazette*, March 7, 2017, http://www.chillicothegazette.com/story /news/crime/high-in-ohio/2017/03/05/44-dead-drug-overdoses-ross -county-ohio-chillicothe-breaks-record-again/98663668.

11. Paris, "How the Democratic Party Takes Black Voters for Granted," *Vice*, July 8, 2016, https://www.vice.com/en_ca/article/how-the-democratic -party-takes-black-voters-for-granted.

12. Simon Hooper, "Could the Muslim Vote Sway the UK's General Election?," Al Jazeera, March 13, 2015, http://www.aljazeera.com/indepth/features /2015/03/muslim-vote-sway-uk-general-election-150311055142181 .html.

13. Esther J. Cepeda, "Latino Voters Taken for Granted," My San Antonio, September 26, 2016, http://www.mysanantonio.com/opinion/commentary /article/Latino-voters-taken-for-granted-9289875.php.

14. Soeren Kern, "UK: What British Muslims Really Think," Gatestone Institute, April 17, 2016, https://www.gatestoneinstitute.org/7861/british -muslims-survey.

15. "Changing Attitudes on Gay Marriage," Pew Research Center, May 12, 2016, http://www.pewforum.org/2016/05/12/changing-attitudes-on -gay-marriage.

16. Eric Bradner and Gregory Krieg, "Inside the Fight That Could Derail the Democratic Party," CNN, August 11, 2017, http://www.cnn.com/2017 /08/11/politics/democrats-bernie-sanders-feud/index.html.

17. Malcolm X, "The Ballot or the Bullet," speech, King Solomon Baptist Church, Detroit, Michigan, April 12, 1964, http://americanradioworks .publicradio.org/features/blackspeech/mx.html.

18. Jon Schroeder, "Ripples of Innovation: Charter Schooling in Minnesota, the Nation's First Charter School State," Progressive Policy Institute, April 2004, https://eric.ed.gov/?id=ED491210.

19. Center for Research on Education Outcomes, "Urban Charter School Study: Report on 41 Regions," Stanford University, 2015, http://urbancharters.stanford.edu/download/Urban%20Charter%20School%20Study%20Report%20on%2041%20Regions.pdf.

20. Geoffrey Canada, "Schools Are for Kids, Not Adults," *New York Times*, March 14, 2010, http://roomfordebate.blogs.nytimes.com/2010/03/14/the-push-back-on-charter-schools.

21. Derek W. Black, "Civil Rights, Charter Schools, and Lessons to Be Learned," *Florida Law Review* 64, no. 6 (December 2012): 1772, http://scholarship.law.ufl.edu/flr/vol64/iss6/6.

22. Black, "Civil Rights, Charter Schools," 1773.

23. Monica R. Almond, "The Great Migration: Charter School Satisfaction Among African American Parents," *LUX: A Journal of Transdisciplinary Writing and Research from Claremont Graduate University* 2, no. 1 (2013), http://scholarship.claremont.edu/lux/vol2/iss1/1.

24. Sarah Carr, "Mississippi Debate over Charters, School Reform Evokes Broader Racial Divide," Hechinger Report, January 8, 2013, http://hechingerreport.org/content/mississippi-debate-over-charters-school-reform-evokes-broader-racial-divide_10786.

25. Valarie Strauss, "NAACP Members Call for Ban on Privately Managed Charter Schools," *Washington Post*, August 7, 2016, https://www.washingtonpost.com/news/answer-sheet/wp/2016/08/07/naacp-members-call-for-ban-on-privately-managed-charter-schools.

26. Lori Higgins, "Concerns over Charter School Performance Persist as More Open in Michigan," *Detroit Free Press*, June 26, 2014, http://www.freep.com/story/news/local/michigan/2014/06/26/concerns-over-charter-school-performance-persist-as-more-open-in/77155450.

27. Center for Research on Education Outcomes, "Urban Charter School Study."

28. Urban Prep Academies, "The Creed," http://www.urbanprep.org/about/creed.

18. MY BROTHER'S KEEPER

1. Paul Galdas, Francine Cheater and Paul Marshall, "Men and Health Help-Seeking Behaviour: Literature Review," *Journal of Advanced Nursing* 49, no. 6 (2005): 621.

2. Quoctrung Bui, "Why Some Men Don't Work: Video Games Have Gotten Really Good," *New York Times*, July 3, 2017, https://www.nytimes.com/2017/07/03/upshot/why-some-men-dont-work-video-games-have-gotten-really-good.html.

3. Philip Zimbardo and Nikita Coulombe, *Man Interrupted: Why Young*

Men Are Struggling and What We Can Do About It (Newburyport, MA: Conari Press, 2016), 8.

4. Amanda Marcotte, "Overcompensation Nation: It's Time to Admit That Toxic Masculinity Drives Gun Violence," *Salon*, June 13, 2016, http://www.salon.com/2016/06/13/overcompensation_nation_its_time_to_admit_that_toxic_masculinity_drives_gun_violence.

5. W. E. B. Du Bois, *Black Reconstruction in America, 1860–1880* (New York: Free Press, 1998), 700.

6. Barack Obama, "Remarks by the President on 'My Brother's Keeper' Initiative," White House Office of the Press Secretary, February 27, 2014, https://www.whitehouse.gov/the-press-office/2014/02/27/remarks-president-my-brothers-keeper-initiative.

7. Broderick Johnson and Jim Shelton, "My Brother's Keeper Task Force Report to the President," May 2014, https://obamawhitehouse.archives.gov/sites/default/files/docs/053014_mbk_report.pdf, 5–6.

8. Johnson and Shelton, "Task Force Report to the President," 7.

9. Edna McConnell Clark Foundation, "Grantees in Action: Youth Guidance," http://www.emcf.org/grantees/youth-guidance.

10. Edna McConnell Clark Foundation, "Grantees in Action."

11. Sara B. Heller, Anuj K. Shah, Jonathan Guryan, Jens Ludwig, Sendhil Mullainathan and Harold A. Pollack, "Thinking, Fast and Slow? Some Field Experiments to Reduce Crime and Dropout in Chicago," National Bureau of Economic Research, May 2015, http://www.nber.org/papers/w21178.pdf, 2.

12. Heller et al., "Thinking, Fast and Slow?," 8.

13. Heller et al., "Thinking, Fast and Slow?," 41.

14. MBK Task Force, "My Brother's Keeper 2016 Progress Report: Two Years of Expanding Opportunity and Creating Pathways to Success," White House Office of the Press Secretary, April 22, 2016, https://www.whitehouse.gov/sites/whitehouse.gov/files/images/MBK-2016-Progress-Report.pdf.

15. Frederick C. Harris, "The Challenges of My Brother's Keeper," Brookings Institution, October 29, 2015, https://www.brookings.edu/wp-content/uploads/2016/07/my_brothers_keeper.pdf, 6–7.

16. Jennifer Pagliaro, "Jane and Finch: Toronto's Most Dangerous Place to Be a Kid?," *Toronto Star*, August 31, 2013, https://www.thestar.com/news/crime/2013/08/31/jane_and_finch_torontos_most_dangerous_place_to_be_a_kid.html.

17. Zoey McKnight, "Black Creek Neighbourhood Deemed Toronto's Least Livable," *Toronto Star*, March 13, 2014, https://www.thestar.com/news/gta/2014/03/13/black_creek_neighbourhood_deemed_torontos_least_livable.html.

18. William Marsiglio, *Men on a Mission: Valuing Youth Work in Our Communities* (Baltimore: Johns Hopkins University Press, 2008), 311.

19. Darlene Superville, "Obama Gives My Brother's Keeper Initiative New Name," Associated Press, January 13, 2017, https://apnews.com/768d9 b1c4ff34da9ae05c9fd82782b50/obama-gives-my-brothers-keeper -initiative-new-name.

20. Kirstin Weir, "The Men America Left Behind," *Monitor on Psychology* 48, no. 2 (February 2017): 34, http://www.apa.org/monitor/2017/02/men -left-behind.aspx.

INDEX

10/19/19